SECONDARY SCHOOL LITERACY

Secondary School Literacy

What Research Reveals for Classroom Practice

EDITED BY

LESLIE S. RUSH
University of Wyoming

A. JONATHAN EAKLE
Johns Hopkins University

ALLEN BERGER
Miami University, Professor Emeritus

Foreword by Elizabeth Noll

National Council of Teachers of English
1111 W. Kenyon Road, Urbana, Illinois 61801-1096

Staff Editor: Bonny Graham
Manuscript Editor: Susan Campanini
Interior Design: Jenny Jensen Greenleaf
Cover Design: Frank P. Cucciarre, Blink Concept & Design, Inc.

NCTE Stock Number: 42936

It is the policy of NCTE in its journals and other publications to provide a
forum for the open discussion of ideas concerning the content and the teaching of English and the language arts. Publicity accorded to any particular
point of view does not imply endorsement by the Executive Committee, the
Board of Directors, or the membership at large, except in announcements
of policy, where such endorsement is clearly specified.

Every effort has been made to provide current URLs and email addresses,
but because of the rapidly changing nature of the Web, some sites and addresses may no longer be accessible.

Library of Congress Cataloging-in-Publication Data

Secondary school literacy : what research reveals for classroom practice /
edited by Leslie S. Rush, A. Jonathan Eakle, Allen Berger ; foreword by
Elizabeth Noll.
     p. cm.
  Includes bibliographical references and index.
  ISBN 978-0-8141-4293-6 (pbk.)
  1. Reading (Secondary)—United States. 2. Language arts (Secondary)—
United States. 3. Literacy programs—United States. I. Rush, Leslie S.,
1962– II. Eakle, A. Jonathan, 1957– III. Berger, Allen.
LB1632.S35 2007
428.4071'2—dc22
                                    2007028949

This book is for
Mark
Rosa Aurora and Maya
Jon, Nate, and Marni

CONTENTS

Contents

FOREWORD

ELIZABETH NOLL
University of New Mexico

M̲ost teacher educators in our field would probably agree that one of the challenges we face in the university classroom is how to convey effectively the reciprocal relationship between research and practice. Our students—English language arts teachers and prospective teachers—want to know "what works"; they may resist learning about research and theory that seem removed from the reality of their teaching lives. Helping them understand how reading and writing research informs and is informed by classroom practice is critical to their growth as educators.

Secondary School Literacy: What Research Reveals for Classroom Practice represents the fourth volume in a series begun fifty years ago as a collaborative effort between the National Conference on Research in Language and Literacy (NCRLL), formerly the National Conference on Research in English (NCRE), and the National Council of Teachers of English (NCTE). Like its predecessors, *Secondary School Literacy* is an authoritative resource for our field. It draws on the knowledge and expertise of outstanding scholars and addresses a wide range of topics that reflects current issues. And, as its title suggests, connections to classroom practice are infused throughout rich discussions of research. I was struck by the authors' thoughtful descriptions of practice that deepened my understanding of the research presented. I fully expect that both secondary and prospective teachers will benefit from the careful balance of research and practice.

Secondary School Literacy distinguishes itself from earlier versions in its broadened scope. Whereas the other versions focused specifically on reading, this version includes both reading and writing, reflecting the editors' and authors' understanding of the integrality of these subjects. What Richard Beach and David O'Brien write in the introduction to their chapter is true of the book as a whole: "[W]e reach beyond the familiar curriculum framework that artificially separates reading, writing, speaking, listening, and viewing to explore how reading and writing may be integrated by engaging students in practices involved in better understanding and producing texts" (p. 218).

I enjoyed the experience of reading this volume: it is not only intellectually thought-provoking, but aesthetically engaging. The language is rich, clear, and accessible, and the reader is invited to take part in the conversation of each chapter. Consider, for example, the invitation that James Damico, Gerald Campano, and Jerry Harste extend to readers:

> Imagine yourself as a high school teacher in the following classroom:
>> Several boys, sitting in the back of the class, draw pictures of lowrider art; two African American girls seated at opposite ends of the room use their eyes and shoulders to communicate silently with each other; two boys use cellular phones to share photos they took of their neighborhoods; and a Hmong refugee girl writes a narrative of her experiences, using her emergent English skills to convey the power of her story. (p. 203)

A sense of story is also evident in a number of the chapters, including one about Tony, an "illiterate" teen, in Donna Alvermann and Cheryl McLean's chapter. The story begins, "It was too late. I'd seen it: the book in the back pocket" (p. 1); the tale is woven throughout the chapter to illustrate the nature of literacies and implications for adolescent literacy instruction.

Secondary School Literacy is the culmination of extensive efforts by exceptional authors, editors, and "behind the scenes" supporters. I would like to acknowledge two individuals in particular: Allen Berger and Russel Durst. It was Allen, one of the coeditors, who recognized and acted on the need for an updated version of this series. In 2004, he sought the support of Russel Durst, then President of the NCRLL. Russel encouraged Allen to pursue the project and helped him secure sponsorship by NCRLL and NCTE. Both individuals were instrumental in bringing this outstanding volume to fruition.

INTRODUCTION

LESLIE S. RUSH
University of Wyoming

A. JONATHAN EAKLE
Johns Hopkins University

ALLEN BERGER
Miami University, Professor Emeritus

The pages that follow are part of a half-century journey. As in all traveling tales, these pages contain turns, pauses, and varying speeds and intensities. Some ideas that readers encounter about literacy here may be familiar, others re-imagined, and still others may be novel. In this vein, beginning the text at hand, we emphasize that the destination is not defined and fixed; rather, its intent is to open possibilities for teaching and learning literacy in the twenty-first century.

A familiar theme in some chapters of this volume involves adolescents who struggle with reading and writing. Most educators recognize this common road post and the challenges that many students have with academic literacy. In the works that follow, leading researchers in literacy education map insights on what to do to engage these students and improve adolescent literacy. It is our hope that readers will take from their crossings through subsequent pages various new ways to teach and motivate these students to master conventional modes of using language-based texts.

On the other hand, adolescents in general provide for us important insights on what counts as literacy, particularly in rapidly changing societies that are rich in multimedia. This position also runs through many of the chapters. In fact, as shown through works in this volume, there are increasing opportunities for young people to teach their elders about what content, form, and literacy pedagogies can be engaging for youth. As Underwood, Woo, and Pearson and others point out, there have been moves in some corners of education from transmission models of teaching toward participatory, critical, and postmodern stances of literacy teaching and learning. A lesson from many of the chapters in this volume is that defining adolescent literacy as a strictly unidirectional skill transmitted from teacher to student is antiquated at best.

As teacher educators, we believe that this revised book is long overdue. Teachers, principals, and other stakeholders concerned with adolescent literacy need up-to-date, crucial information about research, theory, and practice related to adolescent literacy, information that is particularly important in these days of increasing accountability and assessment of literacy levels among young people. We think that this updated edition provides such crucial information, and we would like to take this opportunity to extend our gratitude to the chapter authors for their thoughtfulness, creativity, and diligence in producing this work. For her valuable comments and advice as we compiled this volume, we are also particularly grateful to Margaret J. Early, past president of NCTE. Her essays appear in the first three volumes of this publication; her contribution to this volume was to assist the editors in reviewing the manuscripts.

Purpose and History of the Book

The principal purpose of the individual chapters and of the collection as a whole is to inform secondary school teachers and administrators about current research in secondary school literacy as well as to provide information about how research findings might be applied in secondary school settings. Each of the chapters includes reviews of research on a particular topic and provides instructional implications for classroom teachers. It is our hope that classroom teachers, as well as teacher educators, policymakers, administrators, and education researchers, will find the material in this edited collection both intellectually stimulating and useful in practice. We believe that this collection is a timely one; now more than ever, teachers, principals, and school districts are looking for research-based practices on which to ground their classroom practice and professional development.

This book is the fourth in a long history of collaboration between academic organizations and among individuals—both researchers and teachers—who believe in the importance of basing classroom teaching on the findings of quality research. The first publication in this line appeared during the 1957–1958 academic year. It was subsequently revised in 1969. M. Agnella Gunn of Boston University edited both volumes. Each was published under the auspices of the National Conference on Research in English (NCRE, now known as NCRLL) and NCTE. Energy for a third revision, which appeared in 1982, was generated at a Commission on Reading meeting of the NCTE convention in November of 1979. Edited by Allen Berger and H. Alan Robinson, the third edition provided an expanded examination of research in secondary school reading, including reading achievement, the reading process, readers' strategies, and assessment, as well as other topics. Like the first two volumes, NCTE published the 1982 volume with the support of NCRE and the additional support of NCTE's Commission on Reading.

This fourth volume contains expanded understandings that reflect theoretical and practical changes occurring in the field of literacy education. Authors in this volume include research on both reading and writing in their chapters, an intertwining reflected in the title's emphasis on secondary school literacy. Although many reviews of research on secondary school reading and some on secondary school writing are available, few do an effective job of combining reviews of research on both secondary school reading and writing. Because of the growing acknowledgment of the overlapping, strong connections between these two tenuously defined domains, our belief is that language arts teachers at the secondary level will benefit from this combination; furthermore, we expect that teachers of all content areas will find useful information here as well.

Moving beyond an understanding of the interconnected processes of reading and writing, many of the chapters in this volume are written from what is called in some corners of the academy a "new literacies" perspective (Collins & Blot, 2003; Pahl & Rowsell, 2006). This perspective emphasizes how literacy cannot be separated from culture. We live in a culture of multiplicity and diverse communicative modes, which include digital multimedia technologies, images, and various forms of printed texts. In subsequent "new literacies" chapters, theoretical and pedagogical perspectives and the research on which they are based make it possible for teachers to reconsider youth engagement with literacy in and out of school, the identities and subjects that are constructed through literacy practices, and the role of multiple texts in various settings. The thoughts and resources in these chapters provide a starting point for reconsidering current secondary school teaching and learning.

Finally, this volume presents a unique combination of established scholarship and newer perspectives. In many cases, we invited authors with established track records of publication to coauthor with relatively new researchers. We believe that this combination—also apparent in the editorship of this volume—provides experience and knowledge of the history of research in secondary school literacy, as well as fresh perspectives on current adolescent literacy research. Building on the past and on literacy research and practices that have stood the test of time, we have also invited some authors from the third edition to update their chapters in the present book.

In each chapter, we have asked authors to examine relevant research and to address two questions:

1. What research findings are available in relation to aspects of secondary school literacy?
2. What do these research findings mean for best practices in secondary school literacy?

Structure of the Volume

Our volume begins with Donna Alvermann and Cheryl McLean's chapter, "The Nature of Literacies," which presents a brief history of literacy practices; how our understanding of literacy has changed over time; and how current research in New Literacy

Studies and multimodality might provide new means for envisioning adolescent literacies in classrooms. Drawing on personal narrative accounts and reviews of significant research, the authors suggest ways that teachers might use participatory instruction and connect students' in-school and out-of-school literacies and interests.

"New Literacy Learning Strategies for New Times" by Robert Tierney is an update of his chapter "Learning from Text" from the previous edition of this book. Assuming the position that new forms of literacies demand new instructional practices, Tierney outlines ways in which teachers can help students become informed meaning-makers, inquirers, and evaluators of the myriad of text forms available through digital advancements.

In "What Is New about the New Literacies of Online Reading Comprehension?" authors Donald Leu, Lisa Zawilinski, Jill Castek, Manju Banerjee, Brian Housand, Yingjie Liu, and Maureen O'Neil note the marked absence of research on reading comprehension in online and other digital settings. Defining the range of "New Literacies," these authors cite research to show that differences may exist between skills and strategies needed for online and offline reading comprehension. They also provide suggestions for teachers who are interested in cultivating students' online reading skills. One intriguing aspect of this chapter is its provision of connections to websites with online video excerpts of students engaged in online reading practices. Readers may view these videos and see examples of students with varying differences in skills required for online and offline reading comprehension.

In "Assessment of Adolescent Reading Proficiencies," Richard Allington and Danielle Dennis provide an understanding, from national and international assessment data, of adolescent proficiency in reading. This is followed by a discussion and critique of these formal assessments and a presentation of several informal assessment techniques that provide detailed information on literacy learners' strengths and weaknesses.

In their chapter "Understanding Reading Comprehension in Secondary Schools through the Lens of the Four Resources Model," Terry Underwood, Monica Yoo, and David Pearson examine state standards, standardized tests, and commonly used anthologies through the lens of the Four Resources model of literacy instruction (Freebody & Luke, 1990). Focusing on these issues in California and Massachusetts, the authors argue that, although state standards carry the complexity and sophistication underscored by the Four Resources Model, standardized assessments in those states are based on more limited and narrow understandings of reading comprehension. Faced with these incongruities, the authors provide teachers with a set of guidelines to use for planning and conducting effective reading comprehension instruction.

Kathleen Hinchman's chapter, "I Want to Learn to Read Before I Graduate: How Sociocultural Research on Adolescents' Literacy Struggles Can Shape Classroom Practice," presents a discussion of sociocultural literacy perspectives and provides guidelines culled from research that can shape teachers' classroom practices. She particularly focuses on the importance of combining quality literacy instruction with teachers gaining insight into students' interests, identities, and cultural backgrounds.

In "Literacy, Identity, and the Changing Social Spaces of Teaching and Learning," Kevin Leander and Jessica Zacher begin with the concept that adolescent identities are not stable: they are constantly under construction both in and out of classrooms. They argue that identity construction has important impacts on how students interact with each other, with teachers, and with academic work, and that considering issues of space and time is critical to understanding adolescent literacies. Organizing their chapter into three distinct modes of how literacy can be conceived, they present a review of current research that connects identity and literacy learning. From each mode, they provide education implications for teachers and schools.

In their chapter "Legitimacy, Recognition, and Access to Language and Literacy: English Language Learners at the Secondary School Level," Robert Jiménez and Brad Teague review research related to literacy learning of English Language Learners (ELLs) in secondary schools and provide a discussion of instructional strategies that emerge from this research. They focus particularly on revisioning the literacies of immigrants in regard to the education, language, experience, and cultural capital that they acquired prior to their arrival in U.S. schools and that they are continually refining. The authors also provide helpful information related to necessary professional development for secondary content teachers who teach immigrant children and ELLs.

Alfred Tatum's chapter, "Literacy Development of African American Adolescent Males," reviews research on African American males in schools and, in particular, on teaching African American males. He draws on the importance of Csikszentmihalyi's (1990) concept of "flow" during in-school and out-of-school activities and articulates several ways in which teachers can meet the literacy and curriculum needs of African American male students.

In a chapter titled "From Contexts to Contextualizing and Recontextualizing: The Work of Teaching," James Damico, Gerald Campano, and Jerry Harste have revised Harste's chapter on classroom contexts in the earlier volume. They draw on the complex understandings present in the literacy field concerning new forms of texts and the importance of cultural and linguistic resources, particularly on the ways in which teachers can reshape their classroom contexts to meet the needs of today's young people.

Richard Beach and David O'Brien, in "Adopting Reader and Writer Stances in Understanding and Producing Texts," present an interesting look at the ways reading and writing skills impact each other and how teachers might incorporate the skills of reading in writing instruction and vice versa. Pulling from their own study of struggling middle school students, they advocate engaging students in purposeful, meaningful activities in which reading and writing skills interact.

Jeannine Richison, Anita Hernández, and Marcia Carter, in "Using Scaffolding in Teaching Core Literature," provide an introduction to the constructivist notion of scaffolding as an instructional practice, with a particular focus on the challenges faced by ELLs and their teachers. They also present seven instructional scaffolds that are useful for teaching second-language students and discuss development of themed text sets in secondary English classrooms.

Jill Lewis and Gary Moorman's chapter, "Federal and State Literacy Mandates for Secondary Schools: Responding to Unintended Consequences," provides a historical perspective on the intertwining of literacy instruction and policy mandates. This is followed by a discussion of recent policy mandates and the ways in which these mandates impact literacy instruction in secondary schools.

These chapters provide an excellent blend of important and complex theoretical and research-based understandings, along with the practical application so important to classroom teachers and principals today. We think that readers of this volume will find its chapters, written by leading literacy scholars, not only engaging and intriguing but also useful in their education practices.

References

Collins, J., & Blot, R. K. (2003). *Literacy and literacies: Texts, power, and identity*. Cambridge, England: Cambridge University Press.

Csikszentmihalyi, M. (1990). *Flow: The psychology of optimal experience*. New York: Harper and Row.

Freebody, P., & Luke, A. (1990). Literacies programs: Debates and demands in cultural context. *Prospect: Australian Journal of TESOL, 5*(7), 7–16.

Pahl, K., & Rowsell, J. (Eds.). (2006). *Travel notes from the new literacy studies: Instances of practice*. Clevedon, England: Multilingual Matters.

The Nature of Literacies

DONNA E. ALVERMANN AND CHERYL A. MCLEAN
University of Georgia

The invitation to write this chapter allowed us to reflect on our experiences and interactions as learners, teachers, and teacher educators. Out of our many conversations, Donna and I found common stories that helped deepen our understanding of literacy practices and experiences of adolescent students and teachers in a broadened context. I share one such reflection in the hope that these words may help bring diverse worlds closer.

It was too late. I'd seen it: the book in the back pocket. And, more important, I'd read the title: *Nelson's Primary School Reader*. Tony had casually leaned over to tie the laces of his scuffed gym shoes, and his T-shirt shifted to reveal the well-worn book that was folded and tucked into the back pocket of his jeans. Perhaps it was my sharp intake of breath, or the fact that I had stumbled in midsentence, because my friend's head spun around, he sprang up, and, with swift yet practiced movements, he pushed his secret deeper into his pocket, pulling his T-shirt over his shame.

I remember his eyes furtively searching my face for signs of my having seen the dog-eared text. Here was silent confirmation of what I'd suspected: my childhood friend could not read or write beyond the early elementary level. I remember how, that day, I had accurately and fluently read his sixteen-year-old embarrassment and the fear that came from being labeled "illiterate." I knew that this label was a stigma that brought with it the likelihood of becoming a social and academic pariah in a society that privileged book learning. I knew also that students such as Tony would often counter this stigma either with feigned indifference or fierce defiance toward those who assigned and embraced such labels. So with tacit agreement, I too pushed the book into the back pocket of our friendship and pretended that these labels of literate and illiterate did not matter in our lives.

Many years later, I learned the term *new literacies* through the works of such writers as Brian Street and James Gee, and I became fascinated with how this concept takes a fresh look at literacy. Underlying this notion of new literacies is the view that learning and the nature, ways, and uses of literate practices need redefinition. Even now, in thinking about new literacies, I recall the book in Tony's back pocket and how what is valued in school took us on two separate and different paths that were words and worlds apart.

Situating New Literacies

Historical Perspective

A historical perspective allows us to recognize that the traditional conceptions of what counts as literacy and its connections to education and schooling are propelled by national and global demands that are central to the creation of the workforce. Consequently, there have been a series of movements, such as the Great Divide (Goody, 1986; Goody & Watt, 1963; Olson, 1994), that reflect an ongoing revision of communicative competence: from orality—spoken and context-bound oral modes of expression and transmission of knowledge—to the twentieth-century phenomenon of print and writing; from reading as sacred and confined to the privileged elite, to a more open and universally accessible practice. Within this progression, literacy and the knowledge associated with it have become synonymous with the practices that take place within the structure of schools.

Shaping national and global emphases on the conceptions of education and schooling were two dominant models of literacy: autonomous and ideological (Street, 1984; 1995). Adherents of the autonomous model view literacy as a neutral set of skills. The ideological model conceptualized by Street (1995) offers a contrasting view of literacy, one that, according to Collins and Blot (2003), has helped redefine what reading and writing are and how these practices are conducted and judged. In the ideological model, literacy is looked on as a social practice that is culturally embedded within seemingly absent but always present power structures such as class, race and gender. Implicit in this conception of literacy is the assumption that reading and writing are part and parcel of local ways of living and that these practices are sustained by talk and vary according to time and place (Gee, 1990; Heath, 1983; Scribner & Cole, 1981).

However, despite the broadening and redefining of the traditional notions of literacy since the time of the Great Divide, a dichotomous relationship still persists in regards to what counts as literacy, how it is defined and measured, and why researchers choose particular designs for studying it. Across the field of literacy studies, in its themes, research methods, contexts, and pedagogical practices, a binary exists: a one-dimensional conception of print-centric reading and writing, as contrasted with the intersection of people, texts, modes, practices, and the varied meanings of literacy learning in different situations and cultural contexts.

Contemporary Directions

Despite what may have seemed in the past like an impasse in conceptualizing the nature of literacy, the field of literacy studies is currently brimming with new directions. With the convening of the New London Group (2000), the idea that new literacies are multiple in nature and vary according to contexts began to take shape; as a result, new terms to describe that notion entered the lexicon. One of the terms, *multiliteracies*, denotes "modes of representation much broader than language alone . . . [that are situated within] increasing local diversity and global connectedness" (Cope & Kalantzis, 2000, pp. 5–6). Other terms such as *multiple literacies*, *situated literacies*, and *local literacies* became commonplace and part of a burgeoning literature (e.g., Barton, Hamilton, & Ivanič, 2000). Underlying much of the new vocabulary, however, were concepts related to multimodality and the New Literacy Studies (NLS)—two approaches that have sizeable bodies of literature behind them and whose underlying theories seem to complement one another in several respects.

The social semiotic theory of multimodality that guides the work of Kress and his colleagues (Kress, 1997; Kress & van Leeuwen, 1996) is concerned primarily with communication in its widest sense—gestural, oral, linguistic, digital, visual, kinesthetic, and so on. Underlying the NLS is a theory of literacy as social practice that varies across cultures and contexts (Gee, 1990; Street, 1984). In his keynote address to the National Reading Conference, Street (2005) provided a rationale for considering the complementarity that underlies work in NLS and multimodalities. His remarks there and later in the foreword that he and Kress coauthored for *Travel Notes from the New Literacy Studies* (Pahl & Rowsell, 2006) suggest a need to open communication between the two approaches:

> [While] both approaches look at broadly the same field, from each of the two positions the field has a distinctive look: one that tries to understand what people acting together are doing, the other that tries to understand about the tools with which the same people do what they are doing. Each has defined its objects of study—practices, events, participants on the one hand, semiosis, modes and affordances, genres, signmakers, and signs on the other. (Kress & Street, 2006, p. ix)

Theoretical considerations aside, the new literacies are having a considerable impact on contemporary education and schooling. Faced with challenges such as conceptualizing learning and the production of knowledge from multiple perspectives and definitions of literacies, classroom teachers are becoming more important than ever; at the same time, their roles are changing. Specifically, the new literacies are making it imperative that teachers guide students in navigating and learning from the Internet and other information and communication technologies.

These new technologies present their own set of challenges, which are quite separate from those associated with print media. Becoming adept at orchestrating complex learning opportunities is but one skill that classroom teachers need in a world fast becoming so knowledge-driven that students with access to the same resources as teachers may know as much if not more than their teachers about particular topics and subject areas of study (Leu,

Kinzer, Coiro, & Cammack, 2004). Sensing this same potential for new literacies to affect teachers' lives, Oldham (2005) conducted three case studies of secondary school English teachers and found that the multimodal nature of new literacies has led, in effect, to learning opportunities that call into question several commonplace practices related to assessment and instruction. For example, as Oldham pointed out, traditional methods of assessing students' learning do not take into account dramatic performances, set designs, or other forms of multimodal competencies. Overlooking the area of English studies concerned with drama may mean that students are "actually more (or differently) (multi)literate than assessment suggests" (p. 185). The need to attend to such commonplace practices and to view them within the plurality of perspectives and communities of practice that the new literacies afford is incumbent on teacher educators as they work toward preparing teachers for new literacy classrooms.

Looking Back on Tony

In moving beyond traditional notions of literacy, it is possible to acknowledge even the most academically "incapable" adolescents as consciously discerning literate beings. Using a new literacies perspective as her backdrop, Cheryl calls to mind further remembrances of Tony who, like so many adolescents, lives with multiple labels of illiteracy, despite knowledge and skills that, logic tells us, are evidence of an ability to read signs and symbols beyond the printed word:

> I remember being among the many who marveled at and respected Tony's knowledge of electronics: it was to him that both peers and adults would first turn whenever we needed a television, radio, or tape-recorder repaired. We just accepted that he had this knowledge. And yet, in our narrow *literate* minds we chose to devalue *his* literacies because he could not figure out some printed words on a page. Studies by Kress (1997), Lankshear and Knobel (2003), and Mahiri (2004) have offered insights into how contemporary youth communicate, express themselves, and "make meaning through practices constituting what might be

thought of as counter-literacy—outside of the formal practices of academic literacy, pedagogy, and curriculum" (Street, 2005, p. 106). Now I know that Tony failed because we—school and society—had failed him. Now I know that this young man failed because he could not meet *society's* imposed standards of what literacy should look like.

As a beginning high school English teacher in Trinidad, I daily came face to face with many Tonys—each struggling and striving to make sense [as Freire and Macedo's (1987) work would remind me] of the word, and the word in their world. They were not alone. I also strived to come to meaning: I too was a struggling reader of how our conceptions and practice of literacy shape our students' experiences. I was trying to make sense of the fact that some of my students' fire and passion was extinguished when they opened their textbooks. I was trying to make sense of those compelling voices that I heard engaging in the art of storytelling as they performed their narratives to enraptured peers in corridors, which became muted when asked to tell those stories in Standard English. I was trying to make sense of those eyes that shut down with frustration over a test, and just minutes later would open up with excitement at the Web page they were designing.

Tony stayed with me even though our differently literate lives took us in directions that physically, academically, and socially distanced us. Each day, I continued to question the nature of literacy as I recognized that adolescents had multiple and diverse ways of knowing, and just as many ways of *showing* their knowing. The reality was, however, that certain traditional ways of knowing were valued and privileged. Often I could not help but question *who* was illiterate. Was it really those students to whom we had so readily assigned the label or was it we who, in our academic, pedagogical, professional, and social practices, privileged this narrow concept of reading and writing as literacy, and failed or even refused to acknowledge and validate that there are multiple ways of knowing and learning? At that point, it seemed clear that inherent in our conception of literacy is the power to position learners in certain ways, to privilege some and marginalize others, and to restrict what counts and *who* counts.

Insights for Adolescent Literacy Instruction

In reflecting further on the incident that exposed Tony's identity as a reader—and later informed her own teaching as she interacted daily with other readers like Tony who struggled to conform to society's imposed standards of what literacy should look like—Cheryl has provided an excellent segue way into this section on the implications of a new literacies perspective for teachers and teacher educators.

Participatory Instruction

Teachers who invite students to take an active role in literacy learning base their instruction on students' needs and interests as much as possible. This is done through choosing relevant reading materials, making students aware of their progress toward short- and long-term goals, or simply providing an open forum for discussion. In effect, these are the elements of participatory classroom instruction—a place where most students thrive. But what about those students, such as Tony, who do not see themselves as capable and engaged readers and writers? What about those who are not actively involved in their own learning? How did they get to that place in their few short years of schooling? If we are to believe education anthropologists McDermott and Varenne (1995), all cultures, including school and classroom cultures, are historically evolved ways of "doing" life. That is, they teach people about what is worth working for, how to succeed, and who will fall short. Thus, from their perspective, how people end up inhabiting some positions in a culture and not others is more a matter of being put into those positions than of being incidentally born into them. The question then becomes, how does one escape a negative positioning?

In addressing that question, as former classroom teachers and now teacher educators, we take our cue from Eric Cooper, President of the National Urban Alliance, who reminded us in a recent email, "poverty is a circumstance, not an identity" (personal communication, Eric Cooper, May 29, 2006). We see a parallel here that merits reflection. What if we were to conceptualize "falling short as readers and writers" as nothing more than a circumstance? In an attempt to bring instructional offerings more in line with students' needs, might we reverse the positioning of those youth who have been labeled "incapable" and "unengaged"? What if we viewed such labels as mere circumstances and not identities? Even more intriguing, what if we were to discover that some youth who are so labeled do not accept those identities?

A participatory approach to literacy instruction is no less concerned with content mastery than is a transmission model. However, rather than rely on teachers to transmit facts through skill and drill tactics, a participatory approach calls for teachers to support students' academic literacies by looking for ways to validate their students' in-school and out-of-school literacy practices. In a participatory approach to instruction, students like Tony are encouraged to read for multiple purposes from a mix of trade books, textbooks, magazines, newspapers, student-generated texts, digital texts, hypermedia productions, visuals, artistic performances, and the like. Because many adolescents of the Net Generation find their own reasons for becoming literate—reasons that go beyond reading to acquire disciplinary knowledge—it is important that teachers create opportunities for them to engage actively in meaningful subject matter learning that both extends and elaborates on the literacy practices they already own and value. Such owned and valued practices, not surprisingly, are often ones that young people have acquired through informal learning.

Out-of-School Learning

Much can be learned that has potential implications for classroom teachers from attending carefully to how adolescents who struggle to read, for whatever reason (motivational, linguistic, cognitive, social, or any combination of such), use certain practices to shape their own identities as literate beings when they are using new literacies in informal, out-of-school learning. Although these practices may remain largely invisible to others around them, the youth with whom Donna has worked in after-school media literacy programs (Alvermann, Jonas, Steele, & Washington,

2006; Hagood, 2003; Heron-Hruby, Hagood, & Alvermann, in press) often identify themselves as readers, despite the perceptions others may have of them in this regard. These are youth who are aware of and value their own literacy practices, which are often, but not totally, school related. An example of two such young people follows.

The setting for this example is an after-school program sponsored by The Children's Aid Society (CAS) in New York City. Sarah Jonas, Director of Education Services for CAS, is interviewing Eric Washington, a middle school youth enrolled in the program. Queried as to what he wished others knew about him, Eric replied that he wished his family could appreciate how he viewed himself as a reader: "I would tell 'em that I really like to read. I might not show it sometimes when I'm playing video games a lot. But I really do read, like for 30 minutes, about an hour sometimes." In identifying himself as a reader, according to Holland, Lachicotte, Skinner, and Cain (1998), Eric is well on his way to becoming the type of reader he wants other people to see in him. As Holland and her colleagues have so aptly reminded us, "People tell others who they are, but even more important, they tell themselves and then try to act as though they are who they say they are" (p. 3).

But what about others for whom reading is so challenging that they have virtually given up? It is our contention that these are the young people, such as Tony, whose sense of self-efficacy as readers has been derailed to the point that they sit passively in class, unwilling to participate in activities for which they lack competence or perceive themselves ill prepared to tackle. It could be said that they are the products of a school and classroom culture that imposed and reinforced negative positionings of them as readers. For an up close look at how such positionings occur, we recommend reading a section of the second edition of *Reconceptualizing the Literacies in Adolescents' Lives* (Alvermann, Hinchman, Moore, Phelps, & Waff, 2006) titled "Positioning Youth as Readers and Writers." The chapter authors in this section (Moje & Dillon, 2006; Harper & Bean, 2006; Moore & Cunningham, 2006; Obidah & Marsh, 2006) depict a range of literate actions that youth take in their bid to be viewed by others as competent readers and writers in science classes, persuasive writing, and poetry. In each instance, these youth demonstrate an ability to identify with literacy practices that have some footing in, and are relevant to, their everyday lives. Add to this, O'Brien's (2003) finding that engagement with multimodal texts redefines adolescents' literate competence, and one can readily see the value of making connections between formal and informal learning opportunities.

Connecting Literacies That Span In-School and Out-of-School Learning

We use this section title advisedly for two reasons. First, implying that the literacies young people practice inside school are categorically different from those they practice on the outside makes little sense (Eakle & Alvermann, 2006). Second, dividing up engagement with texts, places, and spaces as if there were no relations among them is an approach that NCTE's 2003 position statement on composing with nonprint media finds objectionable, and with good reason we would add. What makes better sense to us, as Sutherland, Botzakis, Moje, and Alvermann (in press) have suggested elsewhere, is the need for teachers to listen to students for ideas on how to bridge the bogus divide between in-school and out-of-school literacy practices. Because the cultures and identity-making practices in which young people participate are overlapping and multidimensional (consider, for example, school, family, community, and popular cultures), they are potentially useful as conversational spaces in which teachers and students might explore ways of bridging the divide that now exists. That's the positive spin.

A less positive one is this: educators in the United States remain (at best) lukewarm to the idea of connecting students' so-called out-of-school literacies with in-school curricula. Why this is so, in our view, is largely explained by Dyson's (2003) notion of "the 'nothing' assumption—[that is] the decision to make no assumption that [young people] have any relevant knowledge" (p. 101), especially when it comes to knowing things that are pertinent to literacy learning outside an idealized, print-centric environment. At a time when reading a book on one's cell phone is possible (Kageyama, 2005), or when being sent to one's room is no longer viewed as a punishment but as an opportunity to engage with media of various kinds (Armas, 2005), the notion of an idealized, print-centric existence seems an anachronism. A holdover from earlier times, reading the printed word will survive and rightfully so, but it is quickly becoming just one among several other textual practices vying for young people's attention, as Heim (cited in Lankshear & Knobel, 2003) captures:

> The word now shares Web space with the image, and text appears inextricably tied to pictures. The pictures are dynamic, animated, and continually updated. The unprecedented speed and ease of digital production mounts photographs, movies, and video on the Web. Cyberspace becomes visualized data, and meaning arrives in spatial as well as in verbal expressions. (p. 170)

Ironically, visual literacy is largely ignored by today's advocates of "scientific" reading instruction and the Institution of Old Learning (IOL)—a tongue-in-cheek term coined by O'Brien and Bauer (2005) to denote the rigidity of certain historically situated practices and organizational structures in U.S. schools. Predating the No Child Left Behind Act (2001) and its stepchild, "scientific" reading instruction, by nearly a hundred years, the IOL attempts to fit new information communication technologies into its century-old rigid structures and practices. And when the IOL is successful in such attempts, students are quick to take note of discrepancies between what they are expected to do in school and what they do on their own outside of school.

For example, in a report titled *The Digital Disconnect: The Widening Gap between Internet-Savvy Students and Their Schools,* Levin and Arafeh (2002) found that "for the most part, students' educational use of the Internet occurs outside of the school day, outside of the school building, outside the direction of their teachers" (n. p.). They also found that students were disappointed in the quality of the homework assignments teachers made them do online. From the students' perspective, these assignments did not exploit the Web's capacity to teach and could just as well have been done by reading and responding to paper-copy encyclopedias. In the students' view, their own expertise and motivation in locating information on the Web and connecting it to school learning in ways that interested them were not being tapped.

Unfortunately, although it is easy to critique the IOL in relation to newer literacies and technologies, it is quite another matter to loosen its stranglehold on the mindset of U.S. educators at large. Yet, as teachers and teacher educators, we would argue that if we turn our backs on ideas that seem too far outside the IOL—especially ideas that challenge the status quo—we end up supporting a pedagogy that is one-sided, in which teaching in relation to learning is viewed as causative rather than contextual. Nearly a decade ago, Green (1998), using English education as an example, warned against just such a move for the following reasons:

> On the one hand, an important shift is underway from canonic forms and orders of knowledge, culture, and textuality to what can be called the realm of the techno-popular. In terms of English teaching, this means shifting from literature to media, and hence from literary culture to popular culture as the focus for curriculum practice. . . . On the other hand, new and different formations of subjectivity are arguably emerging among young people . . . as they are characteristically immersed in new intensities of media culture, the flow of images and information, and their associated forms of life. . . . Taken together, these aspects of difference represent significant challenges for educational theory and practice. (p. 180)

Although our various positionings as teachers and teacher educators undoubtedly inform our perceptions about how seriously we should (or should not) take Green's (1998) warning, one thing seems clear: we cannot afford to dismiss the importance of understanding and validating young people's literacy practices, especially those that span in- and out-of-school learning. Moreover, it is instructive to note that textual practices in popular literacies are not limited to decoding the printed word. From a new literacies perspective, the ability to analyze media messages presumes that one is at least visually (if not auditorily) literate. Becoming visually literate involves expanding print literacy skills by developing a greater awareness of how things come to have the meanings that they have and why those meanings vary from one individual to the next. As Muffoletto (2001) explained, "Being 'visually literate' means more than having the ability to produce/encode and read/decode constructed visual experiences; it . . . is to be actively engaged in asking questions and seeking answers about the multiple meanings of a visual experience" (n. p.).

Coexisting with Digital Natives

Referring to the youth of today as Digital Natives—that is, "native speakers" of the digital language of computers, video games, and the Internet—Prensky (2001) proceeded to contrast their several years of practice at parallel processing and multitasking to that of the rest of us so-called Digital Immigrants. According to Prensky, like all immigrants, Digital Immigrants retain to some degree their "accent"—their cultural footing in the past. Such "accents," he maintains, can include simple things, such as "turning to the Internet for information second rather than first, or reading the manual for a program rather than assuming that the program itself will teach us to use it" (n. p). But, more to the point, distinguishing between Digital Natives and Digital Immigrants is important for those of us in education for the following reasons:

> Digital Immigrants don't believe their students can learn successfully while watching TV or listening to music because they (the Immigrants) can't. Of course not—they didn't practice this skill constantly for all of their formative years. Digital Immigrants think learning can't (or shouldn't be) fun. Why should they—they didn't spend their formative years learning with *Sesame Street.*
>
> Unfortunately for our Digital Immigrant teachers, the people sitting in their classes grew up on the 'twitch speed' of video games and MTV. They are used to the instantaneity of hypertext, downloaded music, phones in their pockets, a library on their laptops, beamed messages, and instant messaging. They have little patience for lectures, step-by-step logic, and 'tell-test' instruction. (Prensky, 2001, n. p.)

The points are well taken but are not without a critique of our own. Whereas Prensky would have us create a divide between Immigrant Teachers and Digital Students, we would argue that binaries such as this one rarely serve either "side" well. Disjunctures between generational literacies are not new. In fact, in a thought-provoking chapter on how these disjunctures reflect larger technological and sociological forces that continue to change, Hagood, Stevens, and Reinking (2002) argue for moving beyond the confines of generational literacies, such as the current divide between Digital Natives and Digital Immigrants, toward a better understanding of what literacies do across generations. With this in mind, we turn to a similar argument made on behalf of restoring literacy to a "thing-status" (Brandt & Clinton, 2002).

A Caveat Worth Considering

In a seminal article titled "Limits of the Local: Expanding Perspectives on Literacy as a Social Practice," Brandt and Clinton (2002) claimed that challenges to the Great Divide, or autonomous model of literacy, had gone too far. According to them, in rejecting literacy as a deterministic force, critics of the autonomous model of literacy had overreacted to the point where the material, or real-world, dimensions of literacy were virtually shut out of consideration. To remedy this situation, Brandt and Clinton, drawing from the work of Latour (1993), proposed that we treat literacy not simply as an outcome of local practices but as "a thing"—an actor, a participant in those practices. In effect, they argued, "understanding what literacy is doing with people in a setting is as important as understanding what people are doing with literacy in a setting" (p. 337).

Street (2003), who himself had been one of the strongest critics of a deterministic view of literacy, responded to Brandt and Clinton's claim in this fashion:

> Policy makers . . . bringing the "light" of literacy to the "darkness" of the "illiterate," and educationalists . . . similarly arguing for the economic and social benefits of a narrowly defined and disciplined "literacy" can simply argue that all of those counterexamples of the complexity and meanings of literacy in people's everyday lives are not relevant to their agenda. Local, everyday, home literacies are seen within that frame as failed attempts at the real thing, as inferior versions of the "literacy" demanded by

the economy, by educational institutions, by the politics of cen-
tralizing and homogenizing tendencies. (pp. xi–xii)

Although Street's (2003) remarks might appear, on first inspec-
tion, to signal a retreat from the ideological model of literacy,
they are anything but that. Instead, as he goes on to point out in
his foreword to *Literacy and Literacies: Texts, Power, and Identity* (Collins & Blot, 2003), although the NLS movement "has
hit an impasse [on] how to account for the local whilst recognizing also the general—or the global" (p. xii), a way out is possible. The first step, he argues, is to consider carefully (as Collins
and Blot have done) the question, "What is a text?" (p. xiii).
Claiming that this question is especially relevant, given the ubiquitous nature of the new information communication technologies and the growing interest in multimodal representations, Street
concludes that texts, in and of themselves, should be the focus of
attention.

What this means for a chapter on the nature of literacies is
quite clear, at least to our way of thinking. We view it as a call to
explore the impact of texts of all kinds (visual, print, digital, sound,
multimodal, performance) on young people's identity-making
practices and, especially, on how texts mediate young people's
perceptions of themselves as literate beings. For example, as
teacher educators and researchers, we are interested in learning
whether or not students' use of multimodal texts and their perceptions of themselves as readers are inextricably tied to their
teachers' perceptions of "what counts as text" and "who is a
good reader." Do young people value reading against the grain—
sometimes described as reading the subtexts or "hidden" messages of texts that authors may have consciously or unconsciously
concealed? More to the point, have they been taught to read in
this manner, and, if so, do they recognize that texts of all kinds
(print, visual, aural, digital) position them in ways that produce
certain meanings and literate identities from the resources available within certain sociocultural contexts? Finally, and perhaps
most important, might the small but growing trend to do research *with* rather than exclusively *on* youth (Alvermann,
Marshall, McLean, & Kirk, in progress; Vadeboncoeur & Stevens,
2005) signal the field's openness to valuing adolescents' percep-

tions of themselves as readers and writers and the textual self-understandings that mediate those perceptions?

A Parting Thought

In retrospect, perhaps, as teachers, we have always been aware that people learn and come to know differently. What the new literacies perspective tends to highlight for us is the need to consider carefully the things we value differently. To our way of thinking, a new literacies perspective offers insights into a *new valuing* of adolescents as learners. It challenges us as teachers, teacher educators, and researchers to begin, in more formal ways, to validate multiple ways of knowing by thinking about what such knowing might look like and how it might be integrated into our instructional practices. It challenges us to question whose values are taken up and whose are sidelined, marginalized, and even unacknowledged in our schools and classrooms. By providing a framework in which to revisit earlier conceptions of the nature of literacy, a new literacies perspective has challenged our thinking about how learners make sense of the word and the world. We recognize that when we fail to take note of a schooled literacy practice that blocks opportunities for students to use their multiple ways of knowing meaningfully, with almost tacit agreement, we are instructing the Tonys of the world to push the texts of *their* literacies deep in the back pockets of their schooling experiences.

References

Alvermann, D. E., Hinchman, K. A., Moore, D. W., Phelps, S. F., & Waff, D. R. (Eds.). (2006). *Reconceptualizing the literacies in adolescents' lives* (2nd ed.). Mahwah, NJ: Erlbaum.

Alvermann, D. E., Jonas, S., Steele, A., & Washington, E. (2006). Introduction. In D. E. Alvermann, K. A. Hinchman, D. W. Moore, S. F. Phelps, & D. R. Waff (Eds.), *Reconceptualizing the literacies in adolescents' lives* (2nd ed., pp. xxi–xxxii). Mahwah, NJ: Erlbaum.

Alvermann, D. E., Marshall, J. D., McLean, C. A., & Kirk, D. (in progress). *Literacy practices in afterschool Web-based youth communities.* Grant funded by the Robert Bowne Foundation, New York City.

Armas, G. C. (2005, March 10). "Go to your room!" sends many kids to multimedia hub. *The Seattle Times.* Retrieved March 20, 2005, from http://archives.seattletimes.nwsource.com/cgi-bin/texis.cgi/web/vortex/display?slug=mediakids10&date=20050310 &query=Armas

Barton, D., Hamilton, M., & Ivanič, R. (Eds.). (2000). *Situated literacies: Reading and writing in context.* London: Routledge.

Brandt, D., & Clinton, K. (2002). Limits of the local: Expanding perspectives on literacy as a social practice. *Journal of Literacy Research, 34,* 337–56.

Collins, J., & Blot, R. K. (2003). *Literacy and literacies: Texts, power, and identity.* Cambridge, UK: Cambridge University Press.

Cope, B., & Kalantzis, M. (2000). Introduction: Multiliteracies: The beginnings of an idea. In B. Cope & M. Kalantzis (Eds.), *Multiliteracies: Literacy learning and the design of social futures* (pp. 3–8). London: Routledge.

Dyson, A. H. (2003). Popular literacies and the "all" children: Rethinking literacy development for contemporary childhoods. *Language Arts, 81,* 100–109.

Eakle, A. J., & Alvermann, D. E. (2006, April). Dissolving learning boundaries: The doing, redoing, and undoing of school. Paper presented in an alternative format session organized by A. Cook-Sather & D. Thiessen titled "Amplifying student voices in educational research: Lessons from the *International handbook of student experience in elementary and secondary school.*" American Educational Research Association, San Francisco, April 8.

Freire, P., & Macedo, D. (1987). *Literacy: Reading the word and the world.* South Hadley, MA: Bergin & Garvey.

Gee, J. P. (1990). *Social linguistics and literacies: Ideology in discourses.* London: Falmer Press.

Goody, J. (1986). *The logic of writing and the organization of society.* Cambridge, UK: Cambridge University Press.

Goody, J., & Watt, I. (1963). The consequences of literacy. *Comparative Studies in Society and History, 5*(3), 304–45.

Green, B. (1998). Teaching for difference: Learning theory and post-critical pedagogy. In D. Buckingham (Ed.), *Teaching popular culture: Beyond radical pedagogy* (pp. 177–97). London: UCL Press.

Hagood, M. C. (2003). New media and online literacies: No age left behind. *Reading Research Quarterly, 38,* 387–91.

Hagood, M. C., Stevens, L. P., & Reinking, D. (2002). What do THEY have to teach US? Talkin' 'cross generations! In D. E. Alvermann (Ed.), *Adolescents and literacies in a digital world* (pp. 68–83). New York: Peter Lang.

Harper, H. J., & Bean, T. W. (2006). Fallen angels: Finding adolescents and adolescent literacy in a renewed project of democratic citizenship. In D. E. Alvermann, K. A. Hinchman, D. W. Moore, S. F. Phelps, & D. R. Waff (Eds.), *Reconceptualizing the literacies in adolescents' lives* (2nd ed., pp. 147–60). Mahwah, NJ: Erlbaum.

Heath, S. B. (1983). *Ways with words: Language, life, and work in communities and classrooms.* Cambridge, UK: Cambridge University Press.

Heron-Hruby, A., Hagood, M. C., & Alvermann, D. E. (in press). Switching places and looking to adolescents for the practices that shape school literacies. *Reading and Writing Quarterly.*

Holland, D., Lachicotte, W., Jr., Skinner, D., & Cain, C. (1998). *Identity and agency in cultural worlds.* Cambridge, MA: Harvard University Press.

Kageyama, Y. (2005, March 19). Literature on the move. *The Post and Courier,* p. B9.

Kress, G. (1997). *Before writing: Rethinking the pathways to literacy.* London: Routledge.

Kress, G., & Street, B. V. (2006). Foreword. In K. Pahl & J. Rowsell (Eds.), *Travel notes from the new literacy studies: Instances of practice* (pp. vii–x). Clevedon, UK: Multilingual Matters.

Kress, G., & van Leeuwen, T. (1996). *Reading images: The grammar of visual design.* London: Routledge.

Lankshear, C., & Knobel, M. (2003). *New literacies: Changing knowledge and classroom learning.* Buckingham, UK: Open University Press.

Latour, B. (1993). *We have never been modern* (C. Porter, Trans.). Cambridge, MA: Harvard University Press.

Leu, D. J., Jr., Kinzer, C. K., Coiro, J. L., & Cammack, D. W. (2004). Toward a theory of new literacies emerging from the Internet and other information and communication technologies. In R. B. Ruddell & N. J. Unrau (Eds.), *Theoretical models and processes of reading* (5th ed., pp. 1570–1613). Newark, DE: International Reading Association.

Levin, D., & Arafeh, S. (2002, August 14). *The digital disconnect: The widening gap between Internet-savvy students and their schools.* Retrieved June 25, 2006, from http://www.pewinternet.org/pdfs/PIP_Schools_Internet_Report.pdf

Mahiri, J. (Ed.). (2004). *What they don't learn in school: Literacy in the lives of urban youth.* New York: Peter Lang.

McDermott, R., & Varenne, H. (1995). Culture as disability. *Anthropology and Education Quarterly, 26,* 324–48.

Moje, E. B., & Dillon, D. R. (2006). Adolescent identities as demanded by science classroom discourse communities. In D. E. Alvermann, K. A. Hinchman, D. W. Moore, S. F. Phelps, & D. R. Waff (Eds.), *Reconceptualizing the literacies in adolescents' lives* (2nd ed., pp. 85–106). Mahwah, NJ: Erlbaum.

Moore, D. W., & Cunningham, J. W. (2006). Adolescent agency and literacy. In D. E. Alvermann, K. A. Hinchman, D. W. Moore, S. F. Phelps, & D. R. Waff (Eds.), *Reconceptualizing the literacies in adolescents' lives* (2nd ed., pp. 129–46). Mahwah, NJ: Erlbaum.

Muffoletto, R. (2001, March). An inquiry into the nature of Uncle Joe's representation and meaning. *Reading Online, 4*(8). Retrieved February 25, 2003, from http://www.readingonline.org/newliteracies/lit_index.asp?HREF=/newliteracies/muffoletto/index.html

New London Group. (2000). A pedagogy of multiliteracies designing social futures. In B. Cope & M. Kalantzis (Eds.), *Multiliteracies: Literacy learning and the design of social futures* (pp. 9–37). London: Routledge.

No Child Left Behind Act of 2001 (Public Law 107-110). (2002). Retrieved June 25, 2006, from http://www.ed.gov/policy/elsec/leg/esea02/107-110.pdf

Obidah, J. E., & Marsh, T. E. J. (2006). Utilizing student's cultural capital in the teaching and learning process: "As if" learning communities and African American students' literate currency. In D. E. Alvermann, K. A. Hinchman, D. W. Moore, S. F. Phelps, & D. R. Waff (Eds.), *Reconceptualizing the literacies in adolescents' lives* (2nd ed., pp. 107–27). Mahwah, NJ: Erlbaum.

O'Brien, D. (2003, March). Juxtaposing traditional and intermedial literacies to redefine the competence of struggling adolescents. *Reading Online, 6*(7). Retrieved January 20, 2004, from http://www.readingonline.org/newliteracies/lit_index.asp?HREF=obrien2/

O'Brien, D. G., & Bauer, E. B. (2005). New literacies and the institution of old learning. *Reading Research Quarterly, 40,* 120–31.

Oldham, J. (2005). Literacy and media in secondary schools in the United Kingdom. In B. V. Street (Ed.), *Literacies across educational contexts: Mediating learning and teaching* (pp. 170–87). Philadelphia: Caslon.

Olson, D. R. (1994). *The world on paper: The conceptual and cognitive implications of writing and reading.* Cambridge, UK: Cambridge University Press.

Pahl, K., & Rowsell, J. (Eds.). (2006). *Travel notes from the new literacy studies: Instances of practice.* Clevedon, UK: Multilingual Matters.

Prensky, M. (2001). Digital natives, digital immigrants. *On the Horizon, 9*(5). Retrieved November 1, 2005, from http://www.marc prensky.com/writing/Prensky%20-%20Digital%20Natives, %20Digital%20Immigrants%20-%20Part1.pdf

Scribner, S., & Cole, M. (1981). *The psychology of literacy.* Cambridge, MA: Harvard University Press.

Street, B. V. (1984). *Literacy in theory and practice.* Cambridge, UK: Cambridge University Press.

Street, B. V. (1995). *Social literacies: Critical approaches to literacy in development, ethnography and education.* London: Longman.

Street, B. V. (2003). Foreword. In J. Collins & R. K. Blot, *Literacy and literacies: Texts, power, and identity* (pp. xi–xv). Cambridge, UK: Cambridge University Press.

Street, B. V. (Ed.). (2005). *Literacies across educational contexts: Mediating learning and teaching.* Philadelphia: Caslon.

Sutherland, L.A., Botzakis, S., Moje, E. B., & Alvermann, D.E. (in press). Drawing on youth cultures in content learning and literacy. In D. Lapp, J. Flood, & N. Farnan (Eds.), *Content area reading and learning: Instructional strategies* (2nd ed.). Englewood Cliffs, NJ: Prentice-Hall.

Vadeboncoeur, J. A., & Stevens, L. P. (Eds.). (2005). *Re/constructing "the adolescent": Sign, symbol, and body.* New York: Peter Lang.

New Literacy Learning Strategies for New Times

ROBERT J. TIERNEY
University of British Columbia

In an earlier edition of this volume, I wrote a chapter titled "Learning from Text." I now view that previous contribution to be inadequate. I am positing that it is not enough to be meaning-makers in traditional print environments; we need to prepare students to be meaning-makers in today's environments of multiple, digital-based literacies. I would suggest that my view resonates with the claims proffered by the New London Group (1996), Cope and Kalantzis (2000), the International Reading Association (2001), Lankshear and Knobel (2003), Leu (2000, 2005), Street (2003), and others, and more recently the claim made by Lewis and Fabos (2005):

> If we mourn the loss of print literacy as we think we once knew it, then we may find ourselves schooling young people in literacy practices that disregard the vitality of their literate lives and the needs they will have for their literate and social futures at home, at work, and in their communities. (p. 498)

My view is also in agreement with the argument made by Selfe and Hawisher (2004):

> If literacy educators continue to define literacy in terms of alphabetic practices only, in ways that ignore, exclude, or devalue new-media texts, they not only abdicate a professional responsibility to describe the ways in which humans are now communicating and making meaning, but they also run the risk of their curricu-

lum no longer holding relevance for students who are communicating in increasingly expansive networked environments. (p. 233)

With this perspective in mind, my goal in this chapter is to begin to unpack the nature of meaning-making to fit with changing views of literacy. In my view, to be literate means being able to participate in one's world rather than just being an observer of it. Being literate requires being able to make meanings while probing ideas, solving problems, or pursuing new understandings. Meaning-making also requires transacting with people and ideas—both face to face and virtually, by way of written words, audio, and images—in ways that embrace others as potential collaborators and audiences. Being literate involves engagement with the unedited and ever expanding world of ideas 24/7. Meaning-making through these multiple forms of literacies involves a rich and complex array of processes: researching, navigating, and integrating multilayered text, images, and sounds; linking together ideas and patterns; collaborating, considering, and evaluating the meanings that are constructed.

My views of literacy converge with what has been espoused by a number of individuals, including Allan Luke and Peter Freebody, who contributed to the notion of rich literacy tasks and the definition of literacy espoused in Australia for Queensland schools. Their literacy is defined as " . . . the flexible and sustainable mastery of a repertoire of practices with the texts of traditional and new communication technologies via spoken language, print, and multimedia" (Education Queensland, 2000, p. 9). My view converges with discussions of standards for literacy by groups such as the International Society for Literacy, which suggests that digital technologies "enable students to become: capable information technology users; information seekers, analyzers, and evaluators; problem solvers and decision makers; creative and effective users of production tools; communicators, collaborators, publishers, and producers; and, informed, responsible, and contributing citizens" (International Society for Technology in Education, 2002). My view of literacy is tied to meaning-making across a range of texts as readers and writers become involved in ongoing engagements, which are often akin to projects.

Considering These New Literacies

In a recent issue of *Time* magazine, Steven Johnson (2006) describes the youth generation as the *M generation* or *Multitasking generation*:

> Today's kids see the screen as an environment to be explored, inhabited, shared, and shaped. They're blogging. They're building their MySpace Pages. They're constructing elaborate fan sites for their favorite artists or TV shows. They're playing immensely complicated games, like Civilization IV—one of the most popular computer games in the world last autumn—in which players re-create the entire course of human economic and technological history. . . . The skills that they are developing are not trivial. They're learning to analyze complex systems with many interacting variables, to master new interfaces, to find and validate information in vast data bases, to build and maintain extensive social networks across both virtual and real-world environments, to adapt existing technologies to new uses. (p. 42)

In Johnson's view, young people engage with these as spaces for "discovery, for debate, for clarity, and for action" and "for social awakening" (p. 42).

In the same edition, *Time* magazine reporter Wallis (2006) describes an adolescent named Piers:

> Zooming in on Piers's screen gives a pretty good indication of what's on his hyperkinetic mind. OK, there's a Google Images window open, where he's chasing down pictures of Keira Knightley. Good ones get added to a snazzy Windows Media Player slide show that serves as his personal e-shrine to the actress. Several IM windows are also open, revealing some penetrating conversations as this one with a MySpace pal:
>
> MySPACER: suuuuuuup!!! (Translation: What's up?)
>
> PIERS: wat up dude
>
> MySPACER: nmu (Not much You?)
>
> PIERS: same
>
> Naturally iTunes is open, and Piers is blasting a mix of Queen, AC/DC, classic rock, and hip-hop. Somewhere on the screen

there's a Word file, in which Piers is writing an essay for English class. "I usually finish my homework at school," he explains to a visitor, "but if not, I pop a book open on my lap in my room, and while my computer is loading, I'll do a problem or write a sentence. Then, while mail is loading, I do more. I get it done a little bit at a time." (pp. 35–36)

Piers seems to operate across and within these tasks in a fashion that suggests a high degree of agility—an ability to switch from one task to another, enlisting various tools to construct the meanings and texts or projects that he is pursuing. His engagements are not solitary, but involve collaborative engagements (both virtual and face to face; both synchronized and asynchronized) with peers and others. Piers behaves as if he is in a physical space with others as he proceeds with his various activities. He is engaged in maneuvering across activities involving multiple texts (conversations with others, images, and material from Internet sites, etc.) as he uses a range of platforms to interact, develop, and present ideas in a fashion for which genre constructions have yet to be codified or prescribed. On Piers's MySpace site, it is evident that he is using a search engine to locate or relocate sites that contain learning objects that he can import into a space that represents his construction of an actor he admires.[1] It is as if he is creating an identity for himself from found objects (objets trouvés) on the Net, similar to a diary or a personal photo album.

Although school settings may not as yet be as well equipped with technology as in some home settings, we have seen the emergence of expectations that students will be able to access digital platforms and the Internet in the context of learning. Increasingly, teachers are developing a curriculum that integrates the acquisition and use of digital learning strategies with other learning goals. For instance, a class might pursue a project about the wars in Iraq and students might engage in explorations that delve into relevant histories, cultures, geography, and events en route to pulling together dramatizations, displays, media coverage, or documentaries. Such a project could proceed with or without digital access. However, with digital access, the Internet and its resources come into play, as well as the multimedia possibilities. Students who are studying great literary works can access background material, including items such as drafts of revisions by the author or commentary by experts. In mathematics, the teacher might use a range of digital tools to support problem-based learning. In science, tools to support documentation, data collection, analysis, or simulation could be used.

With digitally based technologies and other media, the collective nature, multilayering, and multiple dimensions give the user the opportunity to pursue multiple lines of thought or to entertain varying perspectives (Spiro, Coulson, Feltovich, & Anderson, 2004). Learning assumes the character of being a composite of multiple traverses of a topic. A student project can become a composite of media involving the development and capturing of conversations, observations, scanned images, video clips, or firsthand experiences. The explorations of a specific topic could involve a mix of conversations that are tied to readings, viewing films, or interacting firsthand with informants. Students can amass folders and files of reference materials and sources as vehicles for their own expressions, explorations, or presentations. Storyboarding templates allow the user to try out how images and text work together and complement one another.

It has been my experience that students, in conjunction with being able to explore the integrated use of various graphics (animation, video segments, scanned images, or various ways to depict data graphically), use various media as a way of achieving different perspectives on issues they might be exploring in physics, history, and other subjects. The students explore ways to integrate images with written text to achieve various takes and twists. I have found that the students often see and aspire to a kind of edginess that is "more inviting, dynamic, and open than regular text" (Tierney, Bond, & Bresler, 2006). Students are exploring their world with media that afford the enlistment of multiple symbol systems that create new ways of knowing (Lemke, 1998). As Siegel (1995) has suggested, these multimedia explorations have "a generative power that comes from juxtaposing different ways of knowing . . . as a way of positioning students as knowledge makers and reflective inquirers" (p. 473).

I would characterize meaning-making across and within multiliteracies in a fashion akin to using a multimedia palate. This palate includes projects that enlist one or more texts or other forms of representation (sound and image) linked in different ways during the development and constructions that are manifested. One might envision the multimedia palate to be somewhat equivalent to what is afforded by a combination of electronic and other tools that students can use to search, access, compile, link, inquire, compose, critique, chat, collaborate, document, represent, construct, or present. As learners use these new literacies, they are often engaged with teams of collaborators from the inception to the posting of their pursuits. Once their efforts are posted, they may find themselves receiving feedback locally from their fellow learners or from learners in remote locations who have been granted access to the posting. The feedback may involve critique, advice, or ongoing conversation.

The meaning-making through multiple literacies thus has a collective character. It is collective individually, in that meanings build on meanings for the individual. It is also collective in the sense that meanings are created socially, such as meanings that are positioned in relationship to the meanings of others—members of a group who themselves have different meanings. Meaning-making is collective and multilayered in ways that connect across spaces; and it is collective in respect to the perspectives and understandings that might be gleaned. Examined sociopolitically, these engagements with new literacies interface with emerging identities and ways of bridging between school and the students' lives—especially for disengaged learners (Hull & Zacher, 2004; Rogers and Schofield, 2005). These engagements are also seen as having clearer connections to the tools used in the workplace (Brandt, 2001).

The ideas themselves may assume a different character, depending on how they are positioned. Just as form and function have an interplay in architectured space, the form, patterning, or management of ideas has an impact on the meaning-making that occurs. When designing a text from multiple sources—when multiple layers are linked or traversed—one creates meanings that may be patterned or formed in various ways. Ideas may be linked into complex patterns that may range from stacks of texts and images sectioned off and posted within Web templates, ideas presented in a linear or temporal sequence, or a host of other patterns involving a complex embedding of texts and images and expectations for learners to choose what will be accessed or not. Students might enlist audio and video feeds of Martin Luther King, Jr.'s "I Have a Dream" speech and accompany it with images and statements that spur discussion on a range of issues from different perspectives. Or, as Al Gore has done in his presentations on global warming, images of ice shelves collapsing might be accompanied by graphs and commentary on the changes in temperature over time and projected into the future. Thus, students can choose their learning path and the texts, images, or sounds that they access or skip.

Whereas meaning-making processes may be the same regardless of the environment (e.g., goal setting, questioning, refinement of meaning, predicting, and connecting ideas), some differences arise in conjunction with working within these new digital environments. The search function is one such difference. With access to the Internet and within my own software, I can quickly search all of my documents and compile a listing of all references to a certain topic. In essence, I can compile a stack of materials that bear a relationship to a concept, which I can then examine historically or in a host of other ways. Indeed, even confined to my own computer files, the number of connections may be massive. If I choose to venture more widely and use a search engine (Yahoo, Google, etc.), I am likely to generate thousands of connections, depending on how I define the search. These connections (or worlds of other texts and images that link and inform meaning-making) are at my fingertips. The nature of these connections shifts with the searches employed, the libraries accessed, and the questions and strategies used, including the forward inferencing and organizing or compiling that may be enlisted.

For example, for some time, I have been interested in how the public might resist the accountability mandates of some of the U.S. testing initiatives. I read widely on court cases and the research on parent engagement at the same time as I was linked to a few resistance movements via email, listservs, etc. Some time ago, I encountered mention of strikes by students in Greece, which had occurred in opposition to some of the high school testing there. I searched some of my mainstays for news (*New York Times* online) but had little success. I tried some U.S.-based search engines, but, again, I was not overly successful. Via the Greek media, I was able to find some materials and then, by email with some Greek colleagues, I accessed some of the organizers and interviewed them. Together with a coauthor in Maryland and with some input from some of the parents in the United States, as well as some educators in Massachusetts and New Zealand, I began to draft an account that included links to my sources (newspaper articles and emails). The linking that I pursued across a range of sources went far beyond the intertextual links that have been characterized in the past to developing meanings from a varied range of multiple sources of information (e.g., articles, emails, conversations, images, and my own drafts). My meaning-making remained focused as I enlisted a range of searches and navigated a host of Internet structures. I was able to enlist search strategies successfully while employing a variety of search engines. Perhaps the key was setting my own goals and remaining flexible as I gathered together what I deemed pertinent.

Navigating the architecture of digital versus printed text may also be quite different. The multilayered nature of the meaning-making may represent a huge shift for learners. Most notably, as learners access individual Internet sites, they may be required to navigate across spaces. To do so may require skill in the use of certain tools (e.g., search engines) in the management of ideas and the self-regulation of their activities. Largely, the architecture of the Web and websites is tied to hypertext, which emerged in order to afford multiple ways to link ideas and move around textual space. Learners are faced with having to make more choices about what links they might pursue and which learning pathways they might shift to or from. Learners can become frustrated as they encounter difficulty keeping track of their pathways, determining whether or where there are links, and what link to follow for various purposes (Foltz, 1996; Tripp & Roby, 1990). In addition, they may have difficulty integrating the layers that they encounter across their emerging knowledge structures (Kinzer & Leander, 2003; Spiro, 2004). Digital navigation requires literacy learners to have an understanding of how to compose (read and write) across multiple sources.

What Might I Do to Prepare Learners for the New Literate Times?

My view of the work of teachers in preparing learners for today's forms of literacy is that we need new strategies for new times and a view of learners as inquirers, designers, and public intellectuals. I would posit that, in order to be successful, learners need to become inquirers with a tendency toward being proactive decision makers. Accordingly, I am struck by the need to rethink the notion of what it means to be a strategic reader and writer. Whereas most models of strategic readers and writers remain focused on reading or writing a single text, learners in new times are engaged in being strategic across a range of materials, including multiple texts, embedded pathways, digital media, and their integration or connections. Most models of strategic readers and writers emphasize mastery and independence, yet we see a need to emphasize inquiry-oriented learning, including the agency of the learner as navigator, designer, collaborator, and communicator.

More specifically, I see literate learners engaged in specific ways as they navigate multiple forms of digital literacies. When carrying out research, learners are involved in the following:

◆ Exploring possible areas of inquiry;

◆ Initiating inquiries, such as searching for the right questions to ask and for related materials;

◆ Developing searching strategies, such as digging around and across ideas, gathering materials, developing a plan, managing search engines across and within Internet sites and texts;

◆ Delving into hypotheses and suggesting questions, practicing forward thinking across digital layers;

◆ Inferencing in conjunction with navigating the architecture of multilayered and multimedia spaces for search purposes—using structural clues, links, and context clues;

◆ Gathering and organizing materials, including images;

◆ Weighing the significance of materials;

◆ Seeking input and feedback from others; and

◆ Considering links, gaps, and patterns—criss-crossing from multiple perspectives.

When carrying out development and design, learners are involved in the following practices:

◆ Making connections and developing clusters—looking for patterns;

◆ Developing composites from the collections;

◆ Navigating the architecture of multilayered and multimedia spaces for meaning-making purposes;

◆ Assigning significance to ideas and their representations;

◆ Integrating meanings from a range of sources;

◆ Entertaining possible frameworks and designs—collapsing or building cases, making arguments, generating meanings;

◆ Positioning and constructing self in relationship to the research and projects; and

◆ Self-regulating their meaning-making across and within a range of digital texts.

When conversing, critiquing, and disseminating their work, learners are involved in the following practices:

◆ Sharing or posting ideas, efforts, or projects and obtaining reactions and feedback;

◆ Engaging in ongoing conversations with others—both immediate and remotely located;

◆ Pursuing a voice as a public intellectual alongside others;

◆ Critiquing the ideas and design of ideas; and

◆ Reviewing their own meaning-making strategies.

Just as learners would be able to read and write (search, plan, design, link, compose, and share) as they make meanings and compose multifaceted projects, they also can engage in exchange with others near and far through websites, blogs, wikis, podcasts, chatrooms, listservs, photo galleries, electronic portfolios, etc. They have the tools for dissemination, conferencing, critique, and ongoing conversations in the course of their engagements as learners in re-architectured classrooms without fixed walls and the posting of queries, drafts, and projects to the wiki, blog, chatroom, listserv, or website.

The ramifications are enormous for the tools that we provide students. At a minimum, I suggest that students should have access to reading and writing tools that include hardware and software beyond word processing and data management. The tools should afford Internet access; resource management; multimedia integration; Web-construction or hypermedia-composing tools; tools to capture, organize, edit, and integrate images and sound; as well as tools to collaborate with others, spur conversations, and send and receive feedback online and face to face.

Although we hope that learners always operate with a form of wary consumerism, even when reading state-approved textbooks, the proliferation and ease with which ideas and images can be manufactured and distributed requires recognition that we may be dealing with unedited and raw meaning—synthetic compositions. It heightens the need for a more critical consideration of what we are exploring, compiling, or composing. Likewise, the ideas and compositions of the students can be exposed, and issues concerning the appropriateness of a posting need to be considered. We may want to afford students restricted access as they develop their compositions or engage with one another or themselves. Digital environments have the potential to support a range of collaborative engagements from the outset of the process of researching a project, through to the development of input on design and drafts, and to comments or "hits" by well-known and supportive colleagues, critics, and the public. Issues of intended use and audience quickly emerge as decision areas to be considered. Without fixed walls, we may need to be mindful of the kind of dissemination that is constructive versus destructive.

Finally, as students engage with these new literacies, we need to think anew about how to support and assess them. What practices might support the richness of the strategies and meaning-making with which the students engage? That is, how might we support the research, development, dissemination, and critique of the literacy learners? I would suggest that techniques should be developed and refined in the context of their literacy engagements and related conversations with students (Azevedo & Cromley, 2004; Johnson-Eilola, 1994; Kumbruck, 1998; Kymes, 2005). Teachers and students might move to a combination of approaches:

- The use of conferencing and think-alouds;

- Sharing and critique of digital spaces (websites, etc.);

- The use of digital working portfolios as depositories for students' plans, research materials, early drafts, various clips, etc.;

- Show-and-tell discussions stemming from sharing their projects and describing their process;

- Metaconversations about the genres encountered, the navigation and design of digital spaces; and

- Self-assessment that includes narratives and menu-like rubrics based on looking at their work through a variety of lenses, including the following:

  - Research, especially search approaches and goal refinement;

  - Development and design, especially material management and architecture of the project, perhaps focusing on links, use of media, and collaborations;

  - Dissemination, audience consideration, postings, and ongoing conversations; and

  - Self-critiques and conversations about what they pursued, what they learned, and how they improved their literacy range and expertise through their engagement with the project.

I recommend the use of dynamic and generative assessment tools, such as electronic portfolios and home pages, that can serve "as construction zones where plans, resources, and learning pursuits are housed, and as a space where products can be archived and critiqued" (Tierney & Rogers, 2004). Indeed, I see evaluation as ongoing conversations (Johnston, 2003). I recommend assessment approaches that emerge from, rather than supersede or constrain, classroom learning possibilities—conversations about plans, strategies, progress, and future directions.

Evaluating projects is not straightforward. I suggest that teachers and learners develop criteria and expectations that support the dynamic, creative, and even edgy work that students produce. Each project requires the development of somewhat unique criteria: students' uses of digital technologies and the range of new literacies needs to be evaluated in the context of everyday examples rather than exemplars, and we need to reflect on their work through a variety of lenses and criteria so that we can be attentive to what the new technologies and the students are teaching us.

In closing, being literate is no longer finding the right book or writing a set of papers in a particular genre to specification. It is not simply learning to master a set of skills such as decoding or comprehension or being able to retrieve certain information about characters and plots of narrative or informational texts. Being literate involves research and development as well as collaboration and community engagement. Being literate requires learners who are designers and public intellectuals.

The meaning-making construction zone of literacy learners is the equivalent of a television studio that can generate images from cameras, sound recordings, and scripts or can cut, edit, compile, and paste from a variety of sources. To get there, learners need to engage in a form of research and development that involves skill in defining and refining goals and in searching and selecting various documents, websites, and other sources for relevant material. Learners need skill in gathering relevant material and considering how it connects or is relevant to compositions from these searches. They need a sense of agency as they engage in research and design, as well as ongoing conversations that are complex, multilayered, virtual and face to face, global and local, identity-shaping and informing. Rather than the traditional triad of before, during, and after, a different array of strategies and skills receives emphasis as part of an engagement of multiple literacies associated with project-based ventures incorporating Web searches and other resources, multimedia and multilayered project development, and postings on the Internet for consumption and connections. Without suggesting a rigid sequence or discrete categories, I would propose an approach to meaning-making that views literacy learners as inquirers and public intellectuals engaged in ongoing and recursive research, development, design, dissemination, and discussion. This approach ensures that the new generation of digital architects continue to be empowered within the digital landscape and its cascading flow of information and ideas.

Note

1. Currently, there are the 100 million users of MySpace that exists under the corporate umbrella of NewsCorp with advertising rights managed by Google. *New York Times*, August 9, 2006, C1.

References

Azevedo, R., & Cromley, J. G. (2004). Does training on self-regulated learning facilitate students' learning with hypermedia? *Journal of Educational Psychology, 96*, 523–35.

Brandt, D. (2001). *Literacy in American lives*. Cambridge, UK: Cambridge University Press.

Cope, B., & Kalantzis, M. (Eds.). (2000). *Multiliteracies: Literacy learning and the design of social futures*. London: Routledge.

Education Queensland. (2000). *Literate futures: Report of the literacy review for Queensland state schools*. Retrieved May 1, 2007, from The State of Queensland, Department of Education website: http://education.qld.gov.au/curriculum/learning/literate-futures/pdfs/lf-review.pdf

Foltz, P. W. (1996). Comprehension, coherence, and strategies in hypertext and linear text. In J.-F. Rouet, J. J. Levonen, A. Dillon, & R. J. Spiro (Eds.), *Hypertext and cognition* (pp. 109–36). Mahwah, NJ: Erlbaum.

Hull, G., & Zacher, J. (2004, Winter/Spring). What is after-school worth? Developing literacy and identity out of school. *Voices in urban education, 3*. Retrieved May 1, 2007, from http://www.annenberg institute.org/VUE/spring04/Hull.html

International Reading Association. (2001). *Integrating literacy and technology in the curriculum: A position statement of the International Reading Association.* Newark, DE: Author.

International Society for Technology in Education. (2002). *National educational technology standards for teachers: Preparing teachers to use technology.* Eugene, OR: Author.

Johnson, S. (2006, March 27). Don't fear the digital. *Time, 167,* 56.

Johnson-Eilola, J. (1994). Reading and writing in hypertext: Vertigo and euphoria. In C. L. Selfe & S. Hilligoss (Eds.), *Literacy and computers: The complications of teaching and learning with technology* (pp. 195–219). New York: Modern Language Association.

Johnston, P. (2003). Assessment conversations. *The Reading Teacher, 57,* 90–92.

Kinzer, C. K., & Leander, K. M. (2003). Technology and the language arts: Implications of an expanded definition of literacy. In J. Flood, D. Lapp, J. R. Squire, & J. M. Jensen (Eds.), Handbook of research on teaching the English language arts (2nd ed., pp. 546–65). Mahwah, NJ: Erlbaum.

Kumbruck, C. (1998). Hypertext reading: Novice vs. expert reading. *Journal of Research in Reading, 21,* 160–72.

Kymes, A. (2005). Teaching online comprehension strategies using think-alouds. *Journal of Adolescent & Adult Literacy, 48,* 492–500.

Lankshear, C., & Knobel, M. (2003). *New literacies: Changing knowledge and classroom learning.* Buckingham, UK: Open University Press.

Lemke, J. L. (1998). Metamedia literacy: Transforming meanings and media. In D. Reinking, M. C. McKenna, L. D. Labbo, & R. D. Kieffer (Eds.), *Handbook of literacy and technology: Transformations in a post-typographic world.* (pp. 283–301). Mahwah, NJ: Erlbaum.

Leu, D. J., Jr. (2000). Literacy and technology: Deictic consequences for literacy education in an information age. In M. L. Kamil, P. B. Mosenthal, P. D. Pearson, & R. Barr (Eds.), *Handbook of reading research* (Vol. 3, pp. 743–70). Mahwah, NJ: Erlbaum.

Leu, D. J. (2005, November). *New literacies, reading research, and the challenges of change: A deictic perspective of our research worlds.* Presidential address presented at the meeting of the National Reading Conference, Miami, FL.

Lewis, C., & Fabos, B. (2005). Instant messaging, literacies, and social identities. *Reading Research Quarterly, 40,* 470–501.

New London Group. (1996). A pedagogy of multiliteracies: Designing social futures. *Harvard Educational Review, 66,* 60–92.

Rogers, T., & Schofield, A. (2005). Things thicker than words: Portraits of youth multiple literacies in an alternative secondary program. In J. Anderson, M. Kendrick, T. Rogers, & S. Smythe, (Eds.), *Portraits of literacy across families, communities, and schools: Intersections and tensions* (pp. 205–20). Mahwah, NJ: Erlbaum.

Selfe, C. L., & Hawisher, G. E. (2004). *Literate lives in the information age: Narratives of literacy from the United States.* Mahwah, NJ: Erlbaum.

Siegel, M. (1995). More than words: The generative power of transmediation for learning. *Canadian Journal of Education, 20,* 455–75.

Spiro, R. J. (2004). Principled pluralism for adaptive flexibility in teaching and learning. In R. B. Ruddell & N. J. Unrau (Eds.), *Theoretical models and processes of reading* (5th ed., pp. 654–9). Newark, DE: International Reading Association.

Spiro, R. J., Coulson, R. L., Feltovich, P. J., & Anderson, D. K. (2004). Cognitive flexibility theory: Advanced knowledge acquisition in ill-structured domains. In R. B. Ruddell & N. J. Unrau (Eds.), *Theoretical models and processes of reading* (5th ed., pp. 640–53). Newark, DE: International Reading Association.

Street, B. (2003). What's "new" in new literacy studies? Critical approaches to literacy in theory and practice. *Current Issues in Comparative Education, 5,* 77–91.

Tierney, R. J., Bond, E., & Bresler, J. (2006). Examining literate lives as students engage with multiple literacies. *Theory into Practice, 45,* 359–67.

Tierney, R. J., & Rogers, T. (2004). Process/content/design/critique: Generative and dynamic evaluation in a digital world. *The Reading Teacher, 58,* 218–21.

Tripp, S. D., & Roby, W. (1990). Orientation and disorientation in a hypertext lexicon. *Journal of Computer-Based Instruction, 17,* 120–4.

Wallis, C. (2006, March 27). The multitasking generation. *Time, 167,* 48–55.

What Is New about the New Literacies of Online Reading Comprehension?

DONALD J. LEU, LISA ZAWILINSKI, JILL CASTEK, MANJU BANERJEE,
BRIAN C. HOUSAND, YINGJIE LIU, AND MAUREEN O'NEIL
University of Connecticut

Change defines literacy (Coiro, 2003; Hartman, 2000; Leu, 2000; Rosenblatt, 1938). Our lives change in fundamental ways as we become literate, expanding access to information, communication, and action (Freire, 1972, 1985; LeVine, LeVine, & Schnell, 2001).

Because understanding change is at the core of what we do, it is ironic that our research community has largely ignored the extensive changes to literacy taking place in a digital, networked, multimodal, and multitasking world of information and communication. The nature of literacy is undergoing profound change, and we have little research or solid theory to inform our understanding of the consequences for classroom practice (Reinking, 1998).

New information and communication technologies (ICTs), such as the Internet (Leu, 2000), wikis (Thomas, in press), blogs (Mortensen, in press), search engines (Henry, 2006), instant messaging (Jacobs, in press; Lewis & Fabos, 2005), email (Tao & Reinking, 2000), online gaming worlds (Steinkuehler, in press) require new literacies and have become important new contexts for literacy, learning, and life (International ICT Literacy Panel, 2002). Few, if any, of these new literacies have found their way into the classroom (Cuban, 2001; Madden, Ford, Miller, & Levy, 2005). Indeed, many seem to be resisted overtly, by deliberate educational policies (Leu, 2006), or covertly, by educators who sometimes are not nearly as literate with the Internet as the students they teach (Chandler-Olcott & Mahar, 2003).

The irony of ignorance may be greatest in research on reading comprehension. Although we are beginning to establish extensive theoretical and research literatures on the reading comprehension of traditional texts to inform practice (Biancarosa & Snow, 2004; Kamil, Mosenthal, Pearson, & Barr, 2000; National Institute of Child and Human Development [NICHD], 2000; RAND Reading Study Group [RRSG], 2002), there is hardly any research on the nature of reading comprehension on the Internet or with other ICTs (Coiro & Dobler, 2007). The assumption appears to be that reading comprehension is fully isomorphic—offline and online.

Both speculation (Coiro, 2003; RRSG, 2002; International Reading Association [IRA], 2001) and emerging research (Coiro & Dobler, 2007; Coiro, 2007; Leu et al., 2005) suggest that this assumption is misplaced. As the RRSG (2002) concluded, ". . . accessing the Internet makes large demands on individuals' literacy skills; in some cases, this new technology requires readers to have novel literacy skills, and little is known about how to analyze or teach those skills" (p. 4).

We have failed, however, to provide the educational community with adequate research and theory on the new literacies of reading comprehension on the Internet (Coiro, 2003). That failure has important consequences for education in the twenty-first century, when learning is increasingly dependent on the ability to read and comprehend complex information at high levels (Alexander & Jetton, 2000; Bransford, Brown, & Cocking, 2000), and the Internet is now a central source of that information (Lyman & Varian, 2003). As a result of our collective failure, many students go unsupported in developing the new literacies of online reading comprehension in school (Castek, Leu, Coiro, Gort, Henry, & Lima, in press; Leu, 2006), especially those students who require our support the most—those who have access to the Internet at home the least.

What is new about these new literacies? The answer to this question is only beginning to emerge. We are hampered by a confusing series of overlapping constructs (Coiro, Knobel, Lankshear,

& Leu, in press), a limited body of research (Leu, 2006), and very few scholars who study the issue (Hartman, 2004). Moreover, the continuously changing nature of ICTs suggests that even newer literacies will be required from even newer technologies appearing tomorrow, next month, and next year (Leu, 2000). Thus, a complete understanding of new literacies may be a Sisyphean task, never fully attainable.

The Internet Is a Defining Technology for Literacy and Learning in the Twenty-First Century

We recently passed an important milestone in the history of literacy: in late 2005, the one-billionth individual started reading online (de Argaez, 2006; Internet World Stats: Usage and Population Statistics, n.d.). The rate of this growth has been exponential; most of it has taken place in the past five years (Global Reach, n.d.). In the history of literacy, no other technology for reading, writing, and communication has been adopted by so many people, in so many places, in so short a time.

Although the Internet fills important personal needs, much of the increase in Internet use has been driven by changes taking place in the workplace. Economic units have had to increase productivity in a globally competitive economy (Friedman, 2005). As a result, the world of work has recently undergone fundamental restructuring (Bruce, 1997; Drucker, 1994; Gilster, 1997; Mikulecky & Kirkley, 1998; New London Group, 2000).

Traditionally, industrial-age organizations were organized vertically. Decisions were made at the highest levels and then communicated to lower levels, where they were simply carried out without the need for much thought by bottom-tier employees. This wasted much of the intellectual capital within an organization, limiting productivity (New London Group, 2000).

With restructuring, workplaces have sought to achieve greater productivity by organizing themselves horizontally, empowering teams within lower levels of an organization to make important decisions related to their work (Mikulecky & Kirkley, 1998; New London Group, 2000). Members of these teams must identify important problems, locate useful information related to the problems they identify, critically analyze the information they find, synthesize this information to solve the problems, and then quickly communicate the solutions to others so that everyone within the horizontally structured organization is informed. By requiring all employees to use their ability to read, communicate, and solve problems, economic organizations have increased productivity, allowing some to flourish within intense global competition (Friedman, 2005).

Given these changes, it is no accident that the Internet has rapidly appeared in the workplace; it permits access to the information required to increase productivity (U.S. Department of Commerce, 2002). Of course, using the Internet to take full advantage of the intellectual capital of each employee has also altered the literacy demands of the workplace (Leu, Kinzer, Coiro, & Cammack, 2004; Mikulecky & Kirkley, 1998). Employers now seek individuals who know how to read, write, and communicate on the Internet to solve problems.

These changes are not insignificant. In just one year (August 2000 to September 2001), use of the Internet at work to read, write, and communicate increased by nearly 60 percent among all employed adults twenty-five years of age and older (U.S. Department of Commerce, 2002). Moreover, recent economic data demonstrate the extent to which this restructuring, Internet integration, and changes in literacy practices account for productivity gains during the past decade in the United States, Europe, and other nations (van Ark, Inklaar, & McGuckin, 2003; Matteucci, O'Mahony, Robinson, & Zwick, 2005).

The Internet has also quickly found its way into homes in the United States and other nations. In 2004, nearly 75 percent of all households in the United States had Internet access (Nielson/NetRatings, 2004). Usage is especially frequent among adolescents. Eighty-seven percent of all students between the ages of 12 and 17 in the United States report using the Internet, nearly 11,000,000 daily (Lenhart, Madden & Hitlin, 2005). Similar changes have occurred in other developed nations, some of which are far ahead of those in the United States. In Japan, for example, Bleha (2005) reports that 98 percent of all households have Internet access via broadband that is sixteen times faster than in the United States.

During the past decade, integration of the Internet into school settings has also been rapid. In 1994, only 3 percent of all K–12 classrooms in the United States had Internet access; today, 93 percent have access (Parsad & Jones, 2005). Of course, increasing Internet access does not necessarily mean that students are being taught the skills necessary to locate, read, and think critically about online information. Indeed, although there is nearly ubiquitous Internet access in U.S. classrooms, new technologies such as the Internet are not often integrated into instruction (Cuban, 2001; Madden et al., 2005).

It is clear that the Internet is this generation's defining technology for literacy and learning. It is also clear that classrooms have yet to take up Internet integration systematically, let alone instruction in the new literacies the Internet requires. In fact, those pioneering teachers who have led the way with Internet integration focus on the technology aspects of use, not seeing this as an instructional issue for literacy at all (Karchmer, 2001).

New Literacies, ICT Literacy, and Information Literacy as Contested Theoretical Space

Several research communities have begun to explore the changes to literacy created by new technologies and the social practices they engender. Scholars from disciplines such as cognitive science (Mayer, 2001), sociolinguistics (Cope & Kalantzis, 2003; Gee, 2003; Kress, 2003; Lemke, 1998), cultural anthropology (Markham, 1998; Street, 2003; Thomas, in press), and information science (Bilal, 2000; Hirsch, 1999) have identified changes to literacy as they study the consequences for their individual areas of study. As many new heuristics appear, informing this multidisciplinary work, a new perspective about the nature of literacy is beginning to emerge. This perspective, often referred to as "new literacies," is still in its initial stages, but it is clear to most that it will be a powerful one, redefining what it means to be literate in the twenty-first century (Lankshear & Knobel, 2003; Leu et al., 2004).

"New literacies" is highly contested space, however; the construct means many things to many people. To some, new literacies are new social practices (Street, 1995; 2003) that emerge with new technologies. Others see new literacies as important new strategies and dispositions, required by the Internet, that are essential for online reading comprehension, learning, and communication (Coiro, 2003; Leu et al., 2004). Yet others consider new literacies to be discourses (Gee, 2003) or new semiotic contexts (Kress, 2003; Lemke, 2002) made possible by new technologies. Still others see literacy as differentiating into multiliteracies (New London Group, 2000), or multimodal contexts (Hull & Schultz, 2002), or view new literacies as a construct that juxtaposes several of these orientations (Lankshear & Knobel, 2003). When these uses of *new literacies* are combined with an earlier use of the term by the New Literacies Study Group and with terms such as *ICT Literacy* (International ICT Literacy Panel, 2002) or *informational literacy* (Hirsch, 1999; Kuiper & Volman, in press; Webber & Johnson, 2000), the construct becomes even more challenging to understand. However, most would agree there are at least four defining characteristics of an emerging new literacies perspective.

First, new technologies for information and communication and new envisionments for their use require us to bring new potentials to literacy tasks that take place within these technologies. Although they may differ on which construct they use, each set of scholars would probably agree that the Internet and other new ICTs require new skills, strategies, and dispositions for their effective use.

Second, new literacies are central to full civic, economic, and personal participation in a globalized community. As a result, they become important to study so that we might provide a more appropriate education for all of our students.

Third, new literacies are deictic (Leu, 2000); they regularly change as defining technologies change. The new literacies of the Internet and other ICTs are not just new today; they will be newer tomorrow, even newer next week, and continuously renewed on a schedule that is limited only by our capacity to keep up. Of course, literacy has always changed as technologies for literacy have changed (Manguel, 1996). What is historically distinctive is that, by definition, the Internet permits the immediate, nearly universal, exchange of new technologies for literacy. With a single click, a new technology such as Wikipedia may be distributed to everyone who is online. Thus, what may be important in reading instruction and literacy education is not to teach any single set of new literacies, but rather to teach students how to learn continuously new literacies that will appear during their lifetime.

Finally, new literacies are multiple, multimodal, and multifaceted. Thus, they increase the complexity of analysis that seeks to understand them and benefit from analysis that brings multiple points of view to understand them (Labbo & Reinking, 1999). This may also suggest that the area is best studied within interdisciplinary teams, as questions become far too complex for the traditional, single-investigator model (Coiro, Knobel, Lankshear, & Leu, in press).

Toward an Understanding of the New Literacies of Online Comprehension

The lack of theory and research on the new literacies of online reading comprehension is surprising, given the increasing prevalence of the Internet in our lives. It suggests that our field assumes isomorphism between online and offline reading comprehension. Initial studies, now beginning to emerge, challenge this assumption. One study, among highly proficient sixth-grade students (Coiro & Dobler, 2007), found that online reading comprehension shared a number of similarities with offline reading comprehension—but also included a number of important differences. A second study (Leu et al., 2005) found no significant correlation, among seventh-grade students, between performance on a measure of offline reading comprehension and a measure of online reading comprehension for adolescents, using a blog to provide prompts and record responses (ORCA-Blog). The ORCA-Blog measure demonstrated good psychometric properties. These results also suggest that new skills and strategies may be required during online reading. A third study (Coiro, 2007), using a regression model, found that—although offline reading comprehension and prior knowledge contributed a significant amount of variance to the prediction of online reading comprehension—additional, significant variance was contributed by knowing students' ability in online reading comprehension. The results of this study are also consistent with the conclusion that new skills and strategies are required during online reading comprehension.

Additional research is now taking place on several, federally funded research grants in the United States. One of these, the Teaching Internet Comprehension to Adolescents (TICA) Project (Leu & Reinking, 2005), explores the skills and strategies that proficient online readers at the seventh-grade level report during online reading comprehension. The project website is available at http://www.newliteracies.uconn.edu/iesproject/.

The initial model of online reading comprehension informing this work (Leu et al., 2004) proposes preliminary answers to two questions essential to a theory of reading: What must students acquire to become proficient at online reading? How do students acquire these skills, strategies, and dispositions?

What Must Students Acquire to Become Proficient at Online Reading?

Models of comprehension have traditionally focused their attention on processing internal to the reader, describing major cognitive and linguistic sources of knowledge (metalinguistic, discourse, syntactic, vocabulary, decoding, etc.) and how each functions during comprehension processing. They have not always situated the reading process in the social practices, texts, or contexts that drive the reading act (Coiro, 2003; RRSG, 2002).

Recent work on online reading comprehension (e.g., Coiro & Dobler, 2007; Henry, 2005; Castek, Leu, Coiro, Kulikowich, Hartman, & Henry, 2006; Leu, Kinzer, Coiro, & Cammack, 2004; Leu & Reinking, 2005) expands on traditional comprehension models to include the purposes that drive online reading, the communicative outcomes of online reading, and the continuously changing nature of the skills, strategies, and dispositions that are required during online reading comprehension. This perspective views reading comprehension on the Internet as contextually situated in both purpose and process:

> The new literacies of the Internet and other ICT include the skills, strategies, and dispositions necessary to successfully use and adapt to the rapidly changing information and communication technologies and contexts that continuously emerge in our world and influence all areas of our personal and professional lives. These new literacies allow us to use the Internet and other ICT to identify important questions, locate information, critically evaluate the usefulness of that information, synthesize information to answer those questions, and then communicate the answers to others. (Leu, Kinzer, Coiro, & Cammack, 2004, p. 1570)

Within this perspective, new literacies of online reading comprehension are defined around five major functions: (1) identifying important questions; (2) locating information; (3) analyzing information; (4) synthesizing information; and (5) communicating information. These five functions contain the skills, strategies, and dispositions that are both distinctive to online reading comprehension and, at the same time, appear to overlap somewhat with offline reading comprehension. What is different from earlier models is that online reading comprehension is defined around the purpose, task, and context as well as the process that takes place in the mind of the reader. Readers read in order to find out answers to their questions on the Internet. Any model of online reading comprehension must begin with this basic observation.

IDENTIFYING IMPORTANT QUESTIONS

We read on the Internet in order to solve problems and answer questions that are both large (e.g., "How do we create a better climate for peace in the Middle East?") and small (e.g., "What is the best price for a flight from New York to Orlando on December 21?"). Indeed, the fact that online reading comprehension always begins with a question or problem may be an important source of the differences between online and offline reading. Recent work within traditional texts by Taboada and Guthrie (2006) suggests that reading initiated by a question or problem differs in important ways from reading that does not.

LOCATING INFORMATION

Because the Internet contains vast amounts of information, it requires new online reading comprehension skills and strategies to locate pertinent information (Henry, 2006). Thus, we include in our model of online reading comprehension the strategies that readers use with a search engine—strategies studied by scholars in information science and library and media studies (e.g., Bilal, 2000) and often included by library media specialists in their work on information literacy.

Our initial work has revealed at least four general types of reading skills associated with the location of information on the Internet: (1) knowing how to use a search engine to locate information; (2) reading search engine results; (3) reading a Web page to locate information that might be present there; and (4) making an inference about where information is located by selecting a link at one site to find information at another site. Often, these skills intersect. Each requires additional new comprehension strategies that become important while students are reading online.

The ability to locate information on the Internet is essential to online reading (International ICT Literacy Panel, 2002). Knowing what to look for and how to access task-relevant information on the Internet is not intuitive; it involves a complex set of skills for which many students are not always adequately prepared (Bilal, 2000; Nachmias & Gilad, 2002). Henry (2006) describes the location of information as an important "gatekeeper" skill that largely determines the effectiveness of online reading comprehension.

Perhaps the easiest way to observe the importance of these online reading comprehension skills is to observe adolescents reading the results page from a search engine such as Google. Most do not actually read the items on the results page. Instead, the majority use a simplistic "click and look" strategy. They begin at the top of the list, clicking on each result and quickly viewing the image at each Web page that appears to see if its visual appearance matches their needs (Guinee, Eagleton, & Hall, 2003; Henry, 2006). Indeed, they do not even appear to "read" any of the search result descriptions as they work their way down the list of search engine results. Knowing how to read search engine results often discriminates between good and poor online readers.

CRITICALLY EVALUATING INFORMATION

Critical analysis and evaluation are skills that we want all readers to acquire, for offline and online texts alike. Our work with more proficient online readers in urban and rural classrooms (Leu, 2006) shows that students are frequently fooled about the reliability of the information they locate, even when they know that they cannot trust information on the Internet. Despite telling investigators that one should not trust the information on the Internet, a majority of proficient online readers in this study thought that a spoof site, *Save the Pacific Northwest Tree Octopus* (http://zapatopi.net/treeoctopus/), provided reliable information.

Coiro (2007) has found at least five different types of evaluation that occur during online reading comprehension:

1. Evaluating understanding: Does it make sense to me?

2. Evaluating relevancy: Does it meet my needs?

3. Evaluating accuracy: Can I verify it with another reliable source?

4. Evaluating reliability: Can I trust it?

5. Evaluating bias: How does the author shape it?

Of course, each of these also takes place in offline environments. Some aspects of online evaluation, however, require new skills and strategies because of the new ways in which information is presented on the Internet.

For example, it is important to know how to evaluate search engine results in order to decide which website to visit first. Was the site created by an organization (.org), a company (.com), an academic institution or school (.edu), or by some other group or individual? After the decision about which site to investigate, critical evaluation continues. Where should I go to determine who is the author? What is his or her background? How does the author shape the information that he or she provides on the

Internet? Do any other sites corroborate this information? We want our students to become healthy skeptics as they ask these and many other questions while reading on the Internet. Analysis and evaluation become especially important online because anyone may publish anything on the Internet.

SYNTHESIZING INFORMATION

Although we have found synthesis to be a central component of online reading comprehension, we have also found it to be the most challenging one to study. Much of synthesis takes place in the mind of the reader. The process happens quickly and is not usually visible, so it is extremely difficult to observe in ways that provide visible patterns.

As they seek answers to questions and solve problems, online readers synthesize texts in at least two ways. First, of course, they synthesize the meaning of the texts, as they do with offline texts, putting together an understanding of what they have read. In addition, however, online readers synthesize texts in a second way: they actively construct the texts that they read through the choices they make about which sites to visit, which links to follow, whom to communicate with, and whose messages to read as they seek answers to the questions that direct their online reading. No two readers construct the same physical text online, even though they may have the same question or problem to solve. Although choosing texts to read occurs offline, of course, it does not happen to nearly the same extent, with nearly the same speed, or with units of text that are nearly so short. Intertextuality (Hartman, 1995) defines online reading; far too often, it is merely a possibility offline in school classrooms. We are in need of much more work on the intertextual synthesis of meaning that occurs online.

COMMUNICATING INFORMATION

Many new communication tools become available on the Internet, each with its own affordances and each developing its own social practices. Thus, each tool requires its own set of strategies. Because reading and writing become fused in this fashion on the

Internet, we have included communication within our comprehension model. Email, instant messages, chats, blogs, wikis, discussion boards, and phone and video conferencing are just a few of the tools that individuals use to read and comprehend information on the Internet today.

How Do Students Acquire Skills, Strategies, and Dispositions for Online Reading Comprehension?

How to support students in acquiring the new literacies of online reading comprehension is also little understood. Several observations suggest, however, that these are likely to be acquired best through social exchange and construction rather than formal, direct instruction. Because literacy is deictic (Leu, 2000), no individual, such as a teacher, can keep up with the many new literacies that rapidly and continuously appear online. Instead, each of us has to depend on others to help us acquire the continuously updated literacies of online reading comprehension. One person may know a useful strategy with Google, but another may know an equally useful strategy to communicate information at a wiki.

In the past, instruction has been based on the assumption that teachers were always more literate than students. This assumption is no longer true. The odds that teachers are less literate than the collective knowledge that exists in a single classroom increase as these new literacies become multiple (New London Group, 2000). As ever newer literacies appear and fragment our literacy landscape, it should be increasingly expected that at least one student always knows more than any teacher about some aspect of online reading comprehension. New models of instruction need to take advantage of this intellectual capital that will be increasingly distributed around a classroom—the new literacies that students possess and that teachers may not.

This speculative analysis does not, of course, suggest that teachers will become less important in future classrooms. Indeed, just the opposite will be true. Teachers become more important, although their role changes, within new literacy classrooms. The more socially mediated learning aspects of online reading comprehension create more complex contexts that must be more thoughtfully orchestrated by teachers so that all of the students can bring their special insights about new literacies to the learning task.

Isomorphic and Nonisomorphic Examples of Offline and Online Reading Comprehension

What does online reading comprehension look like? In this section, we briefly describe the reading episodes of three seventh-grade students completing the same set of online reading tasks. To evaluate the extent to which online and offline reading comprehension are isomorphic, we compare their online performance with their levels of offline reading proficiency. To sustain an isomorphic hypothesis, students' online levels should match their offline levels.

The common set of tasks in these videos required students to read three blog entries, each of which contained a request for assistance in an attached Word document that needed to be downloaded. The first blog request asked students to locate two sites, given partial information about each, and post the URLs and the titles of these sites at the blog and then evaluate the two sites, according to a given set of criteria, and determine which one was better, explaining why. The second blog request asked students to locate a site on the Internet with an animated graphic that met several criteria, communicate the name and URL on the blog of the best animated graphic of the digestive system that they had located, and communicate how one should check the accuracy of information at an Internet site such as this one. The third blog request asked students to complete an activity similar to the second one, but to locate and evaluate the best animated graphic about the respiratory system. They were also asked to communicate additional ways to evaluate information on a site such as this for accuracy. You can view these videos of online reading at http://www.newliteracies.uconn.edu/reading.html. They show the complex ways in which elements of online reading intersect, revealing aspects of: question identification, location, evaluation, synthesis, and communication.

The Isomorphic Reading Hypothesis: Riko, a Student Displaying Proficiency in Both Offline and Online Reading

Riko is an example of a high-achieving offline reader who also is highly proficient with online reading comprehension. His example supports the prevailing assumption that online and offline reading are the same. This hypothesis predicts that high-achieving offline readers should also be high-achieving online readers and that low-achieving offline readers should also be low-achieving online readers. Subsequent cases raise questions about this belief.

OFFLINE READING LEVEL

Riko's science teacher reports that he is an outstanding offline reader, able to read and understand a challenging seventh-grade science text with little assistance from a teacher. This evaluation was sustained by his score on the reading portion of the Connecticut Mastery Test (CMT). Riko achieved a total raw score on the CMT of 305. This falls in the range characterized as "advanced." Riko is an excellent offline reader.

ONLINE READING LEVEL

In addition to doing well on the state reading assessment, Riko also did well on the ORCA-Blog assessment of online reading comprehension (Leu et al., 2005). Among eighty-nine students, Riko achieved the highest raw score, 30 out of 33. Viewing the video of Riko's online reading (on the site listed earlier in this chapter), you can see a high level of performance on a number of intersecting elements that are essential to online reading comprehension: locating, evaluating, and synthesizing information, as well as communicating.

While locating information, you see Riko try first to locate the Human Anatomy Online site using a search strategy commonly seen in lower performing online readers, that is, by simply typing in the name of the site he was asked to find plus the ending ".com." (He mistakenly types in www.humananatomy.com

but is blocked by the school filter to this location.) Then, however, he shifts to a search engine and quickly locates the site that was requested, *Human Anatomy Online* (http://www.innerbody.com/htm/body.html).

In terms of evaluation, the tasks in these videos tend to focus primarily on the evaluation of understanding, relevancy, and reliability. On each of these three aspects of evaluation, Riko performs well: he often rechecks his understanding of the document containing the request. He also evaluates sites for relevancy, and he communicates the strategies that he recommends to evaluate reliability.

In both synthesis and communication, Riko performs well. He correctly synthesizes information and clearly communicates it in his blog postings. This blog may be a new Internet context, but Riko appears to figure things out nicely, even when problems appear.

In short, this video shows that Riko is able to traverse effectively a complex set of informational windows and complete the reading tasks successfully. Riko's performance in online reading is what one would expect if online and offline reading were the same.

The Nonisomorphic Hypothesis: Tomas, a Low-Achieving Offline Reader but a High-Achieving Online Reader

Tomas provides an example you would not expect to find if online and offline reading were isomorphic. He is a very weak offline reader, being provided with supportive services as a student with a specific learning disability in reading. Surprisingly, however, he was among the top 15 percent of online readers in our sample.

OFFLINE READING LEVEL

Tomas's science teacher reports that he was a very weak offline reader; seventh-grade science books were too difficult for Tomas to read, even with significant instructional support. His below-level reading skills were a documented component of his specific learning disability. He received daily instructional support from a trained special educator, who worked closely with all of his teachers to develop modified assignments and provide simplified instructional materials. His score on the recent CMT sustained this evaluation. Tomas's total raw score of 167 fell in the range characterized as "below basic."

ONLINE READING LEVEL

Although Tomas performed poorly on the state reading assessment, he performed at a high level on the ORCA-Blog assessment of online reading comprehension. Among 89 students, Tomas achieved the tenth highest raw score, 22 out of 33. (As in all other assessment settings, Tomas was provided with additional time to complete the online assessment. He was given about 40 minutes instead of 30.) The video shows his successful performance on each of the three tasks, including slow, but very skilled patterns on a number of intersecting elements: locating and synthesizing information and communicating. Tomas did less well during the evaluation of information. (See Figure 3.1.)

Although Tomas is slow, it is immediately apparent that he makes strategic and thoughtful decisions while reading online. He carefully organizes multiple windows so that he can traverse quickly between the task description and the search engine. He also enters appropriate key words for each search. In addition, he reads each list of search engine results, usually selecting the correct site. He also knows how to copy and paste the URL for a site into the blog to communicate the location. He uses thoughtful online reading strategies to locate graphics for digestive and respiratory systems, although, perhaps because of a vocabulary issue, he may not have understood what the word *animated* meant. Tomas also figured out the skills required to use this blog. He downloaded each document and posted entries for each of the three tasks. His communication skills, with the exception of some spelling issues, seemed quite adequate.

Tomas's weakest area of online reading comprehension was critical evaluation. Note, for example, the final entry about evaluation that he posted on the blog: "I don't think it mater who

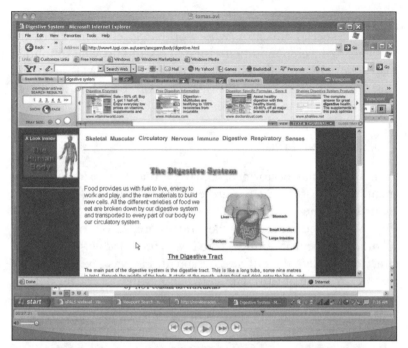

FIGURE 3.1. *A video recording of the online reading comprehension performance by the weakest reader among 89 seventh-grade students. This student was among the highest-achieving online readers. View this video at www.newliteracies.uconn.edu/reading.html.*

made the site aslong as it was good information and no aerver-tisment i don't think you need who made the site." Ignoring the spelling mistakes, we see that Tomas is somewhat naive and not fully aware of how people inevitably bias the information they provide to readers on the Internet.

Despite the more limited understanding of critical evalua-tion skills, this was not a performance one would expect from a student at a "below basic" level who requires instructional sup-port for any assignment in class using offline materials. It sug-gests that readers who struggle with offline materials may not struggle with online materials to the same extent, as long as they have the skills and strategies essential to online reading compre-hension.

The Nonisomorphic Hypothesis: Marcos, a High-Achieving Offline Reader but a Low-Achieving Online Reader

Marcos also provides an example you would not expect to find if online and offline reading were isomorphic. He is a high-achieving offline reader, but a surprisingly low-achieving online reader. His case also provides evidence of additional new reading comprehension skills required during online reading comprehension.

OFFLINE READING LEVEL

Marcos's science teacher reports that he is an outstanding offline reader, able to read independently and understand a challenging seventh-grade science text. His score on the CMT sustained this evaluation; Marcos's total raw score of 302 characterized him as "advanced." Marcos, like Riko, is an excellent offline reader.

ONLINE READING LEVEL

Marcos did not perform well on the ORCA-Blog assessment of online reading comprehension. Among 89 students, Marcos achieved a raw score of 7 out of 33, in the bottom quartile of all online reading comprehension scores.

Comparing Marcos's online performance to Tomas's reminds us of the classic story of the tortoise and the hare. Although Tomas read slowly, he outperformed Marcos with his steady pace because he knew effective strategies for completing the tasks. Tomas located information efficiently and completed all three tasks. Marcos, on the other hand, moved quickly among sites, taking short cuts that hurt his performance. Because he had a difficult time returning to sites he had visited and because he did not know how to copy and paste a URL, he made many errors and, ultimately, ran out of time, failing to complete the third task. Distracted by his inability to locate items, he failed to include the title of the sites in his answers. Finally, because he could not return to some of the sites, he appears to have made up some of his evaluation comments. It looks as though Marcos has some online reading skills but is missing other crucial ones. As a result, he ends up being inefficient during online reading.

What Do These Videos of Online Reading Comprehension Reveal?

These examples teach us several important lessons. First, they reveal that online reading comprehension is typically organized around several elements that often occur simultaneously or recursively. In each video, we see how online reading often begins with a question or a problem and contains elements of locating, evaluating, synthesizing, and communicating that define online reading comprehension.

Second, these examples also illustrate how online reading is, typically, the reading of informational texts, not the reading of narrative texts. The Internet is a major new source of information that can be used to solve problems and answer questions. Online reading comprehension is the comprehension of informational text for learning and discovery.

Third, we see how online reading comprehension appears to require skills, strategies, and dispositions that are likely to contain new elements not required during offline reading comprehension. Both types of reading may involve questions, location, evaluation, synthesis, and communication, but each type contains a somewhat different skill set because each depends on different technologies. A book requires the ability to use an index and a table of contents to locate information; the Internet requires the new skills that a search engine demands.

We also see how intertwined reading and writing become; online reading often has elements of communication that are simultaneous with comprehension. In online environments, we read while we write and we write while we read.

Finally, we see how one should not assume that offline reading and online reading are the same. If they were isomorphic, high-achieving offline readers would always be high-achieving online readers and vice versa. Indeed, the most striking aspect of these cases is that we find a low-achieving offline reader, one who has been formally identified because of reading difficulty, performing at a high level during online reading. This reader achieved scores in the upper quartile of all online readers, a somewhat surprising outcome. Conversely, we saw how one of the highest achieving offline readers was unable to perform the online reading task at the same level as this learning-disabled reader. Isomorphism does not exist between offline and online reading comprehension.

Issues for Research and Practice

This review of research helps us understand that the Internet has become a central context for reading and that—online—reading changes in important ways. It also tells us that far too little research has focused on the nature of online reading comprehension because we have often assumed it to be identical to offline reading comprehension.

The videos of online reading provide visible examples of what online reading looks like, a rich and complex mixture that typically begins with a question and includes locating, evaluating, synthesizing, and communicating, often in unique informational genres and with new online tools such as search engines, blogs, attachments, email, and others. Because online reading comprehension often begins with a question, new literacies are required to accomplish traditional aspects of reading during the comprehension process.

The examples also show us how we should not assume that low-achieving offline readers are necessarily low-achieving online readers or vice versa. To do so is likely to misjudge each student's potential and each student's instructional needs.

The mistaken assumption that online reading comprehension is the same as offline reading comprehension is unfortunate but common throughout the educational system. It is most visible, perhaps, in state reading assessments. Not a single state reading assessment measures students' ability to read search engine results; not a single state reading assessment measures students' ability to evaluate information critically that they read online; and not a single state reading assessment includes the reading of email messages, blogs, or wikis (Leu, Ataya, & Coiro, 2002).

This suggests that current policies, with their focus on testing skills and strategies required for offline reading, but not online reading comprehension, may be exacerbating the problem they seek to solve. Economically challenged school districts currently have little incentive to include online reading comprehension skills in the instructional program because they are under the greatest pressure to raise reading test scores on assessments that have nothing to do with online reading comprehension. As a result, many students go unsupported in developing the new literacies of online reading comprehension in school, especially those students who require support the most—those who have access to the Internet at home the least.

The failure to understand that online reading requires new skills and strategies is not limited to assessments, however. It is a systemic failure. We require teachers who are literate themselves with these new literacies, school leadership teams who understand why it is essential to integrate the Internet into literacy education, state reading and writing standards that include new literacies in their lists of essential skills, and reading and writing curricula that provide instructional support in how best to integrate new literacies into classroom lessons. To continue to ignore this systemic failure is to continue our failure to prepare students for new literacies of the twenty-first century.

What Should We Teach?

Although early work on the nature of the skills required to read and comprehend information online has established a broad outline of what is required, more research is needed to understand completely all of the skills and strategies essential to online reading comprehension. In addition, we need to recall that the rapidly changing nature of the Internet may make a complete taxonomy of these skills a Sisyphean task. Nevertheless, we know that online reading comprehension almost always begins with a question or a problem to solve, is usually limited to informational texts, and requires new skills and strategies to navigate the complex and rich informational space that defines the Internet. Initial research (Coiro, 2007; Coiro & Dobler, 2007; Henry, 2006; Leu, Kinzer, Coiro, & Cammack, 2004), as well as the examples we have presented in this chapter, suggests that new comprehension skills appear in five areas: developing an important question, locating information online, critically evaluating information that readers locate, synthesizing across texts to determine a likely answer, and communicating discoveries to others.

How Should We Teach These New Literacies of Online Reading Comprehension?

The answer to this question is not yet clear because so little research has been conducted to study online reading comprehension in classroom learning contexts. We do know that students at the seventh-grade level acquire online reading comprehension skills as rapidly from exchanging them in small groups as they do through more formal instructional lessons (Castek et al., 2006). This suggests that socially mediated experiences may be especially useful as instructional models are developed for teaching the new literacies of online reading comprehension. Thus, models such as Internet Workshop (Leu, 2002), Internet Project (Harris & Jones, 1999; Leu, 2001), Internet Inquiry (Leu, Leu, & Coiro, 2004), and Internet Reciprocal Teaching (Castek, 2006) may be important starting points. Clearly, however, we require an aggressive research agenda to explore fully the important efficacy issues in teaching the new literacies of online reading comprehension.

The Consequences of Change

This chapter has attempted to show how change is required in our conception of reading comprehension. New online reading comprehension skills and strategies will be required as, increasingly, our reading worlds move to the Internet. Traditional notions of reading comprehension, traditional methods of assessment, and traditional curricular materials will not be sufficient to prepare students adequately for the new literacies required online.

Perhaps the first and most important step is to recognize that changes in online reading comprehension take place on the Internet. Preliminary work (Coiro, 2007; Coiro & Dobler, 2007;

Henry, 2006; Leu, Kinzer, Coiro, & Cammack, 2004) supports this observation; the videos of online reading comprehension presented in this chapter illustrate it. Realizing that we need to reconsider the nature of reading comprehension on the Internet is not a minor accomplishment. From it, many other consequences of change are possible.

This would attract, for example, more researchers to study the issue, providing a more precise roadmap for instruction. It would also make it more likely that we thoughtfully include the new literacies of online reading comprehension within state reading assessments. Additionally, this would make possible greater access to online information. Understanding the nature of the issue would also make it possible to provide current classroom teachers with extensive professional development to enhance their own new literacies skills along with instruction in how best to integrate models such as Internet Workshop, Internet Project, Internet Inquiry, and Internet Reciprocal Teaching into their classroom curriculum. Also, teacher educators could prepare new teachers to understand more fully how best to integrate instruction in online reading comprehension instruction into all subject areas. Most important, however, is the possibility of realizing the goal that every teacher seeks—to ensure that all of our students are fully prepared in reading so that they might each fulfill their personal dreams and make our world a better place through their accomplishments.

Note

1. Portions of this material are based on work supported by the Institute for Education Sciences and the U.S. Department of Education under Award No. R305G050154, the North Central Regional Educational Lab/Learning Point Associates, and the Carnegie Corporation. Opinions expressed herein are solely those of the authors and do not necessarily represent the position of either the U.S. Department of Education, the North Central Regional Educational Lab, or the Carnegie Corporation.

References

Alexander, P. A., & Jetton, T. L. (2000). Learning from text: A multidimensional and developmental perspective. In M. L. Kamil, P. B. Mosenthal, P. D. Pearson, & R. Barr (Eds.), *Handbook of reading research* (Vol. 3, pp. 285–310). Mahwah, NJ: Erlbaum.

Biancarosa, G., & Snow, C. E. (2004). *Reading next—A vision for action and research in middle and high school literacy: A report to Carnegie Corporation of New York*. Retrieved November 2, 2004, from http://www.all4ed.org/publications/ReadingNext

Bilal, D. (2000). Children's use of the Yahooligans! Web search engine: Cognitive, physical, and affective behaviors on fact-based search tasks. *Journal of the American Society for Information Science, 51*, 646–65.

Bleha, T. (2005, May/June). Down to the wire. *Foreign Affairs*. Retrieved December 15, 2005, from http://www.foreignaffairs.org/20050501faessay84311/thomas-bleha/down-to-the-wire.html

Bransford, J. D., Brown, A. L., & Cocking, R. R. (Eds.). (2000). *How people learn: Brain, mind, experience, and school* (expanded ed.). Washington, DC: National Academy Press.

Bruce, B. C. (1997). Literacy technologies: What stance should we take? *Journal of Literacy Research, 29*, 289–309.

Castek, J. M. (2006, April). Adapting reciprocal teaching to the Internet using telecollaborative projects. In D. J. Leu & D. P. Reinking (Chairs), *Developing Internet reading comprehension strategies among adolescents at risk to become dropouts*. Symposium conducted at the meeting of the American Educational Research Association, San Francisco, CA.

Castek, J., Leu, D. J., Jr., Coiro, J., Gort, M., Henry, L. A., & Lima, C. (in press). Developing new literacies among multilingual learners in the elementary grades. In L. L. Parker (Ed.), *Technology-based learning environments for young English learners: Connections in and out of school*. Mahwah, NJ: Erlbaum.

Castek, J., Leu, D. J., Jr., Coiro, J., Kulikowich, J., Hartman, D., & Henry, L. A. (2006). *Exploring the effects of teaching the new literacies of online reading comprehension in a 7th grade science classroom: Literacy and learning with laptops*. Unpublished manuscript, University of Connecticut, Storrs.

Chandler-Olcott, K., & Mahar, D. (2003). "Tech-savviness" meets multiliteracies: Exploring adolescent girls' technology-mediated literacy practices. *Reading Research Quarterly, 38,* 356–85.

Coiro, J. (2003). Reading comprehension on the Internet: Expanding our understanding of reading comprehension to encompass new literacies. *The Reading Teacher, 56,* 458–64. Retrieved May 1, 2007, from *Reading Online*: http://www.readingonline.org/electronic/elec_index.asp?HREF=/electronic/rt/2-03_Column/index.html

Coiro, J. (2007). *Exploring changes to reading comprehension on the Internet: Paradoxes and possibilities for diverse adolescent readers.* Unpublished doctoral dissertation, University of Connecticut, Storrs.

Coiro, J., & Dobler, E. (2007). Exploring the online reading comprehension strategies used by sixth-grade skilled readers to search for and locate information on the Internet. *Reading Research Quarterly, 42,* 214–57.

Coiro, J., Knobel, M., Lankshear, C., & Leu, D. (Eds.). (in press). *Handbook of research on new literacies.* Mahwah, NJ: Erlbaum.

Cope, B., & Kalantzis, M. (2003). *Text-made text.* Melbourne, Australia: Common Ground.

Cuban, L. (2001). *Oversold and underused: Computers in the classroom.* Cambridge, MA: Harvard University Press.

de Argaez, E. (2006, January). One billion Internet users. *Internet world stats news, 14.* Retrieved February 1, 2006, from http://www.internetworldstats.com/pr/edi014.htm#3

Drucker, P. F. (1994, November). The age of social transformation. *Atlantic Monthly, 274,* 53–80.

Freire, P. (1976). *Cultural action for freedom.* Harmondsworth, UK: Penguin.

Freire, P. (1985). *Pedagogy of the oppressed.* Harmondsworth, UK: Penguin.

Friedman, T. L. (2005). *The world is flat: A brief history of the twenty-first century.* New York: Farrar, Straus and Giroux.

Gee, J. P. (2003). *What video games have to teach us about learning and literacy.* New York: Palgrave Macmillian.

Gilster, P. (1997). *Digital literacy.* New York: Wiley.

Global Reach. (n.d.) *Evolution of non-English-speaking online population.* Retrieved October 15, 2005, from http://global-reach.biz/globstats/evol.html

Guinee, K., Eagleton, M. B., & Hall, T. E. (2003). Adolescents' Internet search strategies: Drawing upon familiar cognitive paradigms when accessing electronic information sources. *Journal of Educational Computing Research, 29,* 363–74.

Harris, J. B., & Jones, G. (1999). A descriptive study of telementoring among students, subject matter experts, and teachers: Message flow and function patterns. *Journal of Research on Computing in Education, 32*(1), 36–53.

Hartman, D. (2004, December). *An analysis of the employment opportunities for reading, language arts, and literacy faculty in higher education during the 2003–2004 academic year.* Paper presented at the meeting of the National Reading Conference, San Antonio, TX.

Hartman, D. K. (1995). Eight readers reading: The intertextual links of proficient readers reading multiple passages. *Reading Research Quarterly, 30,* 520–61.

Hartman, D. K. (2000). What will be the influences of media on literacy in the next millennium? *Reading Research Quarterly, 35,* 280–2.

Henry, L. A. (2005, April). Information search strategies on the Internet: A critical component of new literacies. *Webology, 2*(1), Article 9. Retrieved May 3, 2007, from http://www.webology.ir/2005/v2n1/a9.html

Henry, L. A. (2006). SEARCHing for an answer: The critical role of new literacies while reading on the Internet. *The Reading Teacher, 59,* 614–27.

Hirsh, S. G. (1999). Children's relevance criteria and information seeking on electronic resources. *Journal of the American Society for Information Science, 50,* 1265–83.

Hull, G., & Schultz, K. (Eds.). (2002). *School's out! Bridging out-of-school literacies with classroom practice.* New York: Teachers College Press.

International ICT Literacy Panel. (2002, May). *Digital transformation: A framework for ICT literacy.* Retrieved May 1, 2007, from Educational Testing Service website: http://www.ets.org/Media/Tests/Information_and_Communication_Technology_Literacy/ictreport.pdf

International Reading Association. (2001). *Integrating literacy and technology in the curriculum: A position statement of the International Reading Association.* Newark, DE: Author.

Internet World Stats: Usage and Population Statistics. (n.d.). *Internet usage statistics: The big picture.* Retrieved October 25, 2005, from http://www.internetworldstats.com/stats.htm

Jacobs, G. E. (in press). People, purposes, and practices: Insights from cross-disciplinary research into instant messaging. In J. Coiro, M. Knobel, C. Lankshear, & D. Leu (Eds.), *Handbook of research on new literacies.* Mahwah, NJ: Erlbaum.

Kamil, M. L., Mosenthal, P. B., Pearson, P. D., & Barr, R. (Eds.) (2000). *Handbook of reading research* (Vol. 3). Mahwah, NJ: Erlbaum.

Karchmer, R. A. (2001). The journey ahead: Thirteen teachers report how the Internet influences literacy and literacy instruction in their K–12 classrooms. *Reading Research Quarterly, 36,* 442–66.

Kress, G. (2003). *Literacy in the new media age.* London: Routledge.

Kuiper, E., & Volman, M. (in press). The web as a source of information for students in K–12 education. In J. Coiro, M. Knobel, C. Lankshear, & D. Leu (Eds.), *Handbook of research on new literacies.* Mahwah, NJ: Erlbaum.

Labbo, L. D., & Reinking, D. (1999). Negotiating the multiple realities of technology in literacy research and instruction. *Reading Research Quarterly, 34,* 478–92.

Lankshear, C., & Knobel, M. (2003). *New literacies: Changing knowledge and classroom learning.* Buckingham, UK: Open University Press.

Lemke, J. L. (1998). Metamedia literacy: Transforming meanings and media. In D. Reinking, M. C. McKenna, L. D. Labbo, & R. D. Kieffer (Eds.), *Handbook of literacy and technology: Transformations in a post-typographic world* (pp. 283–301). Mahwah, NJ: Erlbaum.

Lemke, J. L. (2002). Travels in hypermodality. *Visual Communication, 1,* 299–325.

Lenhart, A., Madden, M., & Hitlin, P. (2005, July 27). *Teens and Technology: Youth are leading the transition to a fully wired and mobile nation.* Retrieved April 15, 2006, from http://www.pewinternet.org/pdfs/PIP_Teens_Tech_July2005web.pdf

Leu, D. J., Jr. (2000). Literacy and technology: Deictic consequences for literacy education in an information age. In M. L. Kamil, P. B. Mosenthal, P. D. Pearson, & R. Barr (Eds.), *Handbook of reading research* (Vol. 3, pp. 743–70). Mahwah, NJ: Erlbaum.

Leu, D. J., Jr. (2001). Internet project: Preparing students for new literacies in a global village. *The Reading Teacher, 54,* 568–72.

Leu, D. J., Jr. (2002). Internet workshop: Making time for literacy. *The Reading Teacher, 55,* 466–72.

Leu, D. J. (2006). New literacies, reading research, and the challenges of change: A deictic perspective. In J. V. Hoffman, D. L. Schallert, C. M. Fairbanks, J. Worthy, & B. Maloch (Eds.), *55th Yearbook of the National Reading Conference.* (pp. 1–20). Oak Creek, WI: National Reading Conference.

Leu, D. J., Ataya, R., & Coiro, J. (2002, December). *Assessing assessment strategies among the 50 states: Evaluating the literacies of our past or our future?* Paper presented at the meeting of the National Reading Conference, Miami, FL.

Leu, D. J., & Castek, J. (2006, April). *What skills and strategies are characteristic of accomplished adolescent users of the Internet?* In D. J. Leu & D. P. Reinking (Chairs), *Developing Internet reading comprehension strategies among adolescents at risk to become dropouts.* Symposium conducted at the meeting of the American Educational Research Association, San Francisco, CA.

Leu, D. J., Castek, J., Hartman, D. K., Coiro, J., Henry, L. A., Kulikowich, J. M., & Lyver, S. (2005). *Evaluating the development of scientific knowledge and new forms of reading comprehension during online learning* (Final report submitted to the North Central Regional Educational Laboratory/Learning Point Associates). Retrieved May 15, 2006, from http://www.newliteracies.uconn.edu/ncrel_files/FinalNCRELReport.pdf

Leu, D. J., Jr., Kinzer, C. K., Coiro, J. L., & Cammack, D. W. (2004). Toward a theory of new literacies emerging from the Internet and other information and communication technologies. In R. B. Ruddell & N. Unrau (Eds.), *Theoretical models and processes of reading* (5th ed., pp. 1570–1613). Newark, DE: International Reading Association. Retrieved October 15, 2005, from *Reading Online:* http://www.readingonline.org/newliteracies/lit_index.asp?HREF=/newliteracies/leu

Leu, D. J., Leu, D. D., & Coiro, J. (2004). *Teaching with the Internet K–12: New literacies for new times* (4th ed.). Norwood, MA: Christopher-Gordon.

Leu, D. J., & Reinking, D. (2005). *Developing Internet comprehension strategies among adolescent students at risk to become dropouts* (U.S. Department of Education, Institute of Education Sciences Research Grant). Retrieved June 20, 2006, from University of Connecticut, New Literacies Research Team website: http://www. newliteracies.uconn.edu/iesproject/index.html

LeVine, R. A., LeVine, S. E., & Schnell, B. (2001). "Improve the women": Mass schooling, female literacy, and worldwide social change. *Harvard Educational Review, 71,* 1–50.

Lewis, C., & Fabos, B. (2005). Instant messaging, literacies, and social identities. *Reading Research Quarterly, 40,* 470–501.

Lyman, P., & Varian, H. R. (2003). *How much information 2003?* Available from University of California, Berkeley, School of Information Management and Systems website: http://www.sims. berkeley.edu/ research/projects/how-much-info-2003/

Madden, A., Ford, N., Miller, D., & Levy, P. (2005). Using the Internet in teaching: The views of practitioners (A survey of the views of secondary school teachers in Sheffield, UK). *British Journal of Educational Technology, 36,* 255–80.

Manguel, A. (1996). *A history of reading.* New York: Viking.

Markham, A. N. (1998). *Life online: Researching real experience in virtual space.* Walnut Creek, CA: AltaMira Press.

Matteucci, N., O'Mahony, M., Robinson, C., & Zwick, T. (2005). Productivity, workplace performance and ICT: Industry and firm-level evidence for Europe and the US. *Scottish Journal of Political Economy 52,* 359–86.

Mayer, R. E. (2001). *Multimedia learning.* Cambridge, UK: Cambridge University Press.

Mikulecky, L., & Kirkley, J. R. (1998). Changing workplaces, changing classes: The new role of technology in workplace literacy. In D. Reinking, M. C. McKenna, L. D. Labbo, & R. D. Kieffer (Eds.), *Handbook of literacy and technology: Transformations in a posttypographic world* (pp. 303–20). Mahwah, NJ: Erlbaum.

Mortensen, T. E. (in press). Of a divided mind: Weblog literacy. In J. Coiro, M. Knobel, C. Lankshear, & D. Leu (Eds.), *Handbook of research on new literacies*. Mahwah, NJ: Erlbaum.

Nachmias, R., & Gilad, A. (2002). Needle in a hyperstack: Searching for information on the World Wide Web. *Journal of Research on Technology in Education, 34,* 475–86.

National Institute of Child Health and Human Development (NICHD). (2000). *Report of the National Reading Panel: Teaching children to read: An evidence-based assessment of the scientific research literature on reading and its implications for reading instruction* (NIH Publication No. 00-4769). Washington, DC: U.S. Government Printing Office.

New London Group. (2000). A pedagogy of multiliteracies designing social futures. In B. Cope & M. Kalantzis (Eds.), *Multiliteracies: Literacy learning and the design of social futures* (pp. 9–37). London: Routledge.

Nielsen//NetRatings. (2004). *Three out of four Americans have access to the Internet, according to Nielsen//NetRatings.* Retrieved March 18, 2004, from http://www.nielsen-netratings.com/pr/pr_040318.pdf

Parsad, B., & Jones, J. (2005). *Internet access in U.S. public schools and classrooms: 1994–2003* (NCES 2005–015).Washington, DC: U.S. Department of Education, National Center for Education Statistics. Retrieved October 15, 2005, from http://nces.ed.gov/pubs2005/2005015.pdf

RAND Reading Study Group [RRSG]. (2002). *Reading for understanding: Toward an R&D program in reading comprehension.* Santa Monica, CA: Rand.

Reinking, D. (1998). Introduction: Synthesizing technological transformations of literacy in a post-typographic world. In D. Reinking, M. C. McKenna, L. D. Labbo, & R. D. Kieffer (Eds.), *Handbook of literacy and technology: Transformations in a post-typographic world.* (pp. xi–xxx). Mahwah, NJ: Erlbaum.

Rosenblatt, L. M. (1938). *Literature as exploration.* New York: Appleton-Century.

Steinkuehler, C. A. (in press). Cognition and literacy in massively multiplayer online games. In J. Coiro, M. Knobel, C. Lankshear, & D. Leu (Eds.), *Handbook of research on new literacies.* Mahwah, NJ: Erlbaum.

Street, B. (2003). What's "new" in new literacy studies? Critical approaches to literacy in theory and practice. *Current Issues in Comparative Education, 5*, 77–91.

Street, B. V. (1995). *Social literacies: Critical approaches to literacy in development, ethnography and education.* London: Longman.

Taboada, A., & Guthrie, J. T. (2006). Contributions of student questioning and prior knowledge to construction of knowledge from reading information text. *Journal of Literacy Research, 38*, 1–35.

Tao, L., & Reinking, D. (2000). Issues in technology: E-mail and literacy education. *Reading and Writing Quarterly, 16*, 169–74.

Thomas, A. (in press). Cyberspace, cybercommunity, cyberculture, cybercitizenship. In J. Coiro, M. Knobel, C. Lankshear, & D. Leu (Eds.), *Handbook of research on new literacies.* Mahwah, NJ: Erlbaum.

U.S. Department of Commerce. (2002). *A nation online: How Americans are expanding their use of the Internet.* Washington, DC: Author.

van Ark, B., Inklaar, R., & McGuckin, R. H. (2003). ICT and productivity in Europe and the United States: Where do the differences come from? *CESifo Economic Studies, 49*, 295–318.

Webber, S., & Johnson, B. (2000). Conceptions of information literacy: New perspectives and implications. *Journal of Informational Science, 26*, 381–97.

Assessment of Adolescent Reading Proficiencies

RICHARD L. ALLINGTON
University of Tennessee

DANIELLE V. DENNIS
University of South Florida

We must begin by noting that much of the research on the assessment of reading proficiency has focused largely on elementary school students. Nonetheless, there is a substantive body of evidence on assessing adolescent reading proficiency, and we fully expect that that body of evidence will expand with the recent emphasis on adolescent literacy (Rothman, 2005). That said, we begin this chapter with a review of the evidence about adolescent reading proficiencies gathered in national and international assessment programs, programs that use large-scale standardized testing in an attempt to provide snapshots of how well adolescents read. Then we present the research on the most common sort of assessment of adolescent reading development, high-stakes testing with a focus on the impact of these reading assessments. In the third section, we discuss what we know about formal assessment of reading development in adolescence, as well as what we have yet to learn. The fourth section sketches what we know about instructionally useful assessments of reading development, especially assessments useful for planning and adapting instruction in the content areas.

Large-Scale Assessment of Reading Proficiencies

Two assessments of adolescent reading proficiencies, the Programme for International Student Assessment (PISA), conducted with an international pool of adolescents, and the National Assessment of Educational Progress (NAEP), conducted in the United States, have become high profile in the media, with the results from each commonly reported on the front page of newspapers and used in policy debates about the status, or adequacy, of adolescent achievement and what needs to be done.

In the most recent PISA assessments of reading proficiencies, U.S. adolescents have typically performed at or near the average level of performance of adolescents in the thirty or so other nations that have participated (National Center for Education Statistics [NCES], 2001). Of concern is the fact that elementary school students in the United States have historically performed at a much higher level than their peers in other countries, ranking among the world's better readers (NCES, 2002). Why the performance of U.S. adolescents ranks so much lower has become a key question for policymakers.

As for the NAEP, results from 2004 show no change in average reading performance of twelfth graders since the assessment was first administered in 1971 (285 was the average score for the reading scale in both 1971 and 2004). Across this period of more than thirty years, the twelfth grade scores rose a bit in the 1980s and began to slide downward in the early 1990s. During these same periods, middle school reading achievement has remained stable and the achievement of elementary school students has risen modestly. As with the PISA data, the NAEP findings have spurred a national debate about why the trends differ, especially in the most recent assessment periods. These data seem to be a major impetus for the recent initiatives focused on expanding funding for adolescent reading.

These large-scale assessments illustrate one use of standardized tests of reading proficiencies. In this case, results from these assessments perform a monitoring function that is used to depict the general status of reading proficiency across national boundaries and across time. The findings suggest that reading proficiencies of U.S. adolescents are no better—and no worse—

than those of the typical adolescent internationally and that the various initiatives to enhance reading proficiencies have had little in the way of longer term effects.

But these assessments offer no real information that explains these findings. Various hypotheses about adolescent reading proficiencies frame the several debates about what should be done. However, little is known about what the instructional problems of adolescents are, why reading growth slows between the elementary and adolescent years, or why adolescents read less than elementary students. Despite a lack of research and knowledge in these areas, middle and high schools are seeing an increase in the publication of "instructional interventions," as well as standardized assessments to measure student achievement. A major impact of these large-scale assessments of reading is that they have fostered even more assessment—assessments with penalties and rewards attached to them.

Impact of High-Stakes Testing of Reading Proficiencies

Amrein and Berliner (2003) note that policymakers assume that high-stakes testing will raise both student motivation and achievement. They studied eighteen states that use high-stakes testing to grant or withhold diplomas. The evidence demonstrated that such tests actually decrease student motivation and increase the proportion of students who leave school early. "Further, student achievement in 17 of the 18 high-stakes testing states has not improved on a range of other measures of reading proficiency, such as the National Assessment of Educational Progress (NAEP), despite higher scores on the states' own assessments" (p. 32). In a similar vein, Jacob (2001) reported as follows:

> Using data from the National Educational Longitudinal Survey, this analysis is able to control for prior student achievement and a variety of other student, school, and state characteristics. It was found that graduation tests have no significant impact on 12th grade math or reading achievement. . . . Although graduation tests have no appreciable effect on the probability of dropping out for the average student, they increase the probability of dropping out among the lowest ability students. (p. 99)

Both analyses strongly suggest that the act of mandating, as a graduation requirement, some level of reading proficiency—measured by performance on a group achievement test—has been largely impotent as a lever for improving adolescent reading development. We suggest that the impotence of such policies is also reflected in the NAEP twelfth-grade reading assessment. Mandating reading assessments for adolescents has been popular among state educational policymakers for a decade or so. But across this time, the NAEP reading performance of adolescents has remained stagnant, with a small downturn in performance on the most recent assessments (NCES, 2006).

The evidence that high-stakes testing seems to have had no effect on adolescent reading does not, in our minds, mean that we might expect such testing to be eliminated. In fact, federal policymakers seem intent on expanding such annual testing, now mandated for all students in grades 3–8, with a requirement that all adolescents be tested for reading proficiency annually. Early in his second term, President George W. Bush called for greater emphasis on student achievement in high schools. His plan required students to be tested in reading and mathematics in grades 9, 10, and 11. Accountability and testing made up 80 percent of the president's budget for improving high school achievement (Robelen, 2005).

If there is a silver lining to the high-stakes testing research, it is that federal and state policymakers seem to better understand that something beyond testing is needed to enhance the reading of adolescents (Biancarosa & Snow, 2004). Currently, a number of reading intervention studies, focused primarily on supporting struggling adolescent readers, have been funded in order to build a wider evidence base for how we might foster accelerated development of the reading proficiencies of adolescents whose development has lagged behind their peers.

Hargis (2006) used the data from the recent re-norming of the Peabody Individual Achievement Test (PIAT) to illustrate that the maximum score, grade level 12.9, is reached by some students in grade 6 but that, in addition, a quarter of the students in grade 9 are reading at or below the level for grade 7.

Figure 4.1 is adapted from Hargis's article and illustrates the range of reading achievement found in high schools across the

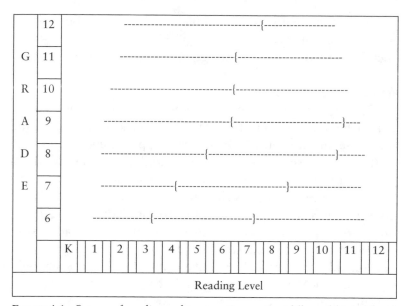

FIGURE **4.1.** *Range of reading achievement among middle and high school students (adapted from Hargis, 2006).*

United States. In the figure, the brackets indicate the range of reading achievement of the middle 50 percent of the students in each grade. To the left of the bracket is the range of scores for the 25 percent of the students who fall outside the middle range. To the right of the bracket is the range of reading achievement for the 25 percent of the students who performed above the middle range of students. The effects of high school dropouts can be seen in that, by grades 11 and 12, the range of low scores gets shorter. This simply reflects the fact that the lowest achieving readers are the most likely to leave school. Nationally, adolescents with reading achievement to the left of the bracket are twenty times as likely to drop out of school as those with achievement to the right of the bracket (Hargis, 2006).

There is no question that reading proficiency is critical to success in high school and in life. But testing, even high-stakes testing, offers no solution to the difficulties with reading development that some students have always experienced and will always experience. We agree with Afflerbach (2004) that ". . .

reading assessment must be conducted with the goal of helping students become better readers" (p. 370). Simply testing—and then labeling or penalizing struggling readers—fails to even begin to address the real issue: supporting and extending the development of reading proficiencies throughout the adolescent years.

It is not just a few adolescents who struggle with reading. Half of high school students read below grade level (because grade level is set at the average level of reading proficiency where half of the students score above that point and half below it). Many of the students who are successful in high school have not developed reading proficiencies that allow them to be successful in college. A recent analysis demonstrated that half of the students who took the ACT assessment as part of the college admission process demonstrated substantial weaknesses, especially in reading complex texts (ACT, 2006). Even more disturbing is that only 21 percent of African American adolescents met the standard of reading complex texts. This report recommends enhancing state reading standards for adolescents, noting that no state sets out the sorts of texts and tasks that high school students should be able to manage. It also recommends a substantial investment in providing all high school teachers with a two-year professional development experience focused on developing complex text-reading proficiencies in science, social studies, English, mathematics, and other content areas.

But it is not just complex text reading that seems problematic for adolescents. McCarthy and Kuh (2006) compared the results of two large surveys, one of high school students, the other of college students. They found that "high school students do not spend a lot of time preparing for their classes. Almost half (47%) of the seniors surveyed said that they spend three or fewer hours per week studying . . . [On the other hand,] half of the first year college students reported they spend more than 10 hours a week studying" (p. 666).

Even though high school students reported little studying, 80 percent reported they always or almost always came to class prepared, having completed assigned reading and other homework tasks. "So high school students in general feel that they are meeting expectations without devoting much time to preparation for class" (p. 666). But, evidently, little time outside of class is needed: nearly half of the students reporting fewer than three hours a week of study time earn mostly A's and B's. And 70 percent of those students reporting even four hours per week of study time report earning mostly A's and B's. It is worrisome that many students will likely carry these study habits on to college with them.

Especially worrisome is that, as McCarthy and Kuh (2006) suggest, only 20 of every 100 first-year high school students earn a four-year degree, even though almost 80 percent expect to. Much of the difficulty that students experience in college has to do with reading, especially preparation for the volume of reading expected in college. As far as reading volume, "Only 2 percent of high school students devoted 11 or more hours per week to assigned reading, approximately enough time to complete comparable book length readings [required in the first year of college]. Clearly, the reading required in college far exceeds what high school seniors do" (p. 667).

Although the high-stakes reading assessments have demonstrated fundamental flaws as tools for improving reading achievement, these standardized assessments might play a useful role in establishing the range of reading proficiencies that teachers are likely to encounter in their high school classrooms. Reading assessments of this nature, however, typically have little to offer as advice on the sorts of texts, or the types of reading tasks, or the volume of reading that would develop the reading proficiencies needed in higher education or in the workplace. In the next section, we provide more information on standardized reading assessments and how they might be used to inform instruction.

Assessing Reading Achievement in the Classroom

Two types of reading assessments may be used in classrooms. Standardized achievement tests, touted by policymakers, are generally norm-referenced, designed to compare an individual's performance to that of a group of students who are, presumably, like that individual (Salvia & Ysseldyke, 2004). Table 4.1 provides a list of commonly used norm-referenced assessments. A more instructionally informative approach includes diagnostic assessments—which provide teachers with information about a specific student, information which can then be used to develop instructional skills and strategies for that student. Both types of assessments are discussed in this section.

What Do We Know about Standardized Reading Assessments?

Standardized assessments are widely used in classrooms, especially in this era of accountability (Darling-Hammond, 2004; Elmore & Fuhrman, 2001; Linn, 2000). Furthermore, newly proposed federal mandates for high school reform include increased measures of standardized student assessment (Rothman, 2005). This increase, of course, is despite the research indicating that increased assessment of students does not produce increased achievement in literacy. Although these measures of student performance can provide information pertaining to growth over time,

TABLE 4.1. Commonly Used Norm-Referenced Reading Assessments (Harp, 2006)

Standardized Assessment	Levels Assessed
Gates-MacGinitie Reading Tests	PreK–Adult
Group Reading Assessment and Diagnostic Evaluation (GRADE)	PreK–Adult
Gray Oral Reading Tests-4 (GORT-4)	K–12
Peabody Individual Achievement Test (PIAT)	Grades K–12
Peabody Picture Vocabulary Test—III (PPVT-III)	Ages 2.5–90
Stanford Diagnostic Reading Test (SDRT)	End of Grade 1–First Semester of College
Test of Word Reading Efficiency (TOWRE)	K–Adult
Woodcock Reading Mastery Tests—Revised(WRMT-R)	K–College Senior

they do not indicate whether teachers are teaching or students are learning. Instead, they provide a snapshot of the entire learning experience.

The research on the effects of high-stakes testing (those that use test scores to make determinations about grade promotion and high school graduation) indicates that the increasing influence of standardized assessments has decreased teacher capacity and effectively "dumbed down" the teaching profession (Casbarro, 2005; Elmore & Fuhrman, 2001). Paris and McEvoy (2000) summarize the findings of five studies of high-stakes testing. This research indicates that many teachers distort their instructional practices and engage in questionable practices when preparing students for high-stakes tests. In other words, high-stakes reading assessments may not simply be unreliable and of low validity; in addition, their very presence may alter instruction in ways that cannot be defended with research or other evidence.

In a survey of teachers in high-stakes states, Abrams, Pedulla, and Madaus (2003) report that 76 percent of teachers surveyed, ". . . reported the state testing programs have led teachers to teach in ways that contradict notions of good educational practice" (p. 24). Over half of the high school students interviewed by Certo, Cauley, and Chafin (2003) noted that teachers' instructional strategies had changed based on the increase in standardized tests. The students felt that teachers were more concerned with breadth than depth and that even the best teachers had become less interesting. Both studies refer to an increase in worksheets and test practice, as well as a change of assessment practices that provide students with more testlike experiences. Furthermore, both studies suggest teachers had less time to work individually with students and that school morale had decreased since the inception of standardized testing programs.

As noted earlier, there is no evidence to support the claim that increased testing at the high school level has a positive impact on student achievement. Instead, high-stakes reading assessments decrease student motivation and increase retention-in-grade and dropout rates. Examples of these findings abound in Florida, Massachusetts, and, most recently, California. In Florida, students must pass the Florida Comprehensive Assessment Test (FCAT) in order to graduate from high school. Florida has the nation's lowest high school graduation rate, 56.8 percent, compared to the national average of 71.5 percent. In other words, students who do not pass this one test will not receive a diploma from a Florida high school, despite the fact the FCAT publishers, CTB/McGraw-Hill, warn against using these scores as the sole factor in making high-stakes decisions about students (Goldberg, 2005).

The Massachusetts Department of Education (2005) reported on high school dropouts from the 2003–2004 school year. Highlights from the report include a 13.6 percent increase in the number of dropouts from the previous year, which was linked to the implementation of the state's Massachusetts Comprehensive Assessment System (MCAS) graduation requirement. In both Florida and Massachusetts, the number of dropouts who are poor, African American, or Latino/Latina is disproportionately represented. In California, the woes of graduation exams are extending to the class of 2006, and nearly 100,000 seniors will potentially be denied the right to graduate, many despite otherwise successful school careers (California Department of Education, 2006).

What Do Standardized Reading Achievement Tests Tell Us about Students?

Standardized reading achievement tests provide several variations of scores. A ninth-grade student's reading performance could be reported as a rank; for example, the thirty-fifth percentile. This means that 65 percent of all ninth graders achieved higher scores than he or she did. So we know that this student doesn't seem to be a strong reader, but what else do we know about his or her reading skills? The performance might be reported as a grade equivalent, for example, a reading level of 7.2. What does that mean instructionally? It might be safe to assume that this student will have difficulty with a ninth-grade earth science text (if only because most science texts are written above grade level, often two or three levels above the grade in which they are being used). The student's performance could also be reported as a stanine, or as a standard score, and so on. None of these scores, however, tells us much about what sort of instruction this student needs. Is the poor reading performance linked to a limited vocabulary? Or is it linked to the fact that he or she has developed no effective use of the comprehension strategies necessary to be a successful adolescent reader? Perhaps this student has never developed strategies for decoding big words or simply was not motivated to work hard on the day that the test was given and thus completed only half of the items. In other words, there are multiple paths to achieving any reading score on any standardized reading test.

A closer look at two popular standardized assessments of reading provides a better sense of what is lacking in terms of instructional knowledge gained through the reporting of these assessments. The *Gates-MacGinitie Reading Test* (MacGinitie, MacGinitie, Maria, & Dreyer, 2000) is a group-administered, norm-referenced test designed to measure reading achievement and to be administered by the classroom teacher. Levels 3 through 10/12 of the *Gates-MacGinitie* are designed to assess vocabulary (determining meaning of words) and comprehension (literal understanding of the passage, as well as some use of drawing inferences) in grades 3 through 12. A Basic Service Report offers classroom teachers a glimpse at the ranking of students as compared to their peers, which is a component of the Building Averages Report that provides administrators with comparative information for the entire school. However, schools may opt to receive additional scoring information, which includes individual scoring reports and lexile reports for each student. These pieces of information may help the teacher in the creation of instructional groups and in measuring growth over time on the skills assessed by the *Gates-MacGinitie* (Harp, 2006). The score reports, however, do not provide teachers with information pertaining to the processes students use while negotiating the text on the assessment. Furthermore, this assessment does not provide content teachers with information about an individual student's ability to access relevant information from classroom resources or information about the types of resources and instructional methods that are appropriate for that student.

Another example of a widely used assessment is the *Woodcock Reading Mastery Tests–Revised* (WRMT-R) (Woodcock, 1998). This standardized reading assessment is normed for students from kindergarten to adults aged seventy-five. There are six subtests on the WRMT-R, including Visual-Auditory Learning, Letter Identification, Word Identification, Word Attack, Word Comprehension, and Passage Comprehension. Although the assessment is individually administered, rather than in a large group like the *Gates-MacGinitie*, it is recommended that only highly trained professionals give the WRMT-R to students. In addition, when given by an experienced administrator, the assessment takes 40 to 45 minutes. Teachers receive score sheets that include a catalog of descriptive statistics. What do all of these numbers tell teachers? Often, they learn nothing that they don't already know: John has trouble with reading grade-level materials. In other words, the WRMT-R reinforces for teachers that the students who struggle in class also struggle on standardized assessments. Those who do well in class often do well on standardized assessments. Professional educators are well aware of the struggling students in their classrooms. Instead of providing general descriptions, assessments should provide teachers with specific information regarding where learning breaks down for individual students. Teachers need assessments that provide instructionally informative results, not assessments that perpetuate a sense of defeat for both student and teacher.

Standardized assessments cannot provide reliable information on the appropriateness of different texts for different students. The test scores, or grade-equivalent scores, that these tests offer cannot be used to select texts of an appropriate level of difficulty. This is because of *standard error of measurement*. Each test score is a crude estimate of a student's reading proficiency: "crude" means that it is best considered a ballpark figure estimated as a range, usually of three to five years. Thus, a grade-equivalent score of 9.0 on a standardized reading test is best thought of as indicating that the student in question would likely be able to read texts with difficulty levels somewhere between grades 7 and 11. We might want to know about our students' reading proficiencies, but there are better ways to determine whether any given student will likely be able to read any particular text with understanding. We discuss such instructionally useful assessments in the next section.

Assumptions Underlying Standardized Reading Achievement Testing

Use of standardized reading tests is based on the assumption that the complex cognitive activity we call *reading* can be adequately evaluated in a single period, with a few short passages accompanied by multiple-choice questions. However, multiple studies challenge this assumption. One classic study by Pressley and Afflerbach (1995) demonstrated the complexity of cognitive activity, the thinking that occurs when proficient readers silently read texts on familiar and unfamiliar topics. Buly and Valencia (2002) conducted further assessments on students who had failed the state-mandated reading test. They found at least six different profiles (e.g., poor comprehension with good decoding, poor decoding with good comprehension, weak vocabulary with accurate reading, very limited decoding skills, slow or inefficient reading) in the poor readers they studied. In other words, although all of these students failed to meet state reading proficiency standards, they failed for many different reasons.

Several studies have reported substantial differences in adolescents' understanding of narrative and informational texts (Caldwell & Leslie, 2004; Saenz & Fuchs, 2002). These studies show that most adolescents found narratives—stories—easier to understand than informational materials such as those found in textbooks. This is a further indication that attempting to reduce "reading proficiency" to a single number is fraught with problems.

Another assumption is that the assessment is an accurate measure of what students are learning in school (Casbarro, 2005). In other words, when test results are reported to the public, the assumption is that the assessments are valid—that they measure what they are supposed to measure (Amrein & Berliner, 2003; Linn, 2000; Salvia & Ysseldyke, 2004). However, most standardized reading tests, including high-stakes state reading tests, measure only the most basic reading proficiencies. Far more emphasis is placed on reading shorter texts, with little emphasis on reading a complete story or news magazine article. Few of the tests have passages that might resemble the texts students are required to read in global studies, biology, mathematics, general agriculture, or French classes. In our view, the evidence available, especially in this era of multimedia texts, indicates that current assessments rate very low on the validity scale. The tests measure one kind of reading, but it is a kind of reading that is seldom observed either in or out of school (unless the school is focusing instruction on test preparation rather than focusing on state curriculum frameworks or student needs). Moje (2002) summarizes this problem quite cogently:

> I watch youth who seem unmotivated to read books in school devouring books out of school. . . . I listen to them comparing types of texts, and at times dismissing texts that progressive educators exhort teachers to offer. . . . Perhaps more important, I watch youth engaging in the skills that Guthrie and Metsala (1999) argued are necessary for high reading achievement: integrating information across multiple texts, relating textual meaning to personal experience, and composing complete messages in the form of stories and reports for actual audiences. And yet standardized assessments of youths' literacy skills suggest that youth struggle with these skills. Why is there such a disparity in what we observe youth doing in ethnographic studies with literacy outside of school, as they engage with particular kinds of texts, and what we observe them doing in formal, standardized, constrained literacy activities? (p. 220)

Instructionally Informative Reading Assessments

Diagnostic assessments acknowledge teachers as evaluation experts (Johnston, 1998). We are calling for a high school reform that develops teachers as experts of evaluation, resulting in improved teacher capacity (Elmore & Fuhrman, 2001) and, presumably, improved motivation and morale for both students and teachers. If the goal of high school reform is to better prepare students for entry into the world of the twenty-first century, we must provide them with authentic opportunities for learning and assessment. Most jobs do not require employees to fill in bubbles and answer decontextualized questions in a five-paragraph format. Therefore, high school reform must not lend itself to such practices. Instead, we offer a few methods for teachers to create classroom assessment plans that meet the needs of all learners, while providing instructionally informative results for classroom teachers.

Before teachers are able to begin instruction, they must first determine where their students are instructionally. Within schools, there is much talk about reading levels, but what does this really mean for teachers? For content area teachers, this typically means, "Can my students read the textbook provided for them?" Teachers can determine this in several ways. In this section, however, we address the informal reading inventory (IRI), cloze testing, silent reading and comprehension testing, and the think-aloud strategy.

An IRI is an "individual assessment that allows a teacher to determine the reading level, identify good reader behaviors, and determine individual progress" (Caldwell, 2002, p. 73). An IRI can be provided as a published instrument, such as the *Qualitative Reading Inventory* (Leslie & Caldwell, 2006), or as a teacher-made classroom assessment. Caldwell (2002) suggests that IRIs are most effective when familiar text is used. Thus, it is appropriate for teachers to use passages from the classroom text to assess their students' reading abilities.

Two components of the IRI process are used to provide teachers with information about accuracy and comprehension in word identification (Caldwell, 2002). Word identification scores are determined by counting the number of reading miscues, or errors, that students make while reading orally. The number of questions that students answer correctly, after reading a passage, determines comprehension scores. Although the word identification and comprehension levels may differ, teachers should take a total score to determine students' ability to access the classroom text. By taking the time to assess students from the onset, teachers will have a better understanding of the individual needs of students, because they are able to analyze where learning breaks down and work to provide instruction tailored to those needs. Additionally, IRIs demonstrate a component of students' achievements that is not measured through standardized assessments: their strengths. This allows teachers to build from what students know in order to provide instruction that closes the learning gaps of individual students. Therefore, they will be better able to provide alternative resources to students who need them. Teachers may complete IRIs periodically, throughout the year, to determine student growth and adjust instruction accordingly. IRIs may also be given as a group instrument, although Caldwell (2002) cautions that this may provide a less sensitive measure of students' ability.

Another method for assessing students' ability to access content area text is use of a cloze passage (Walker, 2000). In a cloze, teachers choose a 300-word passage from the classroom text or any other book they may use in the classroom. The teacher deletes 50 words from this passage (50 is easily converted to percentages) and replaces those words with blanks. While reading the passage, the student attempts to replace the blanks with appropriate words. According to Walker (2000), the passage fits the student's reading level if the student can accurately replace at least 40 percent of the blanks. This assessment can be administered to an entire class at once, but it should not be timed. For construction of a cloze test, the teacher chooses a passage that represents the classroom text but does not include references to illustrated information such as graphs or charts. Then the teacher retypes the passage, replacing every fifth word with a blank of equal length, being careful to not delete the first word of any sentence. Figure 4.2 provides an example of a cloze test.

To score the cloze test, teachers may use the following guidelines (Walker, 2000, p. 144).

1. Score only exact replacements as correct responses.

2. Convert the numeric score to a percentage by making a ratio of correct responses over the total number of blanks (27/50 = 54%).

3. Use the following criteria to determine whether the material is appropriate for the student:

   ◆ Independent Level – students can read and comprehend without assistance = 60 percent or higher

   ◆ Instructional Level – students can read and comprehend with assistance = 40 to 59 percent

   ◆ Frustration Level – students are unable to read the text = 39 percent or lower

During the battles in Sicily and mainland Italy the American and British war planners were deciding which was the best spot in northern France to land an invasion force that would be able to drive quickly into Germany. There _____ many challenges. The landing _____ had to be within _____ of protective Allied fighter _____ based in England. They _____ to be in an _____ where defense fortifications were _____ or incomplete. And, perhaps _____ of all, the invasion _____ to be where the _____ would least expect one. The _____ chosen was the shore _____ Normandy, France.

On June 6, 1944, _____ American and British armies _____. This landing was not _____ the biggest amphibious operation _____ history but the most _____ planned and practiced. In _____ for going ashore on _____, 170,000 soldiers, British and _____ and American, participated in _____ from January through May _____. Every one of them _____ what was expected of _____ and what he could _____ in the way of _____ resistance. They knew that _____ had erected defenses called _____ Atlantic Wall to stop _____. The Atlantic Wall consisted _____ reinforced concrete forts, trenches, _____, and anti-landing craft _____ of all kinds, and _____ was backed up by _____ divisions and was manned _____ battle-hardened Nazis.

The _____ soldiers were carried across _____ English Channel by ship _____ plane and were commanded _____ the best officers their _____ could produce. They would _____ supported by more than 5,000 _____, including four-engine bombers _____ all types of fighters, _____ 500-pound bombs or firing _____ or strafing with .50-caliber _____ guns, and by over 2,000 _____ ships firing cannon on the _____ positions.

FIGURE **4.2.** *Example of a cloze test from* The Good Fight *(2001) by Stephen E. Ambrose.*

Silent reading and comprehension, a component of the IRI process, is another option for teachers who are assessing their students to inform instruction. This assessment allows the teacher to determine whether or not the student is actively engaged with the text (Walker, 2000). Teachers choose a 300–400 word passage that represents the classroom text and ask students to read the text silently. Then, students are asked a series of questions about the text, including multiple-choice, fill-in-the-blank, and short-answer essay questions. Comprehension is measured by the percentage of questions answered correctly. According to Caldwell (2002), comprehension scoring should follow these guidelines for accuracy in answering questions:

Independent Level = 90 to 100 percent

Instructional Level = 70 to 89 percent

Frustration Level = less than 70 percent

Teachers interested in learning more about students' reading behaviors may also choose to ask a student to think aloud while reading the classroom text. According to Caldwell (2002), "Think-alouds are a reader's verbalizations in reaction to reading a selection" (p. 191). When provided with the text, a student is asked to think aloud about the process he or she uses to comprehend while reading (Caldwell & Leslie, 2004). This provides the teacher with information pertaining to the types of comprehension strategies the student does or does not use. These strategies may include reading for meaning, inferring, retelling, questioning, reacting, connecting prior knowledge, and noting mis/understanding (Caldwell, 2002). The think-aloud strategy must be modeled by teachers and practiced by students before it becomes an instructionally informative assessment tool.

Assessment is an ongoing process that provides the teacher with information pertaining to a student's current instructional level. In order for formative assessment to be useful, the information gathered from students must be used to inform instruction. Thus, teachers need access to materials other than the classroom text—materials from which students at varying levels can access content information. Assessment should represent a longitudinal record of student learning (Daniels, Bizar, & Zemelman, 2001). Teachers can accomplish this by using portfolios to demonstrate growth over time and rubrics generated by the students to demonstrate competencies on standards.

Final Thoughts

The evidence available suggests that we must expand our efforts to help students meet the literacy demands of an ever changing society. That evidence also indicates that implementing more high-stakes testing is not likely to aid in this effort. Unless assessment leads to instructional interventions that improve reading and content learning, there appears to be no reason to allocate time and money to assessment activity. Too much money has been spent on testing programs that do not provide teachers with the information necessary to meet the needs of all students. There must be a redirection of funds to activities that develop the expertise of teachers in using instructionally informative assessments to adapt instruction to better meet the needs of the students they teach.

References

Abrams, L. M., Pedulla, J. J., & Madaus, G. F. (2003). Views from the classroom: Teachers' opinions of statewide testing programs. *Theory into Practice, 42,* 18–29.

ACT. (2006). *Reading between the lines: What the ACT reveals about college readiness in reading.* Iowa City, IA: Author.

Afflerbach, P. (2004). Assessing adolescent reading. In T. L. Jetton & J. A. Dole (Eds.), *Adolescent literacy research and practice* (pp. 369–91). New York: Guilford Press.

Ambrose, S. E. (2001). *The good fight: How World War II was won.* New York: Atheneum.

Amrein, A. L., & Berliner, D. C. (2003). The effects of high-stakes testing on student motivation and learning. *Educational Leadership, 60*(5), 32–38.

Biancarosa, G., & Snow, C. E. (2004). *Reading next—A vision for action and research in middle and high school literacy: A report to Carnegie Corporation of New York.* Washington, DC: Alliance for Excellent Education.

Buly, M. R., & Valencia, S. W. (2002). Below the bar: Profiles of students who fail state reading assessments. *Educational Evaluation and Policy Analysis, 24,* 219–39.

Caldwell, J., & Leslie, L. (2003–2004). Does proficiency in middle school reading assure proficiency in high school reading? The possible role of think-alouds. *Journal of Adolescent & Adult Literacy, 47,* 324–335.

Caldwell, J. S. (2002). *Reading assessment: A primer for teachers and tutors.* New York: Guilford Press.

California Department of Education. (2006). *High school graduation requirements.* Retrieved July 10, 2006, from http://www.cde.ca.gov/ci/gs/hs/hsgrgen.asp

Casbarro, J. (2005). The politics of high-stakes testing. *The Education Digest, 70*(6), 20–23.

Certo, J. L., Cauley, K. M., & Chafin, C. (2003). Students' perspectives on their high school experience. *Adolescence, 38,* 705–24.

Daniels, H., Bizar, M., & Zemelman, S. (2001). *Rethinking high school: Best practice in teaching, learning, and leadership.* Portsmouth, NH: Heinemann.

Darling-Hammond, L. (2004). Standards, accountability, and school reform. *Teachers College Record, 106,* 1047–85.

Elmore, R. F., & Fuhrman, S. H. (2001). Research finds the false assumption of accountability. *The Education Digest, 67,* 9–14.

Goldberg, M. (2005). Test mess 2: Are we doing better a year later? *Phi Delta Kappan, 86,* 389–95.

Hargis, C. H. (2006). Setting standards: An exercise in futility? *Phi Delta Kappan, 87,* 393–5.

Harp, B. (2006). *The handbook of literacy assessment and evaluation* (3rd ed.). Norwood, MA: Christopher-Gordon.

Jacob, B. A. (2001). Getting tough? The impact of high school graduation exams. *Educational Evaluation and Policy Analysis, 23,* 99–121.

Johnston, P. (1998). Teachers as evaluation experts. In R. L. Allington (Ed.), *Teaching struggling readers: Articles from* The Reading Teacher (pp. 46–50). Newark, DE: International Reading Association.

Leslie, L., & Caldwell, J. (2006). *Qualitative reading inventory* (4th ed.). Boston: Allyn and Bacon.

Linn, R. L. (2000). Assessments and accountability. *Educational Researcher, 29*(2), 4–16.

MacGinitie, W. H., MacGinitie, R. K., Maria, K., & Dreyer, L. G. (2000). *Gates-MacGinitie reading tests: Manual for scoring and interpretation.* Itasca, IL: Riverside.

Massachusetts Department of Education. (2005). *Dropouts in Massachusetts public schools: 2003–04*. Malden, MA: Author.

McCarthy, M., & Kuh, G. D. (2006). Are students ready for college? What student engagement data say. *Phi Delta Kappan, 87*, 664–9.

Moje, E. B. (2002). Re-framing adolescent literacy research for new times: Studying youth as a resource. *Reading Research and Instruction, 41*, 211–28.

National Center for Education Statistics (NCES). (2002). *Highlights from the 2000 program for international student assessment* (NCES Publication No. 2002-116). Retrieved February 18, 2002, from http://nces.ed.gov/pubsearch/pubsinfo.asp?pubid=2002116

National Center for Education Statistics (NCES). (2006). *The nation's report card*. Retrieved March 23, 2006, from http://nces.ed.gov/nationsreportcard

Paris, S. G., & McEvoy, A. P. (2000). Harmful and enduring effects of high-stakes testing. *Issues in Education: Contributions from Educational Psychology, 6*, 145–59.

Pressley, M., & Afflerbach, P. (1995). *Verbal protocols of reading: The nature of constructively responsive reading*. Hillsdale, NJ: Erlbaum.

Robelen, E. W. (2005, February 9). Bush's high school agenda faces obstacles. *Education Week*, pp. 22, 24.

Rothman, R. (2005). No adolescent left behind? *Harvard Education Letter, 21*(3), 4–7.

Saenz, L. M., & Fuchs, L. S. (2002). Examining the reading difficulty of secondary students with learning disabilities: Expository versus narrative text. *Remedial and Special Education, 23*(1), 31–41.

Salvia, J., & Ysseldyke, J. E. (2004). *Assessment in special and inclusive education* (9th ed.). Boston: Houghton Mifflin.

U.S. Department of Education. (2001, December 4). *U.S. students average among international peers: U.S. 15-year-olds' abilities to apply learning to "real world" examined in 32-nation study* [Press Release]. Retrieved May 8, 2007, from http://www.ed.gov/news/pressreleases/2001/12/12042001a.html

Walker, B. J. (2000). *Diagnostic teaching of reading: Techniques for instruction and assessment* (4th ed.). Upper Saddle River, NJ: Merrill.

Woodcock, R. W. (1998). *Woodcock reading mastery tests—revised: Examiner's manual*. Circle Pines, MN: American Guidance Service.

CHAPTER FIVE

Understanding Reading Comprehension in Secondary Schools through the Lens of the Four Resources Model

TERRY UNDERWOOD
Sacramento State University

MONICA S. YOO AND P. DAVID PEARSON
University of California, Berkeley

What it means to teach reading comprehension has changed in profound ways. As we document in this chapter, state standards embrace a more complex notion of comprehension than the field has seen in the past. Even the standards-driven anthologies that teachers use as curricular resources similarly derive from a more complex perspective on comprehension. The only element that has *not* changed in order to integrate more complexity into the comprehension model is testing: the standards-based and standardized tests employed to measure comprehension belie a different view of reading than underlies either the standards or literature anthologies.

With that background, we attempt to provide insights for teachers trying to come to terms with state standards, curricular materials, and standardized tests that are now largely nonnegotiable aspects of their daily work. We begin by offering what we think is a full-bodied model of reading, the Four Resources Model (Freebody, 1992; Freebody & Luke, 1990), grounded in the best current scholarship, to give teachers a conceptual framework for thinking through reading comprehension as a construct. We then examine, in turn, state standards, standardized tests, and widely used anthologies through the lens of this comprehension model. We conclude by offering principles to guide teacher decision making in this area. Our hope is that the chapter supports teachers in their work of implementing standards, negotiating anthologies, and raising standardized test scores through an integrated, balanced design.

The Four Resources Model of Reading

In 1990, Freebody and Luke named their emerging model of literacy instruction, which they have since fine-tuned, "the four resources model of reading" (Freebody, 1992; Freebody & Luke, 1990; Luke & Freebody, 1997). The model suggests that, depending on a wide range of contextual variables (e.g., pedagogical context, purpose, perceptions of consequences), readers pass through four necessary roles:

- ◆ Code breaker (cracking the code or cipher that maps spellings to sounds and vice versa)

- ◆ Meaning-maker (focusing on the message of the text, including the knowledge required to understand it)

- ◆ Text user (focusing on the pragmatics of use—what function a text serves in a social context)

- ◆ Text critic (a critical competence that entails unpacking social, economic, and political *assumptions* behind and *consequences* of using a text)

In an important online paper, Luke and Freebody (1999) unpack each of these resources (or roles as they sometimes label them) as "descriptions of the normative goals of classroom literacy programs" (n.p.). These descriptions have been widely circulated throughout the world and instantiated as the official curriculum in at least one Australian state for some time:

- ◆ *Break the code* of written texts by recognizing and using fundamental features and architecture, including alphabet, sounds in words, spelling, and structural conventions and patterns;

◆ *Participate in understanding and composing* meaningful written, visual, and spoken texts, taking into account each text's
interior meaning systems in relation to the reader's available
knowledge and experience of other cultural discourses, texts,
and meaning systems;

◆ *Use texts functionally* by traversing and negotiating the labor
and social relations around them—that is, by knowing about
and acting on the different cultural and social functions that
various texts perform inside and outside school and understanding that these functions shape the texts' structure, tone, degree
of formality, and sequence of components;

◆ *Critically analyze and transform texts* by acting on knowledge
that texts are not ideologically neutral—that texts represent particular points of views, while silencing others, and influence
people's ideas—and that text designs and discourses can be critiqued and redesigned in novel and hybrid ways (1999, n. p.;
emphases added).

The competent reader is one who recognizes that, on different occasions, different resources occupy center stage and others
play supporting roles from the wings. So, breaking the code is
likely to be a part of any encounter with text, but it plays the
starring role only when the cipher is obscure (really unfamiliar
words and patterns) or knowledge is weak.

Historically, these four resources correspond to the succes-
sive rise and fall of different theoretical views of the reading process over the past fifty years. Prior to the mid-1970s, the field
was dominated by "perceptual" views of reading that emphasized what some (e.g., Gough & Hillinger, 1980; Juel, 1988) have
dubbed the simple view—that reading comprehension is the product of decoding and listening comprehension. In the simple view,
reading is essentially a process of decoding print to speech and
listening to the product to achieve understanding. This is quint-
essential reader as code breaker.

The 1970s brought to center stage the psycholinguistic and
cognitive perspectives (see Anderson & Pearson, 1984; Pearson
& Stephens, 1993) and, with them, the reader as meaning-maker.
What mattered most was the reciprocal relationship between
knowledge and comprehension. We use our knowledge in active

ways to control the reading process, always seeking congruence between what we know and what passes before our "eyes" in reading. Knowledge is the cause and the consequence of comprehension.

The sociolinguistic perspectives of the 1980s (see Heath, 1983; Wells, 1986) championed functional views of reading, and we wanted to know how the social and cultural contexts in which the reading was done shaped our sense of what was "appropriate." Thus, retelling a story to a friend who asked what the book was about requires a different "performance" than giving a formal "plot-theme-characters" retelling in a ninth-grade literature class. In the text-user role, the reader literally has to learn to "read context" as well as text.

Although critical perspectives that challenge the structuralist assumptions in "modern" views of epistemology and ontology have been available for centuries, it was not until the 1990s that postmodern perspectives (Foucault, 1980; Giroux, 1991) assumed a dominant role in the discourse of reading education; by that time, the term *reading* had been nearly universally replaced by the broader and more contextualized term *literacy* (see Gee, 1987). A key understanding in the critical resource is that texts are inherently "interested," written by individuals (or groups) with intentions, conscious or unconscious, to convey through text. Furthermore, texts are read by "interested" individuals, who bring histories to the reading act at many levels—idiosyncratic, social, and cultural. Hence, all acts of literacy—in addition to being verbal acts of communication—are social, political, or economic. To understand an act of literacy fully requires the asking and answering of many questions of power and control: In whose interests is this text written? Who are the champions? Who are the goats? Who is invisible?

These four resources become our rubric, our guide for evaluating the curriculum enacted in schools every day—through standards, tests, and literature anthologies. We ask of each of these elements whether it represents all of the resources in some plausibly balanced approach—and, if it doesn't, where it falls short.

Reading Comprehension Standards in California and Massachusetts

The federal reauthorization of the Elementary and Secondary Education Act of 1965 (No Child Left Behind, 2001 [NCLB]) has resulted in a proliferation of academic standards in virtually every state, including standards related to reading comprehension. But evidence of considerable variability in these standards has been reported in the literature (Cross, Rebarber, & Torres, 2004; Linn, 2000). Although an analysis of similarities and differences in reading comprehension standards with the Four Resources Model as an analytical tool is beyond the scope of this chapter, such an analysis could be done within each state to validate individual standards vis-à-vis a widely known scholarly model of reading. Such an analysis would undoubtedly reveal the existence of academic standards that narrow rather than expand opportunities for children to grow along each dimension of the Four Resources Model, but we argue in this section that reading comprehension standards in California and Massachusetts, which we have selected as exemplars, open up instructional possibilities for reading comprehension along the dimensions of the model to a greater degree than they constrain them.

When we look at the tests employed to measure reading comprehension in these states, however, it is clear that the instructional possibilities suggested by the standards are diminished to the degree that teachers teach to the tests rather than to the standards. In essence, when teachers gear instruction to features of the reading comprehension tests that states use as accountability measures, the breadth and complexity of state standards disappear, and comprehension instruction becomes a matter of teaching students to break the code and make meaning in some shallow sense, but not to develop their capacities as text users and text critics. More optimistically, we argue in a later section that secondary English textbooks may not stretch the boundaries of the text-user and text-critic aspects of the model, but they often imply a curriculum that could offer authentic opportunities to students to develop along these dimensions.

California Standards

California's English Language Arts Content Standards (California Department of Education, 2005a) for the high school level depict reading as behavior that cuts across each dimension of the Four Resources Model. In California, students are expected to have become accomplished meaning-makers by ninth grade, where the standards move beyond behaviors such as monitoring comprehension of single texts or summarizing information toward behaviors such as ". . . generat[ing] relevant questions on issues that can be researched" and ". . . synthesiz[ing] the content from several sources or works by a single author dealing with a single issue" (Grades 9 and 10 Standards 2.3, 2.4). Clearly, the California reader uses texts to move forward an intellectual agenda with the intention of creating original ideas and understandings (i.e., synthesis).

Unlike standards in other states—such as Texas, for example, where teachers are directed to give students opportunities to use texts in social settings (e.g., participate in discussions, share journal entries)—the California standards are not explicit about this expectation. But, in the first years of high school, students are expected to use a *lot* of texts individually: by ninth and tenth grades, they should ". . . make substantial progress toward [the] goal [of] read[ing] two million words annually on their own, including a wide variety of classic and contemporary literature, magazines, newspapers, and online information" (Grades 9 and 10 Standard 2.0). Moreover, students should become text users, in that they should learn to "compare and contrast the ways in which media genres (e.g., televised news, news magazines, documentaries, online information) cover the same event" (Grades 9 and 10 Standard 1.2). Presumably, these events are part of students' life experiences; by implication, students ought to become text critics in the face of questions such as *Who* benefits from the way a particular media text is made?

An entire section of the California standards is devoted to "expository critique"—becoming text critics—wherein students in the first two years of high school are expected to "critique the logic of functional documents" and "evaluate the credibility of an author's argument or defense of a claim" (Grades 9 and 10 Standards 2.7, 2.8). By graduation, students should be able to "critique the power, validity, and truthfulness of arguments set forth in public documents; their appeal to both friendly and hostile audiences; and the extent to which the arguments anticipate and address reader concerns and counterclaims (e.g., appeal to reason, to authority, to pathos and emotion)" (Grades 11 and 12 Standard 2.6). This standard comes close to the core of the text-critic dimension of the Four Resources Model, wherein readers ask not only "What does the text mean?" but also "Whose interests does it serve?"

Massachusetts Standards

Massachusetts standards for reading comprehension (Massachusetts Department of Education, 2001) are organized in a section of a curriculum framework titled "reading and literature" and are spelled out as "general standards," with subsections delineating expectations for grade-level clusters. General Standard 8, titled "understanding a text," is divided into two categories: "imaginative/literary texts" and "informational/expository texts." This standard is clear about the expectation that students are to develop skill as meaning-makers: "Students will identify the basic facts and main ideas in a text and use them as the basis for interpretation." At the high school level, however, being a meaning-maker is linked to being a text user and a text critic, according to standards in the subsection for grades 9 and 10: "For example, students read two political columnists in *The Boston Globe* . . . and identify the authors' main argument. Then they discuss the strengths and weaknesses of the arguments and cite the authors' best evidence as set forth in the columns" (Standard 8.31).

General Standard 9 requires students to act as meaning-makers with regard to individual texts but extends the cognitive work of the reader beyond negotiating an understanding of texts to making connections with the context in which texts were produced: "Students will deepen their understanding of a literary or non-literary work by relating it to its contemporary context or historical background." The example given for grades 11 and 12 makes clear that the intent is to expect students to become text users: " . . . [S]tudents read *The Scarlet Letter* . . . [and] poems by Anne Bradstreet, transcripts of the Salem witch trials. . . . Then students relate what they have learned to events, characters, and themes in *The Scarlet Letter*" (Standard 9.6). This sort of reading work seems ideally suited to help Massachusetts students develop as text users in settings where a myriad of other texts affords them grounds for analysis.

The Massachusetts standards are so rich that we could take up an entire chapter detailing them, but, for our purposes, two more examples serve to illustrate how these standards map the Four Resources Model. The standard for genre texts (General Standard 10: Genre) is built from the assumption that the structure, language, and content of texts are shaped and interpreted socially by participants (text users and critics) in recurrent events—past, present, and future. In Massachusetts, readers use texts with awareness of what they are—not because of mechanistic rules governing correct textual behavior in English class, but because of their purposes as elements of social and cultural forces playing out in history. Here is an excerpt from that standard for grades 9 and 10:

> 10.5 *Compare and contrast the presentation of a theme or topic across genres to explain how the selection of genre shapes the message.*
> For example, students compare and contrast three reactions to Lincoln's death: Walt Whitman's poem, "O Captain, My Captain," Frederick Douglass's eulogy, and the report in the *New York Times* on April 12, 1865. They make specific contrasts between the impersonal newspaper report and the personal poem and eulogy and between the two personal genres.

Another exemplary standard, General Standard 18: Dramatic Reading and Performance, requires students to ". . . plan and present dramatic readings, recitations, and performances that demonstrate appropriate consideration of audience and purpose" and reference standards in the Theater strand of the Arts curriculum. The rationale for this standard derives from a view of readers as text users: "The excitement and satisfaction of performing in front of an audience should be part of every student's school experience."

As these examples illustrate, whether an English teacher practices in California or Massachusetts, the standards authorized by the legislatures and sanctioned by the federal government call for an instructional focus grounded in the dimensions of the Four Resources Model. This call is not reinforced, however, by the reading comprehension tests mandated in these states, as our next section shows.

Reading Comprehension Tests in California and Massachusetts

The complex history of reading comprehension tests has been discussed at length elsewhere (e.g., Sarroub & Pearson, 1998; Pearson & Hamm, 2005), and innovative approaches to comprehension assessment, ranging from oral reading analyses to think-alouds to curriculum-embedded events to portfolios, have been developed in the past few decades. Although some of these innovative approaches could lead to the development of techniques useful in measuring student reading performances across the dimensions of the Four Resources Model, our analysis of the reading comprehension tests actually used in California and Massachusetts suggest that few if any of the lessons learned from the performance-based assessment work of the 1980s and 1990s show up in test design. Although these tests may have the veneer of assessing text-user or text-critic dimensions, at best they measure readers as code breakers and meaning-makers.

California Standards Test

California's Department of Education releases test items on a yearly basis, as does Massachusetts. We examined the California Standards Test (California Department of Education, 2005b) for use in tenth grade through the lens of the Four Resources Model. According to test specifications spelled out in material that prefaces the items, the CST measures many aspects of meaning-making, e.g., "analyze the structure and format of functional workplace documents" (10RC2.1) and "analyze interactions between main and subordinate characters in a literary text" (10RL3.3). The specifications also call for measurement of the cognitive behaviors of text users and text critics. For example, the test claims to measure how well students "synthesize . . . content from several sources by a single author dealing with a single issue" (10RC2.4) and how they "evaluate the credibility of an author's argument or defense of a claim" (10RC2.8). Note that the specifications for literary response and analysis contain fewer indications of the intent to measure text-user and text-critic behaviors. One specification comes close: "Analyze the way in which a work of literature is related to the themes and issues of its historical period" (10RL3.12).

What does the CST (2005) reading test for tenth grade actually look like? To their credit, California test designers took seriously the charge that short snippets of text, characteristic of earlier comprehension tests, are inadequate to measure reading in the real world. The CST consists of authentic texts of substance, including personal essays by Mark Twain and Louise Erdrich; several functional documents, including advertisements; several lengthy poems; and even rough drafts of essays written by students. All test questions are presented in a multiple-choice format; however, it is impossible to find an item that engages students in synthesis or evaluation of the sort called for in the state standards (and in the text-user and text-critic roles of the Four Resources Model). The closest that the test comes to measuring anything but behavior of meaning-makers appears in an item testing comprehension of Mark Twain's essay "My Watch: An Instructive Little Tale." In the text, through his experiences with watchmakers, Twain teaches us not to fix what isn't broken; in the test item, readers are asked to link the text to its historical period:

> One indication that this was *not* written in the present time is the comparison of the watch to a
>
> A. pair of scissors.
>
> B. musket.
>
> C. spider's web.
>
> D. bee.

The argument could be made that this item gets at the text-user dimension because it assumes that readers ought to recognize where and how texts link to the context of their production, but this item does not necessarily test this behavior. The fact that the item can be answered without having read the passage is not the biggest problem with the validity of the item. The distractors (scissors, bee) *are* mentioned in the text and in the test item to "trick" the reader. Good readers who are not careful with the question stem might easily select "spider's web," which was *not* in the text, entirely on the basis of their reading of the test item, not the Twain passage.

Measures in Massachusetts

The Massachusetts standards document acknowledges that many of its standards are not measurable using its state assessment system. These standards are accompanied by asterisks and readers find in a footnote that they must be assessed locally. An analysis of the English Language Arts Test Grade 10 sample test released in 2005 confirms that the asterisks are well placed. Like tests in California, the Massachusetts test is built from lengthy passages that engage readers in sustained acts of negotiating meaning. Although the Massachusetts test includes constructed response, almost all of the items are traditional multiple-choice format. For instance, "What is this article mainly about?" is followed by four options. Even constructed response items probe students' capacity to make meaning and not to use or critique text: "Describe how Professor Dragoo shows his affection for skunks. Use relevant and specific information from the text to support your answer."

Tests in General

Momentum in the use of large-scale, high-stakes, standards-driven tests has intensified steadily over the past decade, but no parallel source of energy has been directed toward improving the nature of these tests. As Linn, Baker, and Betebenner (2002) explained, NCLB increased testing requirements for all states and linked these requirements to federal grants, but the relationship between tests and state standards was never specified. The legislation did not stipulate whether open-ended (constructed) responses or multiple-choice formats should be used in the design of comprehension tests. The absence of a position on test design is a significant issue; researchers have repeatedly demonstrated that the nature of a test influences instruction (Frederiksen & Collins, 1989; Resnick & Resnick, 1991). In fact, this issue was at the heart of the development of major initiatives in alternative reading assessment during the 1990s (Claggett, 1996; Myers & Pearson, 1996; Simmons & Resnick, 1993). Given the goal of the improvement of teaching and learning, this failure to bring test design into the mix is clearly a problem for the standards movement. The vision of the standards movement takes in much of the complexity of reading as scholars currently construe the phenomenon, although the tests do not, and so teachers find themselves in the crossfire. What help do they get from their anthologies?

Enacting the Standards: Accountability in the Language Arts

Use of Anthologies

Although the wide range of state standards for California and Massachusetts encourage breadth and complexity in the teaching of language arts, the pressures faced by teachers to help students perform well on standardized tests constrain possibilities for instruction (Smith, 1991), especially when high stakes are attached to tests. In schools with concerns about issues such as their AYP (NCLB's provision for Adequate Yearly Progress—toward a magical goal of 100 percent proficiency by 2014), the curricular focus for students struggling in language arts is often on breaking the code and on meaning-making, rather than on developing students' abilities as text users and text critics. Increasing demands for accountability have prompted schools and districts to align their language arts curriculum with standards; and, in some states, this has led to mandates requiring schools and districts to choose a language arts programs from a handful of publishers. With the move toward comprehensive, state-adopted programs for language arts in kindergarten through eighth grade, textbook publishers have attempted to build in accountability at the high school level by revising textbooks to reflect a focus on standards. On the face of it, given our salutary review of standards in the previous section, this new focus would not be all bad.

In their recent incarnation, anthologies for high school language arts and their accompanying materials serve as bridges between curriculum, standards, and assessments. Lesson and unit objectives are geared toward helping students gain mastery over standards preselected by textbook writers and editors. In this section, we examine how the teachers' editions of ninth-grade language arts textbooks produced by Holt, Rinehart, and Winston, Prentice Hall, and Glencoe McGraw-Hill address the standards in California and succeed or fail to provide opportunities for student learning along the dimensions of the Four Resources Model. We have chosen to look at anthologies for ninth-grade language arts because ninth grade is the year prior to students' first opportunity to take the California High School Exit Exam (CAHSEE). In many California schools, ninth grade is also when students receive reading intervention instruction to prepare them with skills they may need to pass the CAHSEE in the tenth grade. Because the publishers Holt, Rinehart, and Winston, Prentice Hall, and Glencoe McGraw-Hill have footholds in Massachusetts as well as California, we operate under the premise that there are similarities between the treatment of standards and their relationship to the curriculum, regardless of the state in which a textbook has been adopted. Although each state employs experts to oversee and ensure the alignment of standards to curriculum, the basic format, selection of literary works, and questions on core comprehension that are written for students largely remain the same for each publisher.

Comparing Anthologies

Because the anthologies published by Holt, Rinehart, and Winston, Prentice Hall, and Glencoe McGraw-Hill contain several of the same classic pieces of literature and acknowledge the incorporation of standards from each state, one might assume that these three publishers would draw upon the same set of standards as foci for the pieces of literature. Using the California teacher's editions of the three anthologies, we compared the three publishers' treatments of "The Cask of Amontillado" by Edgar Allan Poe and found that each text differed in its choice of state standards and important story elements for literary analysis.

In these three anthologies, each literary selection is prefaced by prereading activities—focusing on the frontloading of key concepts, themes, and vocabulary—and followed by a review section that includes comprehension questions, writing activities, vocabulary development, and short grammar lessons. This format is reminiscent of the "into, through, and beyond" sequence that dominated language arts instruction in the 1990s (after Langer, 1990). Key questions in teacher and student editions echo an overarching emphasis on particular standards; yet the standards highlighted seem somewhat arbitrary, especially because they are so different across the three publishers.

By comparing the three anthologies, we do not intend to determine which best speaks to the components of the Four Resources Model. Instead, we aim to examine how anthologies in general take stock of state standards and a variety of literacy and thinking skills. The figures in this section represent language arts standards adopted by each publisher for Poe's "The Cask of Amontillado" and sample questions related to those standards from the student and teacher editions. Although the anthologies do not explicitly connect these particular questions to the acknowledged standards, links can be drawn by means of the content in the questions as well as the proximity of the standard mentioned to the location of the questions in the textbook.

In Poe's "The Cask of Amontillado," the narrator Montresor describes how he led Fortunato, the victim, to an unfortunate demise. The Holt anthology's "Before you Read" section identifies the unreliable narrator as a "literary focus" for this selection. Throughout the duration of reading the story, the teacher is directed, by means of suggestions in the annotated margins of the teacher's edition, to indicate, allude to, and question the words and actions coming from the narrator in order to help students realize his positioning and influence as a storyteller. Likewise, this focus is pursued in the review questions listed at the end of the selection in the student edition.

Although the standards-related question asks students to "think about whether or not Montresor is an unreliable narrator," previous prompts from the teacher and the text have already led students to the answer that Montresor is not to be wholly trusted on his views regarding Fortunato and his version of events in the story. The supporting questions are "think and search" questions (Raphael, 1982, 1984, 1986) that uphold the positioning of Montresor. Both the standard and its representative questions fall into the meaning-making dimension of the Four Resources Model. Yet, if the teacher has followed the activities in the teacher's edition, most of the meaning has already been made *for* the students by the prompts given prior to the start of the story and by the teacher's scaffolding during the story's reading. The questions in Figure 5.1 invoke a transmission model of reading in which meaning is transmitted from the author to the reader, as a passive receiver, rather than a transactional one in which the reader dynamically transacts with the text and creates meaning through an interpretation based on his or her own background knowledge, experiences, purposes, and goals (Rosenblatt, 1938, 1978; Schraw & Brunig, 1996). In a transmission model (Schraw & Brunig, 1996), the teacher and the questions in the anthology act as brokers between text and student, ensuring that, given the right kinds of scaffolding, students will take away the author's intended meaning instead of make the meaning themselves.

Similar to the way that the Holt anthology attends to the unreliable narrator as a literary device, the Prentice Hall edition prefaces mood as a primary literary element and centers on returning to this focus throughout the teaching of the story. In Prentice Hall's "Prepare to Read" pages, the text states, "In 'The Cask of Amontillado,' Edgar Allan Poe carefully chooses words and details to create a mood of eerie suspense" (p. 5). Students are told up front what the mood is, rather than being invited to ascertain the mood for themselves. Questions about the unreliable narrator presented in the Holt text are similar to those students are asked in the Holt text: to examine how the text makes meaning about the mood and to discuss the changes in meaning

California Language Arts Standards	Representative Standards-Related Questions
Reading—Literary Response and Analysis Grades 9 and 10 Standard 3.9 "Explain how voice, persona, and the choice of a narrator affect characterization and the tone, plot, and credibility of a text."	"Think about whether or not Montresor is an unreliable narrator. Do any details suggest that he might have imagined 'the thousand injuries' and the insult—or even the whole story? Can you find evidence in the story to support Montresor's claim that Fortunato did in fact injure and insult him? To support your answers consider Montresor's actions, statements, and voice." (p. 181)(*Student edition, review question*)

FIGURE 5.1. Holt Literature and Language Arts, Third Course *(Beers & Odell, 2003).*

as the story unfolds. Although the actual questions asked at the end of the selection might encourage a transaction between reader and text, the supposed transaction implied in the questions is somewhat misleading: the prereading section spells out the mood and thus limits other possible answers, a clear constraint on text-use behaviors.

Although the first question in Figure 5.2 from the teacher's edition is a "right there" question, asking students to locate details from a particular section of the text, questions in the review guide of the student edition are "author and you" questions, in which the students must base their answers on what they can interpret about the mood change based on what the author has written (Raphael, 1982, 1984, 1986). Although the standards-related questions in Figures 5.1 and 5.2 might be within the making-meaning categorization of the Four Resources Model, the depth of the questions varies insofar as they each call for different demands on cognitive reasoning.

Although the prereading section of "The Cask of Amontillado" in the Glencoe anthology features background information, questions regarding the revenge motif, and frontloaded vocabulary in a fashion similar to the Prentice Hall and Holt

California Language Arts Standards	Representative Standards-Related Questions
Reading—Literary Response and Analysis Grades 9 and 10 Standard 3.6 "Analyze and trace an author's development of time and sequence, including the use of complex literary devices (e.g., foreshadowing, flashbacks)."	"Ask students to define the mood created by the first two paragraphs. Which specific details create this mood?" (p. 7)(*Teacher's edition, scaffolding question*)"(a) Describe the mood of the scene in which Montresor first tells Fortunato about the Amontillado. (b) How does the mood change as the story unfolds?" (p. 13).(*Student edition, review question*)

FIGURE 5.2. Prentice Hall Literature: Timeless Voices, Timeless Themes, Gold Level *(Kinsella, Feldman, Stump, Carroll, & Wilson, 2002).*

texts, it does not contain a focus on one or two main literary elements such as mood or narrative technique. Furthermore, the Glencoe text addresses standards in a different manner. Instead of highlighting one or two main standards to unify the teaching focus of a particular literary work, it lists standards on every couple of pages, while adding to or deleting standards as necessary to accommodate the text, guiding questions and activities prescribed in the teacher's edition. In short, it adopts a distributed rather than a massed approach to unpacking the standards. Perhaps this less intense focus on teaching one or two standards and literary devices leads to more opportunities for students to determine their own transactions with the text. Based on the questions sampled as being representative of a standards focus, we consider that the questions listed in this anthology allow room for students to contribute their points of view rather than echo answers already supplied by text and teacher.

As in the two other anthologies, the questions in the Glencoe text could be classified as meaning-making questions in accordance with the Four Resources Model. Yet, on examining the questions more closely, we find that these meaning-making questions predominately fall within the parameters of the "author and you" type, where the expectation of independent contributions from the reader is greater, rather than the more text-centric, "right there," and "think and search" forms. This sampling of questions also touches somewhat on the text-user and text-critic functions, as well as the meaning-making. Whereas the question on mood in the Prentice Hall text is a meaning-making one, the mood question in Figure 5.3 calls on students to consider themselves as text users in order to think about what they "are led to see and hear" in their imaginations (p. 93). Furthermore, one of the questions that is representative of the standards might actually touch on the text-critic function in addition to meaning-making as it asks, "In your opinion, why did Poe choose to write from the first-person point of view . . . ?" (p. 93). In the case of this question, the student is asked to evaluate why a particular point of view is chosen by the author over another one. Inherent in this question is the consideration of the role, persona, and perspective of the victim Fortunato and a consideration of what the author had to gain by choosing Montresor's first-person point of view.

This is not to say that the Holt and Prentice Hall anthologies neglect the text-user and text-critic dimensions of the Four Resources Model. In the Holt textbook's review section for "The Cask of Amontillado," students are asked to consider whether the text is merely a "story told for entertainment" or one that "reveals some truth about people who are consumed for a desire for revenge" (p. 181). Although, at the onset, this seems like a meaning-making question, it also has possibilities for considering the text-user dimension. A question in the Prentice Hall anthology asks students to evaluate the situation in the story and then probes, "Montresor acts as judge and executioner in this story. Explain whether you think individuals are ever justified in taking justice into their own hands" (p.12). Although this falls under the meaning-making parameters of the Four Resources Model, it also has possibilities for extensions into the text-critic category. If they were to compare social, political, and moral dilemmas regarding justice to the events of the story, students could analyze whether or not Montresor had the best justifications for taking Fortunato's life. Most of the questions in all three texts remain close to the meaning-maker dimension, although a few questions might touch on the text-user and text-critic dimensions.

California Language Arts Standards	Representative Standards-Related Questions
Reading—Literary Response and Analysis Grade 9 and 10 Standards 2.0 3.0, 3.3, 3.4, 3.7, 3.8, 3.9, 3.11 3.3 "Analyze interactions between main and subordinate characters in a literary text (e.g., internal and external conflicts, motivations, relationships, influences) and explain the way those interactions affect the plot."	"How does Montresor get Fortunato to come with him to his vaults? What is Montresor's main motive for leading Fortunato there?" (p. 93) (*Student edition, review question*)
3.4 "Determine characters' traits by what the characters say about themselves in narration, dialogue, dramatic monologue, and soliloquy."	"What can you infer about the character of the narrator from his dialogue with Fortunato?" (p. 88). (*Teacher's edition, scaffolding question*)
3.8 "Interpret and evaluate the impact of ambiguities, subtleties, contradictions, ironies, and incongruities in a text."	"Describe the conversation between Montresor and Fortunato as they walk in the catacombs. What is ironic about Montresor's concern for Fortunato's health?" (p. 93) (*Student edition, review question*)
3.9 "Explain how voice, persona, and the choice of a narrator affect characterization and the tone, plot, and credibility of a text."	"In your opinion, why did Poe choose to write from the first-person point of view, describing only Montresor's thoughts and not Fortunato's?" (p. 93) (*Student edition, review question*)
3.11 "Evaluate the aesthetic qualities of style, including the impact of diction and figurative language on tone, mood, and theme, using the terminology of literary criticism. (Aesthetic approach)."	"How does Poe create the mood? Consider his word choice and think about what you are led to see and hear in your imagination" (p. 93). (*Student edition, review question*)

FIGURE 5.3. Glencoe Literature: The Reader's Choice, Course 4 *(Chin et al., 2002)*.

Although the Holt and Prentice Hall textbooks do not list as many standards for "The Cask of Amontillado" as the Glencoe version does, this does not mean that the questions and activities in the teacher's edition are related to only the one or two standards and literary devices emphasized for the lesson. For example, one of the review questions in the student edition of the Holt text asks, "Think about Poe's decision to set his story during carnival. What is ironic about the setting? In what ways does the setting suit the plot of the story?" This particular question aligns with the Reading: Literary Response and Analysis Grades 9 and 10 Standard 3.8 (see Figure 5.3) more so than with Grades 9 and 10 Standard 3.9 (see Figure 5.1). The anthologies are thus much more inclusive of standards than they claim to be. In other words, they deliver more than they promise.

Yet the avowed focus on particular standards increases the likelihood that more of the teacher's guide and review questions reflect the listed standards and thereby narrow the breadth of curricular possibilities. In a comparison of the review questions in the 1997 Holt anthology and the more recent 2003 version analyzed in this chapter, the bulk of the questions and the unreliable narrator as one of the story's major literary devices remain the same (see Probst, Anderson, Brinnin, Leggett, & Irvin, 1997). Based on this comparison, the content of the curriculum seems to have remained largely intact, although the standards have been added. For example, Grades 9 and 10 Standard 3.9, regarding the narrator's effect on "the tone, plot, and credibility of a text," has led to the inclusion of two additional questions about character and the deletion of two questions regarding the story's use of irony in the student review section. Aligning standards with curriculum has meant that textbooks have largely "plugged in" standards to match lessons and units that were already part of the anthologies. Aligning assessments with curriculum, however, has been a different story.

Including Assessment Practices in the Curriculum

To adjust to accountability measures placed on schools and districts by NCLB, language arts anthologies have added more short nonfiction pieces to their collections. The average one- to two-page length of such pieces mimics the length of the nonfiction pieces typically found on the CAHSEE. These pieces are often informational or expository texts related to a theme, topic, or setting connected to one of the literary selections or its author. For example, following "The Cask of Amontillado," the 2003 Holt anthology includes an excerpt from a biography about Edgar Allan Poe and a series of three short newspaper articles that question the cause of Poe's death.

As the Holt anthology correlates these four nonfiction pieces about Poe's death with the California Grade 9 and 10 Standards in Section 2: Reading Comprehension (Focus on Informational Materials), the questions and activities in the teacher and student editions center less on an aesthetic stance toward reading, brought out by interpretive responses supported by the text, and more on an efferent stance in which the focus is on facts and information (Rosenblatt, 1978). Yet the purposes defined for efferent reading, as stated in the California standards, are not directed toward learning the facts for the sake of remembering them for an exam, but rather toward learning how to use the facts in order to analyze, evaluate, and synthesize information from primary and secondary sources (see CA Grades 9 and 10 Standards 2.1, 2.4, and 2.5). Several standards in Section 2 tend to combine elements of the meaning-making and text-using functions of the Four Resources Model, lying at the border of their parameters—where meaning-making intersects with the purpose of achieving a form of academic literacy.

Most of the sample questions on the anthology's practice test address only the meaning-making dimension of the Four Resources Model, although there are some exceptions. The free-response questions for informational reading tend to go beyond the meaning-making function, whereas the multiple-choice questions tend to limit efferent reading practices to finding bits of information for the sake of eliciting right answers. The multiple-choice format also shows up in the three anthologies in the grammar and vocabulary practice lessons at the end of the review section accompanying a literary work. Although the multiple-choice questions only take up a slim portion of each of the anthologies, this format and that of other "skill and drill" type formats are prevalent and predominant in reading comprehension instruction for struggling high school students receiving reading intervention.

Code-Breaking Skill and Drill

One program implemented for students who struggle with decoding at the high school level is SRA Corrective Reading, published by SRA-McGraw Hill. Its main components are a student book, workbook, and scripted teacher's guide. This particular program focuses only on the code-breaking and meaning-making components of the Four Resources Model. Although this program can be used with students in grade 3 and higher, the materials are neither differentiated nor created to take into account the interest of students at various ages. Most of the student lesson activities require students to read in the student book and fill in the blanks for "right there" questions about short fictional stories (see Engelmann, Meyer, Carnine, Becker, Eisele, & Johnson, 1999). Code-breaker activities in the workbook ask students to fill in blanks while identifying and either combining or dissecting word parts according to their meanings or sounds. A typical code-breaker activity gives students a set of words with endings that affect the word morphology and directs them to write the same words without endings.

Implementation and Enactment: The Teacher's Role

Despite all of the intentions of state and district officials to align standards, curriculum, and assessments, what teachers ultimately do in their classrooms and how they implement curricular materials vary. Teachers have to make difficult choices in how they address mandated reforms. These choices include following instructions wholesale and implementing materials selected by their district without changes to the program, participating in a local plan for the department that is consistent with the district's directives but flexible enough to accommodate and adjust to the needs of the students and the school, substituting other teaching materials and techniques to address the gaps that exist in the district-adopted materials, and "schooling" the system or acting in mock compliance by following the letter of the law but not its spirit. The choices made by teachers likely depend on their experience, beliefs, and personalities. For example, beginning teachers may feel more pressure than experienced ones to follow orders given in school directives. Given their lack of experience, beginning teachers may even feel comforted by scripts and suggestions offered by particular texts and programs. In comparison, teachers with experience and insight recognize that there are inadequacies in any program and that the curriculum needs to be flexible enough to meet the needs of individual students. Furthermore, they often have or can find materials to supplement what they have been given by their schools.

Some teachers are renegades. Some may teach the multiple-choice exercises one day and engage students in other stimulating literacy learning opportunities during the rest of the week. Others may have students participate in prescribed curriculum while asking them to examine critically why they are being required to participate in certain kinds of literacy activities. These teachers stimulate students' thinking and also demand that students employ skills as text critics, regardless of whether or not the materials account for this particular dimension of the Four Resources Model.

Instructional Principles

In our view, there is a clear and powerful incongruity between the tests used to measure reading comprehension and the standards and curriculum materials that teachers are expected to use. This incongruity makes effective instructional decision making more difficult than it needs to be. Based on our analysis of this situation, we offer the following four principles to serve as a foundation for discussion around what ought to occur in the secondary school English classroom in the name of reading comprehension instruction:

1. Curricular planning at all levels—the individual course, the set of courses across all of the secondary school years, and remedial courses—ought to begin with standards. Using the Four Resources Model as an organizer, teachers can map learning opportunities that treat all aspects of reading in a balanced and coherent way.

2. Anthologies should be used as resources, not as curricula. Our examination showed that anthologies provide rich and varied learning opportunities for students to develop on each of the four dimensions, but the publishers appear to have simply "plugged in" standards rather than revising content from the ground up. Teachers may need to update the pedagogy described in the anthologies on their own.

3. Standardized tests ought not to serve as starting points for instruction. The model of comprehension at the core of these tests is antiquated and narrow, and using it as a basis for design severely limits opportunities for students to develop toward state standards. Teachers have a range of options in dealing with these tests: ignore them and teach well, incorporate activities implied by tests sparingly, and become politically active to get testing practices changed. Using standardized tests to guide instruction is not an option if teachers are serious about teaching to standards.

4. Teach *students*, and not cognitive strategies, or novels, or modes of writing. This idea is not new, but it is centrally important. If teachers embrace this notion and follow it faithfully—provided that their understanding of what it means to teach *students* is robust and informed by a defensible conceptual framework such as the Four Resources Model—they can resolve issues raised by standardized tests and outdated curricula.

References

Anderson, R. C., & Pearson, P. D. (1984). A schema-theoretic view of basic processes in reading comprehension. In P. D. Pearson, R. Barr, M. L. Kamil, & P. Mosenthal (Eds.), *Handbook of reading research* (pp. 255–91). New York: Longman.

Beers, K., & Odell, L. (2003). *Holt literature and language arts: Third course* (Annotated teacher's edition). Austin, TX: Holt, Rinehart, & Winston.

California Department of Education. (2005a). *The California English language arts content standards.* Sacramento, CA: Author.

California Department of Education. (2005b). *Released test questions: English language arts grade 10.* Sacramento, CA: Author.

Chin, B. A., et al. (2002). *Glencoe literature: The reader's choice, course 4* (Teacher wraparound edition). Columbus, OH: Glencoe McGraw-Hill.

Claggett, F. (1996). *A measure of success: From assignment to assessment in English language arts.* Portsmouth, NH: Heinemann Boynton/Cook.

Cross, R. W., Rebarber, T., & Torres, J. (Eds.). (2004). *Grading the systems: The guide to state standards, tests, and accountability policies.* Washington, DC: Fordham Foundation.

Engelmann, S., Meyer, L., Carnine, L., Becker, W., Eisele, J., & Johnson, G. (1999). *SRA corrective reading: Decoding strategies, B2* (Workbook). Columbus, OH: SRA McGraw-Hill.

Foucault, M. (1980). *Power/knowledge: Selected interviews and other writings, 1972–1977* (C. Gordon, Ed.). New York: Pantheon Books.

Frederiksen, J. R., & Collins, A. (1989). A systems approach to educational testing. *Educational Researcher, 18*(9), 27–32.

Freebody, P. (1992). A socio-cultural approach: Resourcing four roles as a literacy learner. In A. J. Watson & A. M. Badenhop (Eds.), *Prevention of reading failure* (pp. 48–60). Sydney, Australia: Ashton-Scholastic.

Freebody, P., & Luke, A. (1990). Literacies programs: Debates and demands in cultural context. *Prospect: Australian Journal of TESOL, 5*(7), 7–16.

Gee, J. P. (1987). What is literacy? *Teaching and Learning, 2,* 3–11.

Giroux, H. A. (Ed.). (1991). *Postmodernism, feminism, and cultural politics: Redrawing educational boundaries.* Albany: State University of New York Press.

Gough, P. B., & Hillinger, M. L. (1980). Learning to read: An unnatural act. *Bulletin of the Orton Society, 30,* 179–96.

Heath, S. B. (1983). *Ways with words: Language, life and work in communities and classrooms.* Cambridge, UK: Cambridge University Press.

Juel, C. (1988). Learning to read and write: A longitudinal study of 54 children from first through fourth grades. *Journal of Educational Psychology, 80,* 437–47.

Kinsella, K., Feldman, K., Stump, C. S., Carroll, J. A., & Wilson, E. E. (2002). *Prentice Hall literature: Timeless voices, timeless themes, gold level* (California teacher's edition). Upper Saddle River, NJ: Prentice Hall.

Langer, J. A. (1990) The process of understanding: Reading for literary and informative purposes. *Research in the teaching of English, 24,* 229–60.

Linn, R. L. (2000). Assessments and accountability. *Educational Researcher, 29*(2), 4–16.

Linn, R. L., Baker, E. L., & Betebenner, D. W. (2002). Accountability systems: Implications of requirements of the No Child Left Behind Act of 2001. *Educational Researcher, 31*(6), 3–16.

Luke, A., & Freebody, P. (1997). The social practices of reading. In S. Muspratt, A. Luke, & P. Freebody (Eds.), *Constructing critical literacies: Teaching and learning textual practice* (pp. 185–225). St. Leonards, NSW, Australia: Allen & Unwin.

Luke, A., & Freebody, P. (1999). Further notes on the four resources model. *Reading Online.* Retrieved August 12, 2006, from http://www.readingonline.org/research/lukefreebody.html

Massachusetts Department of Education. (2001). *Massachusetts English language arts curriculum framework.* Malden, MA: Author.

Myers, M., & Pearson, P. D. (1996). Performance assessment and the literacy unit of the New Standards Project. *Assessing Writing, 3,* 5–29.

No Child Left Behind Act of 2001 (Public Law 107-110). (2002).

Pearson, P. D., & Hamm, D. N. (2005). The assessment of reading comprehension: A review of practices—past, present, and future. In S. G. Paris & S. A. Stahl (Eds.), *Children's reading comprehension and assessment* (pp. 13–69). Mahwah, NJ: Erlbaum.

Pearson, P. D., & Stephens, D. (1993). Learning about literacy: A 30-year journey. In C. J. Gordon, G. D. Labercane, & W. R. McEachern (Eds.), *Elementary reading: Process and practice* (pp. 4–18). Needham Heights, MA: Ginn Press.

Probst, R., Anderson, R., Brinnin, J. M., Leggett, J., & Irvin, J. L. (1997). *Elements of literature: Third course* (Annotated teacher's ed.). Austin, TX: Holt, Rinehart, & Winston.

Raphael, T. E. (1982). Question-answering strategies for children. *The Reading Teacher, 36,* 186–91.

Raphael, T. E. (1984). Teaching learners about sources of information for answering comprehension questions. *Journal of Reading, 27,* 303–11.

Raphael, T. E. (1986). Teaching question-answer relationships, revisited. *The Reading Teacher, 39,* 516–22.

Resnick, L. B., & Resnick, D. P. (1991). Assessing the thinking curriculum: New tools for educational reform. In B. R. Gifford & M. C. O'Connor (Eds.), *Changing assessments: Alternative views of aptitude, achievement and instruction* (pp. 37–75). Boston: Kluwer.

Rosenblatt, L. M. (1938). *Literature as exploration.* New York: Appleton-Century.

Rosenblatt, L. M. (1978). *The reader, the text, the poem: The transactional theory of the literary work.* Carbondale: Southern Illinois University Press.

Sarroub, L., & Pearson, P. D. (1998). Two steps forward, three steps back: The stormy history of reading comprehension assessment. *The Clearing House, 72,* 97–105.

Schraw, G., & Brunig, R. (1996). Readers' implicit models of reading. *Reading Research Quarterly, 31,* 290–305.

Simmons, W., & Resnick, L. (1993). Assessment as the catalyst of school reform. *Educational Leadership, 50*(5), 11–15.

Smith, M. (1991). Put to the test: The effects of external testing on teachers. *Educational Researcher, 20*(5), 8–11.

Wells, G. (1986). *The meaning makers: Children learning language and using language to learn.* Portsmouth, NH: Heinemann.

CHAPTER SIX

I Want to Learn to Read Before I Graduate: How Sociocultural Research on Adolescents' Literacy Struggles Can Shape Classroom Practice

KATHLEEN A. HINCHMAN
Syracuse University

I recently received an email from a high school guidance counselor. A young man had walked into her office, asking if someone could teach him to read before he left school. Seventeen years old, and identified as a special education student, this young man knew that his time in school was rapidly coming to an end—despite the fact that he had not yet received the instruction he most desired. The guidance counselor's email went on for several paragraphs, venting, asking how this could have happened.

There are many such students walking middle and high school hallways. Many more young people are not in school but instead are unemployed or working in low-wage jobs. They do not have the requisite skills for better employment. Such individuals cannot read well enough to understand study guides, textbooks, literary texts, test questions, homework, and various other documents and electronic sources that pave the road to academic success. In this chapter, I explore how research on adolescents' literacy provides a response to the guidance counselor's question by considering the state of adolescent literacy in the United States, sociocultural research on adolescents' literacies, and the applicability of this work to classroom practice.

Adolescent Literacy in the United States

The Alliance for Excellent Education, an organization dedicated to reducing high school dropout rates and improving the preparation of all students for college, provides information on its home page (www.all4ed.org) regarding U.S. high school graduation rates, including the following:

◆ 71 percent of all high school students graduate with a diploma;

◆ 52 percent of Hispanic and 56 percent of African American students graduate on time; and

◆ Graduation rates dip to 50 percent or lower in many urban areas.

Youth who drop out of school have also been portrayed as the latest cause célèbre for such popular culture icons as Oprah Winfrey, *Time* magazine, and Bill Gates (Oprah, 2006; Thornburgh, 2006). Even though many of the young people who find themselves dissatisfied enough to leave school can read at satisfactory levels, many others leave school because they struggle with the academic literacy tasks required for school success.

In the report, "Every Child a Graduate," the Alliance for Excellent Education notes that "approximately 25 percent of all high school students read at 'below basic' levels. Affecting more than their achievement in English and language arts classes, low literacy levels also prevent students from mastering content in other subjects" (Joftus, 2002). Older youths' reading achievement has retained roughly the same profile for the last quarter of a century, including persistent gaps in performance between most youth of color and youth who are white or Asian, despite massive federal and state efforts to address initial reading and writing development in young children. Indeed, the National Assessment of Educational Progress's most recent analysis (NCES, 2005) suggests that seventeen-year-old youth in the United States have shown no significant changes in reading performance between 2004 and the average scores of 1971 or 1999.

But such statistics represent only youth who take achievement tests. Many students, like the young man described at the opening of this chapter, are classified as in need of special education or extra language instruction for nonnative speakers of English. As a result, they may not have been asked to participate in assessment that informs them, their parents, school personnel, and community about their literacy levels (USDE, 2006). Some would consider such an omission to be a blessing: because they are designed to assess the literacy abilities of the majority, such assessments may not adequately represent the strengths of youth who are not part of the majority (Stobart, 2005). On the other hand, unreliable assessment administration has left many youth languishing in resource rooms, unsatisfied. These instructional settings typically help them complete homework and, sometimes, learn academic content; they do not often provide needed literacy interventions (Risko, 2005; Utley, Obiakor, & Kozleski, 2005).

Adolescent Literacy and Identity Construction

Statistics also belie specific life circumstances of those youth called "adolescents." Much of the literature on the sociocultural aspects of literacy explores the ties between the lived realities of young people and their literacies (see, for example, the following reviews: Alvermann, 2002; Alvermann, Hinchman, Moore, Phelps, & Waff, 2006; Bean, 2000; Hull & Schultz, 2001; Moje, Young, Readence, & Moore, 2000; Moore, 1996). Between the ages of twelve and twenty, such individuals are often referred to by the term *adolescent*, a word that, at least in the United States, has come to connote an overgeneralized image of immature, emotional, hormone-driven young people who are not quite adults. In contrast, sociocultural theory suggests that young people live increasingly complex lives—lives at least as complex as those of the older people around them—solving problems and trying to meet often disparate expectations of an increasing number of affinity groups, including those of parents, peers, careers, passions, college, sports, and academic study (Lesko, 2001).

What do such competing and shifting affinities mean for young people? All of us are members of a variety of social groups. Membership in these groups may be selected or it may be a matter of birth or social position. Such membership may be marked by income or appearance or restricted to less visible membership. Some group markers with special significance in U.S. culture at large include those tied to gender, race, class, and disability (Fine, Weis, Powell, & Wong, 1997; Hinchman & Moje, 1998; hooks, 1990). Our affinity groups, or "our people," have expectations, both implied and obvious. They tell us how to relate to family, peers, career, and school.

Expectations vary across groups, yielding a maze of contradictions within any individual's construction of identity. Such differences can be especially intense for young people who belong to an increasing number of such groups as they get older. They struggle with choices about enacting identities that are connected to but separated from families, that align with those of friends, and that will address their aspirations for a successful life (Holland, Lachicotte, Skinner, & Cain, 1998; Vadeboncoeur & Stevens, 2005).

Youth work to develop literacies that are needed for communicative competence—the ability to use language appropriately—within such affinity groups (Gee, 1996). Much research has demonstrated varied in- and out-of-school literacies that young people develop, including those related to 'zine reading among girlfriends (Finders, 1997), 'zine writing (Knobel & Lankshear, 2002), gang membership (Moje, 2000), car repair (Smith & Wilhelm, 2002), instant messaging (Lewis & Fabos, 2005), and other technologies (Chandler-Olcott & Mahar, 2003). Such demonstrations of skills and strategies show what young people can do when they need and desire to participate in particular groups.

Young people's school performance shapes and is shaped by such identity construction, woven inextricably into their literacy development. When youth lack the academic literacies needed for school success, they can come to see themselves as unworthy or incapable of completing literacy tasks under any circumstances. Although some have called this lack "learned helplessness" (Seligman, 1975), Alvermann (2001) pointed out the relative and social nature of such constructions. Noting that "culture can construct what counts as reading and who counts as a reader" (p. 676), Alvermann explained how she came to see Grady, a ninth grader, as a "knowing other," when his literate activities occupied social and cultural space that was familiar to him—even though he was identified by his school and parents as struggling with literacy.

Most youth are able to enact situated literacies that serve them within the contexts they find most important. However, more abstract academic literacies can matter a great deal to a young person who spends five or more hours a day in school—even to the young person who claims that academics are unimportant. When this person struggles with reading and writing required for school success because of an inability to read texts of appropriate difficulty, he or she may take on an identity as a "struggling reader," that is, of an individual who bears "the residuals of having been part of a group of people described by both achievement tests and school personnel as the 'have-nots' in terms of access to cultural capital through literate means" (Alvermann, 2001, para. 17).

Somehow, the young man I described at the beginning of this chapter identified himself as in need of reading instruction—with confidence in his ability to benefit from it and with a sense that he deserved this much before he left high school. He appeared to display the identity of someone who was willing to learn to read and had a desire to do needed work. If naming himself a "struggling reader" would help him get this instruction, he was willing to be so named. Perhaps, like Grady, he enacted personal literacies in other contexts, with other affinity groups, and this gave him confidence.

But imagine the numbers of young people who want to avoid being labeled as one of the academic "have-nots" that Alvermann described. They may be silent about their struggles, adopting a manner that leaves them without query by adults around them, appearing to teachers and parents as uncaring, lazy, or worse. Or they may be among those who leave school so that they no longer have to confront their lack of competence in this setting. Such individuals do not usually "open up" to instruction unless they are confident that they are with someone to whom they matter and, better, someone who can offer needed help.

Understanding youths' affinities, the communicative competencies they develop within affinity groups, as well as the particular literacies of individuals in any one classroom, is essential knowledge for effective teachers. At a minimum, teachers should respect and build instruction to use youth's varied repertoire of situated literacy skills and strategies. Teachers can also help youth enhance these skills and strategies by tying them to the academic reading and writing strategies needed for school success—without impinging too greatly on the private literacy spaces of their personal friendships, of course (Luke, 1997).

Situated Literacy Instruction

One reaction to the insight that young people may be stigmatized because they lack the academic literacies needed for school success might be to avoid such confrontations in favor of projects that allow youth to work in more familiar contexts. However, such a polarized reaction will not help these individuals gain access to desired competencies. Alvermann (2001) suggested coaching Grady so that he could begin to see that such literacies can be developed, given what he already knows how to do, and given that he maintains his identity as a reader and his faith in his ability to be competent as he learns to apply skills in new contexts.

The challenge may be greater than can be imagined by Grady or the young man I described at the beginning of this chapter. Gee (2002) argued persuasively that success in the next millennium will come to those young people who are what he described as "shape-shifting portfolio people" (p. 62). Such individuals are entrepreneurs, who switch jobs often—building up a variety of heavily classed skills and experiences that can be arranged and rearranged to suit diverse and ever changing circumstances and technologies of employment as they move from job to job. According to Gee's theory, Grady and my young man need to have many experiences to enhance existing literacies, showing increasing flexibility in their application. Being positioned to have such experiences is so closely tied to socioeconomic status that both young men may also need to "study up," that is, emulate the experiences of those who have more opportunities for experiences—without, of course, losing their sense of existing competence to ground their work.

Once a teacher establishes a relationship with such individuals, she or he needs to plan the varied experiences that lead to the development of Gee's portfolios. But what should these experiences look like? Moje and her colleagues (Moje, Ciechanowski, Kramer, Ellis, Carrillo, & Collazo, 2004) experimented with something they called a "hybrid framework," inviting middle school youth to engage in the discourses of science class. Called hybrid for its blending of sociocultural and cognitive perspectives toward literacy instruction, this framework grounded reading, inquiry, and instruction within youth's existing funds of knowledge (Moll & Gonzalez, 1994); teachers provided scaffolds to support students' work through modeling, demonstrations, and study guides (Vygotsky, 1978). By conducting experiments that mattered to the youth in their study, these projects combined researchers' and teachers' knowledge and enthusiasm with youths' knowledge of themselves and their community, creating new instructional space.

One can easily imagine Moje and her colleagues' hybrid framework being used to develop similar projects in social sciences, literature study, and mathematics. But Grady and the young man also need teachers who create hybrid instructional spaces that tie newly learned, very basic literacy strategies to existing knowledge. It is a challenge to find a way to blend teachers' and students' knowledge and passions when the youth may need instruction in such emergent skills—and, at the same time, to avoid stigma and help youth become shape-shifting portfolio people, as Gee suggested. The preceding suggests that youth belong to such an idiosyncratic array of affinity groups as they age that, when they struggle significantly with reading and writing needed for school success, instruction may be best co-constructed for individuals or small groups rather than for a whole class.

In addition to knowledge about young people's identity construction generally, as well as respectful relationships with specific young people in order to negotiate issues of stigma, interest, and creating new space, teachers need other very specific kinds of expertise to develop the linguistic and cognitive aspects of reading and writing in ways that are situated in this portfolio of academic and real-world tasks. Such instruction helps youth figure out unfamiliar words in context and develop fluency, comprehension, and composition strategies needed for academic reading and writing (see, for example, reviews by Alexander & Jetton, 2000; Alvermann & Moore, 1991; Hattie, Biggs, & Purdie, 1996; Hinchman, Alvermann, Boyd, Brozo, & Vacca, 2003/2004; Jetton & Dole, 2004; National Institute of Child Health and Human Development [NICHD], 2000; Pajares, 1996; Phelps & Hanley-Maxwell, 1997; Snow, Griffin, & Burns, 2005; Sturtevant, Boyd, Brozo, Hinchman, Moore, & Alvermann, 2006; Vacca, 2002; Wade & Moje, 2000). The following sections describe four pedagogical principles that can be derived from blending research from a sociocultural perspective with work from linguistic and cognitive perspectives.

Passion Persuades

Because of their developing affinities, young people typically juggle a lot. With requests from peers, family, and academic contexts to attend to such obligations as babysitting siblings and cousins, playing sports for the chance to earn a college scholarship, working in low-wage jobs, and fostering relationships with friends, young people may ignore schoolwork or extra reading for a number of reasons: it's not a relative priority, it's forgotten even though it's a priority, it's completed during late evenings as they fall into bed, or it's copied from classmates at early morning bus stops. Youth help each other through drug abuse, eating disorders, pregnancy, and STDs; good academic intentions can be waylaid by these other commitments.

One of the things that youth find attractive, however, is an adult who shares a passion for his or her career choices (Moje, 1996). One young woman told Patricia Zalewski and me that she liked the teacher, and she liked understanding the homework, but that she didn't always have time for understanding (Hinchman & Zalewski, 1996). With daily summer vacation and after-school marching band practices, babysitting obligations, and homework in six subjects, this high school sophomore had reduced the completion of her global studies homework so that it did not require comprehension—even while she maintained a "B" average. Once the teacher understood, she began to take this viewpoint into account in her instructional planning. Her instructional activities and homework assignments gave students more time to talk through understandings in class, followed with homework to reinforce ideas that students clearly understood as they exited her classroom door (Hinchman & Zalewski, 2000).

Teachers who develop realistic, impassioned answers to students' question, "Why should we know this stuff?" find themselves displaying enthusiasms that are appealing to preoccupied youth. A teacher can find joy in youth's own literacies, as Alvermann did in Grady's literacies (2001), or in sharing his or her own subject matter in new and different ways: the physics teacher who designs projects with students and delights in their problem solving, the English teacher who co-constructs a poetry project with students and exclaims in wonder at their writing, the global studies teacher who effuses over youth's insights regarding their own investigations of cross-cultural perspectives, and the music teacher who invites students to choose music and then proclaims over the symphony band's melding sounds after hours of practice. All such teachers motivate students and learn much more from them as a result (Alvermann, 2005).

As Moje and her colleagues (2004) found, tasks that begin with students and then mix students' interests and teachers' passions may be most effective for learning new content. If we respect our learners, we can design inquiry projects that allow us to combine discovery of new applications of what we know about our disciplines with young people's desire for relevance and connection in ways that use and provide a chance to enhance the portfolios of skills and experiences that students are trying to develop in and out of school.

Practice Does Not Necessarily Make Perfect

It makes some sense to assume that students cannot develop proficient reading and writing without practice. However, research suggests that reading practice does not always yield the results that teachers desire (NICHD, 2000). Older struggling readers and writers may fall into one of several traps (Broaddus & Ivey, 2002). They may be asked to "practice" reading texts with unfamiliar content. They may be required to write essays using an unfamiliar argument pattern. They may be asked to read texts that contain unfamiliar vocabulary, sentence structures, or other genre conventions, and they may struggle as a result. They may be asked to produce texts about content they do not fully understand. They may not yet have developed the integration of reading or writing skills and strategies needed for fluent silent reading or for writing within a specific discipline.

Whatever the reasons, the aforementioned research on literacy and identity construction suggests that academic literacy struggles feed inextricably into youth's identity constructions—no matter what kind of out-of-school successes they are able to tally. Such struggling over the reading or writing of frustration-level texts is not likely to improve youth's reading. But when youth have some choice in reading and writing texts that match some combination of their interests and reading ability, they are able to complete activities with increased competence (Allington, 2005).

Like students in Moje and her colleagues' (2004) classrooms, youth can be invited to complete inquiry projects, finding answers to self-generated questions, using texts they select, and creating products they design, to represent growing understandings of discipline-specific content. They can send instant messages, search the Web, create collaborative blogs, and collaborate with others across classrooms and, as a result, achieve heightened academic success.

Within such contexts, a teacher may provide appropriate supports to help with the reading and writing that students are likely to encounter. For instance, before students begin reading, a teacher might offer support through organizing vocabulary study, flipping through pages of an assigned text to introduce its new ideas, or providing study guides. Before writing, a teacher might discuss possible topics, work with students to develop graphic organizers of main ideas, or model several approaches to completing needed tasks.

Thinking of O'Brien's (2001) notion of redefining competence to include visual representations to mediate understandings, tutors who worked with the young man described at the beginning of this chapter invited him to engage in Internet inquiry projects. They selected topics together and took turns reading their online discoveries, with tutors doing most of the reading and note taking as the young man dictated. They eventually turned these notes into PowerPoint presentations, complete with video clips, photographs, and outlined information, organized with carefully selected background designs and letter fonts. He also dictated narratives to accompany the presentation that he practiced to deliver fluently. During such projects, the student practiced many academic literacy skills and learned that he had ideas worth communicating.

Simplicity Rules

Youth must draw a number of inferences from the use of scaffolding tools to understand how to complete academic literacy tasks independently across disciplines. Teachers can encourage understanding of this process with explanations of how to apply various reading, writing, and problem-solving strategies in a variety of contexts. The effectiveness of such explanations are, of course, increased when teachers are familiar with and can make connections to youth's out-of-school interests and personal literacy practices (Hinchman et al., 2003/2004).

Explicit instruction should be straightforward and brief. Yet it must include information about how a strategy can be used, as well as a model of such use within the context of a variety of texts. Such explanations should be followed by responsive, guided student practice, also in a variety of texts. During this practice, teachers can observe youth's attempts and keep anecdotal records. Teachers can confer with students, providing helpful feedback and ongoing guidance, like a coach or driving teacher. Over time, a teacher can plan for responsive, gradual release of responsibility so that youth can learn to apply such strategies independently to a variety of reading and writing tasks (Underwood & Pearson, 2004).

Teachers can plan such mini-lessons to explain and model a variety of comprehension and composition strategies (Block & Pressley, 2003). The National Reading Panel Report (NICHD, 2000) suggests that students be taught to monitor their comprehension while reading, to engage in cooperative learning, to use graphic organizers, to generate questions while reading, to use text structure as an aid to comprehension, and to summarize what they have read. The Denver-area Public Education Business Coalition recommends attending to making connections, questioning, visualizing, determining importance, synthesizing, and monitoring to ensure comprehension (Harvey & Goudvis, 2000). Block and Pressley (2003) suggest teaching reading comprehension strategies that can be used before, during, and after reading.

Which strategies should be taught to young writers is less clear from extant research. Proficient writers use a reflexive process that involves planning, organizing, drafting, revising, and editing—working with several pieces until they seek eventual publication (Smagorinsky, 2005). Writing workshops that involve young people in study of teachers' writing models, peer editing, and emulating proficient writers' processes are often successful (Atwell, 1998; Calkins, 1994). More authentic publications seem to generate heightened enthusiasm and commitment from writers, even new ones, such as letters or reports to be shared with someone other than a teacher. A number of teachers have discovered that sharing expectations in the form of scoring rubrics before writing helps emerging writers build bridges from personal literacies to academic ones, making clear teachers' expectations for such traits as ideas, organization, voice, word choice, sentence fluency, conventions, and presentation (Northwest Regional Educational Laboratory [NWREL], 2001).

Research on written language acquisition and development also tells us that good readers and writers are able to recognize word patterns as clues to decoding unknown words and to spelling (Bear, Invernizzi, Templeton, & Johnston, 2003). Vocabulary is learned through incidental exposure and direct instruction (NICHD, 2000). Even though most research in this area involved younger children, one might infer that systematic, explicit instruction can benefit older youth who lack such knowledge, especially instruction in recognizing common word patterns (e.g., consonant-vowel-consonant, silent *e*, consonant-vowel, *r*-controlled, consonant *le*, and vowel teams). Older readers can be taught to determine pronunciation and meaning of unknown words—even discipline-specific technical terminology—from the combined use of decoding and context clues, making more difficult texts seem less so (Snow et al., 2005).

Sociocultural research tells us to approach such strategy instruction with caution. Sounding out words and knowing their meanings is not all there is to reading and writing. Placing too much emphasis on such language bits can seem abstract, monotonous, and meaningless when youth are already discouraged about academic literacy struggles. Teachers of science, mathematics, social studies, and English may explain and model comprehension and composition strategies specific to their respective disciplines. However, research suggests that these subject-area specialists do not have the expertise or time to help youth who struggle with basic reading and writing skills (Alvermann & Moore, 1991). As a result, knowledgeable reading specialists are also needed to help youth who struggle with reading and writing, with time allotted during the school day for such work. Such instruction should be simple and straightforward, grounded in and sensitive to youth's insights and understandings.

Research suggests that such instruction is most effective when it takes place individually or in small groups and when teachers are careful to make explanations brief, using understandable examples. When youths' eyes glaze over, this is likely the result of a too long or abstract explanation. When a youth is offended, this may be the result of an explanation representing information that is either too evident or incomprehensible (Block & Pressley, 2003).

In addition to working on inquiry projects, our high school student also studied types of syllables (Snow et al., 2005). He began slowly, by learning consonant-vowel-consonant words; he argued with one tutor about whether or not there could be a syllable with no vowel in it and, eventually, realized how the pattern generalized to other words and wondered why no one had ever taught him this rule before. He was so fascinated by this straightforward combination of simple word work and inquiry that, in less than a year, he moved from reading words dysfluently at a preprimer level to reading passages at the fifth-grade instructional level.

Time Matters

One of the best-known correlations in educational research is that time on task affects learning (Fuller, 1969). If we want youth to be able to read and write, they must spend time in extended reading and writing, in a variety of sources, so that they can develop a wide array of skills and strategies for their portfolios. If we want them to develop discourses specific to disciplines, such as those tied to mathematics, science, and social studies, students need to spend time immersed in contexts that encourage them to do so. If youth need to develop word skills, comprehension, and composition strategies to facilitate their completion of academic literacy tasks, we need to spend time showing them how such strategies work and helping them find connections between existing personal literacies and those academic literacies needed for success in school and in life.

However, finding the time for strengthening the literacy skills and strategies needed by specific young people in grades 7 through 12 is no easy task. Today's middle and high school schedules are filled with required classes designed to teach subject-specific content for efficient entrée into the study of liberal arts and postsecondary education. The substance and boundaries of such classes have changed little over decades—despite many years of tinkering around the edges and despite the fact that today's secondary schools welcome a vastly more divergent population of students than was the case when the curricula were introduced (Deschenes, Cuban, & Tyack, 2001). Schedules heavy with subject-area study leave youth little time to enhance personal literacy practices, especially in ways that benefit academic literacies, or other related literacies that can most yield success in today's world.

Did our young man make such outstanding progress because he finally decided to take responsibility for his learning, because someone took time to explain the bits of written language to him that he was ready to know, or because of a combination of both? Which schooling experiences will contribute most to his life portfolio? Could someone find time to provide needed literacy instruction for such older youth in school?

Only since No Child Left Behind (NCLB) laws mandated disaggregated reporting of annual reading tests have we begun to realize that traditional curricular requirements may not be serving huge chunks of the population. Students from a variety of minority ethnic backgrounds show significant gaps in performance on NCLB testing compared to European American and Asian peers. Students designated as learners with special needs—a population whose reading performance has not been measured reliably for quite some time—have performed especially poorly on such tests (USDE, 2006). Theorists have argued, conflictingly, that such assessments may be helpful or harmful and that they may measure skills that are too narrow to account for the literacy needs of the next millennium and, at the same time, too broad to provide useful diagnostic information to classroom teachers (Allington, 2005). Even so, such assessment results make it clear that the instruction that is provided is not working for all older students and that more of our time needs to be spent on this work (Ladson-Billings, 2006).

Conclusion

Sociocultural research on adolescent literacy notes the social nature of the constructions by which youth can be viewed as "struggling readers." This body of literature also explains youth's propensities for developing literacies suited to favorite affinity groups—and that this can exclude those academic constructions within which they feel least capable. Such research provides us with grounding for new conceptualizations of instruction that meld together youth's interest and understanding with that of teachers. Such blending creates the potential for new curriculum representations and for youth to develop a broadened portfolio of literacy skills and strategies.

Likewise, teachers who join sociocultural ideas with what we know about helping youth learn to deal with various aspects of the reading process may see analogous instructional benefits. Re-envisioned instruction should demonstrate passion, invite youth to engage in authentic applications, include simple and explicit instruction, and value youth's time by tying instruction to their existing competence and life goals. Only in this way can individuals who are on the margins because they struggle with academic literacies be brought in from the margins and given opportunities to develop the literacies they need for success in school and in life.

References

Alexander, P. A., & Jetton, T. L. (2000). Learning from text: A multidimensional and developmental perspective. In M. L. Kamil, P. B. Mosenthal, P. D. Pearson, & R. Barr (Eds.), *Handbook of reading research* (Vol. 3, pp. 285–310). Mahwah, NJ: Erlbaum.

Allington, R. L. (2005). *What really matters for struggling readers: Designing research-based programs* (2nd ed.). Boston: Allyn and Bacon.

Alvermann, D. E. (2001). Reading adolescents' reading identities: Looking back to see ahead. *Journal of Adolescent and Adult Literacy, 44,* 676–90. Retrieved August 1, 2006, from *Expanded Academic ASAP* database. Thomson Gale. Syracuse University Library.

Alvermann, D. E. (2002). Effective literacy instruction for adolescents. *Journal of Literacy Research, 34,* 189–208.

Alvermann, D. E. (2005). Exemplary literacy instruction in grades 7–12: What counts and who's counting? In J. Flood & P. L. Anders (Eds.), *Literacy development of students in urban schools: Research and Policy* (pp. 185–201). Newark, DE: International Reading Association.

Alvermann, D. E., Hinchman, K. A., Moore, D. W., Phelps, S. F., & Waff, D. R. (Eds.). (2006). *Reconceptualizing the literacies in adolescents' lives* (2nd ed.). Mahwah, NJ: Erlbaum.

Alvermann, D. E., & Moore, D. W. (1991). Secondary school reading. In R. Barr, M. L. Kamil, P. B. Mosenthal, & P. D. Pearson (Eds.), *Handbook of reading research* (Vol. 2, pp. 951–83). New York: Longman.

Atwell, N. (1998). *In the middle: New understandings about writing, reading, and learning.* Portsmouth, NH: Boynton/Cook.

Bean, T. W. (2000). Reading in the content areas: Social constructivist dimensions. In M. J. Kamil, P. B. Mosenthal, P. D. Pearson, & R.

Barr (Eds.), *Handbook of reading research* (Vol. 3, pp. 629–44). Mahwah, NJ: Erlbaum.

Bear, D. R., Invernizzi, M., Templeton, S., & Johnston, F. (2003). *Words their way: Word study for phonics, vocabulary, and spelling instruction* (3rd. ed.). New York: Prentice Hall.

Block, C. C., & Pressley, M. (2003). Best practices in comprehension instruction. In L. M. Morrow, L. B. Gambrell, & M. Pressley (Eds.), *Best practices in literacy instruction* (2nd ed., pp. 111–26). New York: Guilford Press.

Bowles, S., & Gintis, H. (1976). *Schooling in capitalist America: Educational reform and the contradictions of economic life.* New York: Basic Books.

Broaddus, K., & Ivey, G. (2002). Taking away the struggle to read in the middle grades. *Middle School Journal, 34*(2), 5–11.

Calkins, L. M. (1994). *The art of teaching writing.* Portsmouth, NH: Heinemann.

Chandler-Olcott, K., & Mahar, D. (2003). "Tech-savviness" meets multiliteracies: Exploring adolescent girls' technology-mediated literacy practices. *Reading Research Quarterly, 38,* 356–85.

Deschenes, S., Cuban, L., & Tyack, D. (2001). Mismatch: Historical perspectives on schools and students who don't fit them. *Teachers College Record, 103,* 525–47.

Finders, M. J. (1997). *Just girls: Hidden literacies and life in junior high.* New York: Teachers College Press.

Fine, M., Weis, L., Powell, L. C., & Wong, L. M. (Eds.). (1997). *Off white: Readings on race, power, and society.* New York: Routledge.

Fuller, F. F. (1969). Concerns of teachers: A developmental conceptualization. *American Educational Research Journal, 6,* 207–26.

Gee, J. P. (1996). *Social linguistics and literacies: Ideology in discourses* (2nd. ed.). London: Taylor & Francis.

Gee, J. P. (2002). Millennials and bobos, *Blues Clues,* and *Sesame Street*: A story for our times. In D. E. Alvermann (Ed.), *Adolescents and literacies in a digital world* (pp. 51–67). New York: Peter Lang.

Harvey, S., & Goudvis, A. (2000). *Strategies that work: Teaching comprehension to enhance understanding.* Portland, ME: Stenhouse.

Hattie, J., Biggs, J., & Purdie, N. (1996). Effects of learning skills interventions on student learning: A meta-analysis. *Review of Educational Research, 66,* 99–136.

Hinchman, K. A., Alvermann, D. E., Boyd, F. B., Brozo, W. G., & Vacca, R. T. (2003/2004). Supporting older students' in- and out-of-school literacies. *Journal of Adolescent & Adult Literacy, 47,* 304–10.

Hinchman, K. A., & Moje, E. B. (1998). Locating the social and political in secondary school literacy. *Reading Research Quarterly, 33,* 117–28.

Hinchman, K. A., & Zalewski, P. (1996). Reading for success in a tenth-grade global studies class: A qualitative study. *Journal of Literacy Research, 28,* 91–106.

Hinchman, K. A., & Zalewski, P. (2000). "She puts all these words in it": Interpreting the language of tenth-grade global studies. In E. B. Moje & D. G. O'Brien (Eds.), *Constructions of literacy: Studies of teaching and learning in and out of secondary schools* (pp. 171–92). Mahwah, NJ: Erlbaum.

Hirsch, E. D., Jr. (1988). *Cultural literacy: What every American needs to know.* New York: Vintage Books.

Holland, D., Lachicotte, W., Jr., Skinner, D., & Cain, C. (1998). *Identity and agency in cultural worlds.* Cambridge, MA: Harvard University Press.

hooks, b. (1990). *Yearning: Race, gender, and cultural politics.* Boston: South End Press.

Hull, G., & Schultz, K. (2001). Literacy and learning out of school: A review of theory and research. *Review of Educational Research, 71,* 575–611.

Jetton, T. L., & Dole. J. A. (Eds.). (2004). *Adolescent literacy research and practice.* New York: Guilford Press.

Joftus, S. (2002). *Every child a graduate: A framework for an excellent education for all middle and high school students.* Washington, DC: Alliance for Excellent Education. Retrieved April 4, 2006, from http://all4ed.org/publications/EveryChildAGraduate/every.pdf

Knobel, M., & Lankshear, C. (2002). Cut, paste, publish: The production and consumption of zines. In D. E. Alvermann (Ed.), *Adolescents and literacies in a digital world* (pp. 164–85). New York: Peter Lang.

Ladson-Billings, G. J. (2006, April). *From the achievement gap to the education debt: Understanding achievement in U.S. schools.* Presidential address presented at the annual meeting of the American Educational Research Association, San Francisco, CA.

Lesko, N. (2001). *Act your age! A cultural construction of adolescence.* New York: Routledge Falmer.

Lewis, C., & Fabos, B. (2005). Instant messaging, literacies, and social identities. *Reading Research Quarterly, 40,* 470–501.

Luke, C. (1997). Media literacy and cultural studies. In S. Muspratt, A. Luke, & P. Freebody (Eds.), *Constructing critical literacies: Teaching and learning textual practice* (pp. 19–49). Cresskill, NJ: Hampton Press.

Moje, E. B. (1996). "I teach students, not subjects": Teacher-student relationships as contexts for secondary literacy. *Reading Research Quarterly, 31,* 172–95.

Moje, E. B. (2000). "To be part of the story": The literacy practices of gangsta adolescents. *Teachers College Record 102,* 651–90.

Moje, E. B., Ciechanowski, K. M., Kramer, K., Ellis, L., Carrillo, R., & Collazo, T. (2004). Working toward third space in content area literacy: An examination of everyday funds of knowledge and discourse. *Reading Research Quarterly, 39,* 38–70.

Moje, E. B., Young, J. P., Readence, J. E., & Moore, D. W. (2000). Reinventing adolescent literacy for new times: Perennial and millennial issues. *Journal of Adolescent and Adult Literacy, 43,* 400–410.

Moll, L. C., & Gonzalez, N. (1994). Lessons from research with language-minority children. *Journal of Reading Behavior, 26,* 439–56.

Moore, D. W. (1996). Contexts for literacy in secondary schools. In D. J. Leu, C. K. Kinzer, & K. A. Hinchman (Eds.), *Literacies for the 21st century: Research and practice* (45th Yearbook of the National Reading Conference, pp. 15–46). Chicago: National Reading Conference.

National Center for Education Statistics (NCES). (2005). *NAEP 2004 trends in academic progress: Three decades of student performance in reading and mathematics: Findings in brief* (NCES Publication No. 2005-463). Retrieved April 24, 2006, from http://nces.ed.gov/nationsreportcard/pdf/main2005/2005463.pdf

National Institute of Child Health and Human Development (NICHD). (2000). *Report of the National Reading Panel: Teaching children to read: An evidence-based assessment of the scientific research literature on reading and its implications for reading instruction* (NIH Publication No. 00-4769). Washington, DC: U.S. Government Printing Office.

Northwest Regional Educational Laboratory (NWREL). (2001). *6 + 1 trait writing.* Retrieved August 1, 2006, from www.nwrel.org/assessment/department.php?d=1

O'Brien, D. (2001, June). "At-risk" adolescents: Redefining competence through the multiliteracies of intermediality, visual arts, and representation. *Reading Online, 4*(11). Retrieved August 1, 2006, from http://www.readingonline.org/newliteracies/lit_index.asp?HREF=/newliteracies/obrien/index.html

Oprah (2006, April 11). Failing grade: Lisa Ling tours dropout nation. *Oprah.com.* Retrieved April 17, 2006, from www.oprah.com/tows/slide/200604/20060411/slide_20060411_284_105.jhtml

Pajares, F. (1996). Self-efficacy beliefs in academic settings. *Review of Educational Research, 66,* 543–78.

Phelps, L. A., & Hanley-Maxwell, C. (1997). School-to-work transitions for youth with disabilities: A review of outcomes and practices. *Review of Educational Research, 67,* 197–226.

Risko, V. J. (2005). A loss of equity, excellence, and expectations through overrepresentation of culturally and linguistically diverse students in special education: A response to Cheryl Utley, Festus Obiakor, and Elizabeth Kozleski. In J. Flood & P. L. Anders (Eds.), *Literacy development of students in urban schools: Research and Policy* (pp. 345–60). Newark, DE: International Reading Association.

Seligman, M. E. P. (1975). *Helplessness: On depression, development, and death.* San Francisco: W. H. Freeman.

Smagorinsky, P. (Ed.). (2005). *Research on composition: Multiple perspectives on two decades of change.* New York: Teachers College Press.

Smith, M. W., & Wilhelm, J. D. (2002). *"Reading don't fix no chevys": Literacy in the lives of young men.* Portsmouth, NH: Heinemann.

Snow, C., Griffin, P., & Burns, M. S. (Eds.). (2005). *Knowledge to support the teaching of reading: Preparing teachers for a changing world.* San Francisco: Jossey-Bass.

Stobart, G. (2005). Fairness in multicultural assessment systems. *Assessment in education: Principles, policy and practice, 12,* 275–87.

Sturtevant, E. G., Boyd, F. B., Brozo, W. G., Hinchman, K. A., Moore, D. W., & Alvermann, D. E. (2006). *Principled practices for adolescent literacy: A framework for instruction and policy.* Mahwah, NJ: Erlbaum.

Thornburgh, N. (2006, April 17). Dropout nation. *Time, 167*(16). Retrieved April 24, 2006, from www.time.com/time/archive/preview/0,10987,1181646,00.html

Underwood, T., & Pearson, P. D. (2004). Teaching struggling adolescent readers to comprehend what they read. In T. L. Jetton & J. A. Dole (Eds.), *Adolescent literacy research and practice* (pp. 135–61). New York: Guilford Press.

U.S. Department of Education. (2006). No Child Left Behind: Fact sheets, op-eds. Retrieved August 10, 2006, from www.ed.gov/news/opeds/factsheets/index.html?src=gu

Utley, C. A., Obiakor, F. E., & Kozleski, E. B. (2005). Overrepresentation of culturally and linguistically diverse students in special education in urban schools: A research synthesis. In J. Flood & P. L. Anders (Eds.), *Literacy development of students in urban schools: Research and Policy* (pp. 314–344). Newark, DE: International Reading Association.

Vacca, R. T. (2002). Making a difference in adolescents' school lives: Visible and invisible aspects of content area reading. In A. E. Farstrup & S. J. Samuels (Eds.), *What research has to say about reading instruction* (3rd ed., pp. 184–204). Newark, DE: International Reading Association.

Vadeboncoeur, J. A., & Stevens, L. P. (Eds.). (2005). *Re/constructing "the adolescent": Sign, symbol, and body.* New York: Peter Lang.

Vygotsky, L. S. (1978). *Mind in society: The development of higher mental processes* (M. Cole, V. John-Steiner, S. Scribner, & E. Souberman, Eds.). Cambridge, MA: Harvard University Press.

Wade, S. E., & Moje, E. B. (2000). The role of text in classroom learning. In M. L. Kamil, P. B. Mosenthal, P. D. Pearson, & R. Barr (Eds.), *Handbook of reading research* (Vol. 3, pp. 609–44). Mahwah, NJ: Erlbaum.

Literacy, Identity, and the Changing Social Spaces of Teaching and Learning

KEVIN M. LEANDER
Vanderbilt University

JESSICA C. ZACHER
California State University, Long Beach

In this chapter, we consider identity as it is related to common practices in English classrooms, focusing in particular on classroom interactions. As we conceive of it, identity is an individual or group's sense of self that is constructed through social interaction. Identity shifts in different contexts, and people typically relate to more than one identity or have several "senses of self." We begin with a perspective on identity that complicates identity as given in advance by stable social and cultural categories, whether in regard to nation, class, race, ethnicity, gender, religion, and so forth. From this perspective, we might think of the classroom as a kind of container that holds certain kinds of identities: "teachers," "observing administrators," "good students," and "poor students."

Yet, we challenge this identity-container perspective in two key ways, on both the "identity" and "container" sides of the equation. First, the classroom does not merely hold identities placed within it; rather, social practices within the classroom, such as reading and writing, actively produce identities. Second, although the classroom appears to be a container, it has recently been more productively described as a crossroads—a site that flows as people, culture, materials, and different discourses move through and make contact with one another. Thus, the classroom contains and produces resources for identity that come into it from many directions.

In order to describe the complex relationship between identity production and the classroom as a site, English education scholars have begun to understand the classroom as a social space that is internally diverse and connected to other social spaces. In the following sections, we draw on contemporary research to describe three modes of thinking about the classroom as a social space where identities are produced through literacy practices. Each of these modes is informed by a different perspective, or dominant metaphor or mode, on the classroom as social space. The first mode conceives of the classroom as a site where different discourses and materials interact and intersect. It provides a critique of classrooms as primarily containing teacher-directed talk and considers how various student and teacher discourses can be simultaneously alive and constituting diverse spaces in the classroom.

The second mode is guided by contrasting what youth do and who they are when they are out of school with their in-school actions and identities. That is, the second mode works to juxtapose sites of practice and identity, raising questions about how classroom practices and identities are related to those out of school, in after-school programs, and so forth. A third mode considers how the classroom is a site related to other sites, but one that reaches beyond home-school relations to conceive of larger-scaled relations, including those of the state, and how these relations shape student and teacher identities.

While these three modes of understanding identity and literacy are still being formulated, they offer powerful ways of critiquing and reshaping routine teaching and learning practices in English language arts. In each of the following sections, we consider a small set of studies that have made important contributions to these modes or ways of thinking. Rather than representing the "field" at large, we selected these studies because they share novel and dynamic orientations to literacy, interaction, and identity while also providing for productive tensions with one another. We follow each select review with implications for practice that emanate from the studies.

Mode I: Looking at How Identities Are Formed in Classroom Literacy Events

A shared orientation of studies in this first mode involves seeing the classroom as permeable, open to the cultures, discourses, practices, and materials that might seem to exist "outside" of them. Classrooms are highly dynamic social spaces in which power circulates in unpredictable, idiosyncratic ways. School curriculum and pedagogy provide resources for the production of identity, but the resources are frequently taken up only in their relations with everyday life and popular culture. Identities produced along with classroom cultures are imagined not as fixed entities, but as intersections where the traffic of multiple resources are brought together and reorganized.

Teacher Scripts, Student Scripts, and "Third Space"

Gutiérrez, Rymes, and Larson's (1995) work is notable for moving outside of accounts of classroom interaction that are teacher-focused or teacher-dominated; it considers instead how students actively shape the directions of classroom interaction, including the cultural resources used in them and possible identities that may emerge from them. Gutiérrez et al. draw on Bakhtin's (1981) notion of social heteroglossia (or "multivoicedness"). This notion provides a way of understanding how language-in-use, or discourse, is always shaped by the people who have used it in the past, by their purposes, and by their histories. Therefore, even when a single speaker has the floor in interaction, the presence and influence of others and of their histories can be traced within his or her talk. Heteroglossia helps us understand how using language involves assuming a social position. In other terms, using language in interaction always involves identity work, as speakers (and hearers) assume stances with respect to voices that have shaped the language they are using.

However, although we might expect the presence of many voices within any interaction, classroom interaction presents a case in which a single voice—that of the teacher and the institution behind him or her—tends to dominate. Gutiérrez et al. (1995)

contrast this dominance of a single, institutional teacher voice and dominant cultural values backing this voice with more free-wheeling student dialogue that is informed by many different voices and cultural resources. This contrast informs their analysis of the contact zone between the "teacher script" and the "student script" (or "counterscript"). They trace the students' progression as they first "rekey," or play with, joke, and deliberately misread the teacher's talk. At first, it appears that the teacher and students are not connecting with one another at all. Later in the interaction, however, both the teacher and the students let go of this separation and meet in a relatively fleeting and transitional phase of interaction that looks like neither of their familiar scripts. Gutiérrez et al. (1995) term this phase and meeting point the *third space*. Although teacher talk and student talk seem to occur in mutually exclusive spaces, this "third space" brings them together into "authentic interaction and heteroglossia" (p. 446).

The ninth-grade classroom context of their investigation comprises primarily African American and Latino students, with several European American students as well. The key interaction was a recitation period about current events; Gutiérrez et al. (1995) argue that the teacher was guided by a curriculum script of "Keeping up with the world" (p. 454), in which he presented news story information as if it were commonsensical and readily available to all of the students. The teacher moved into a recitation on *Brown v. Board of Education*, during which students rekey and deliberately misread his talk about "Brown" to include comments concerning "James Brown" (the musician), as well as "Richard Brown," "Al Green," and others. The pivotal moment of the interaction, opening up to a third space in terms of the authors' analysis, is when a student poses the question: "What if the kid's half White and half Black / where do they g-what *school* do they go to?" (p. 465).

When this question is asked, the attentions of students and teacher are momentarily organized together; the teacher is not following an authoritative script and the students are not resisting or deliberately misreading the teacher's script. The interaction seems to hold genuine interest and importance for all and might have been a site for beginning to think about racial politics and identities. In the midst of this, a student remarks, "Tania [is] confused," in reference to a student in that particular class who was half black and half white. Such a moment, what Wortham (1994) calls a "participant example," might have had high importance for the class to reconsider racial identity. However, the moment ended, and the teacher returned to his monologue.

Although the article by Gutiérrez et al. (1995) is more focused on the structures of classroom interaction than on the particulars of identity work, it does lay some important groundwork for reconceiving learning and identity processes. The authors push us to consider how effective teaching practice does not merely involve bringing students into the teacher's script, culture, or discourse, but instead means creating a set of social relations—or a kind of social space—in which the teacher's and students' "cultures, discourses, and knowledges" can circulate, come into contact, and form new hybrids. Effective practice is essentially disruptive of scripts and plans for *both* teacher and student. The next article we review by George Kamberelis pushes the idea of hybridity further.

Heterogeneous Resources and Hybrid Social Identities

The key construct that Kamberelis (2001) develops throughout his article is the "hybrid discourse practice," which is a way of accounting for how children and teachers draw their routine and not-so-routine forms of talk, material practices, and social interactions from many social and cultural worlds. In so doing, children and teachers "constitute interactional spaces that are intertextually complex, interactionally dynamic, locally situated accomplishments" (p. 87). Like Gutiérrez et al. (1995), Kamberelis focuses on and celebrates possibilities of such heterogeneity, using the term *free spaces* (Fine, Weis, Centrie, & Roberts, 2000) to accentuate how the multivoicedness of classroom cultures can create "(micro) cultures" in which the identities of students and teachers can be constructed as hybrids.

Of particular interest to us is the way in which Kamberelis's (2001) work extends the relations of classroom interaction to public media and everyday knowledge. Kamberelis frames and explores the relationship of school-ratified and nonratified discourses through Bakhtin's (1981) contrast of "authoritative" vs. "internally persuasive" discourse. Although these are more of a continuum than exclusive categories, authoritative discourse is "rooted in external authority" (p. 87) and is described as not being easily divided up or assimilated by an individual. An example of authoritative discourse used elsewhere (Leander & Brown, 1999) is the scientific equation for simple harmonic motion. This type of language carries the weight of culture and institutions (e.g., science, schooling), is not typically open for debate, and is also not easily appropriated or digested by individuals. By contrast, internally persuasive discourses are those that people feel they have ownership over, are "sensible," personalized, and malleable for them. For the transformation of teaching practice, Kamberelis describes and imagines frequent and rapid circulation among authoritative (school) discourses and internally persuasive (everyday, media) discourses. The classroom (micro)-cultures developed through such traffic can be seen as a practiced, intentional extension of the "third spaces" described by Gutiérrez et al. (1995).

We draw on one of Kamberelis's (2001) two key data examples, a study of preadolescents (fifth graders) in a racially and culturally mixed urban school with a high percentage of working-class and poor students. Two European American students, Kyle and Max, from working-class families, had "quasi-outsider" status with respect to the others at the beginning of the school year. Kamberelis follows the two through a literacy-related biology activity in which the students, working in pairs, were to dissect owl pellets, reconstruct the skeletons of the animals contained in the pellets, and write reports of their experiences. To analyze the heterogeneous resources that Kyle and Max are drawing on as they shape hybrid identities and knowledges, Kamberelis considers first the genres of the activities in which they are involved. These genres, or typified activities, informed by histories that change over time, include a "surgery activity genre," a Beavis and Butthead reenactment, a (school) "science activity genre," a "mad scientist activity genre," and a "task-related Star Trek activity genre." Similarly, the boys draw on social languages from popular culture *and* school discourse, including surgery discourses from television, superhero discourse, the teacher's instruction, and science textbook discourse.

The effects of the contact between heterogeneous practices and discourses are evident in the data within the owl pellet report that Kyle and Max eventually authored, which were successfully infused with many links to popular culture that they had developed during the dissection. Kamberelis suggests in this article how opening up the classroom (by teacher and students) to heterogeneous practices and discourses had long-term positive identity effects for students such as Kyle and Max. In the next section, we review an article that looks even more closely at how identities are produced.

Material Spaces and Objects as Identity Artifacts

An article by one of the authors of this chapter (Leander, 2002) considers how different signs and sign systems are used within classrooms to create identities. Semiotics—the study of signs and sign systems—prompts us to look beyond language and to myriad ways in which people "code" and recode their identities. Although they are focused on language and literacy learning, English classrooms are increasingly conceived as sites where multiple resources are used for learning and identity construction, including gesture, bodily movements, images, physical spaces, objects, and so forth (Jewitt, 2006; Rowe & Leander, 2005; Sheehy, 2002).

In this chapter, Leander is concerned, as is Wortham (2004), with how identities are stabilized. If identities can be made and remade in interactions, why do some appear to be produced over others and to have staying power? Rather than tracing identity development over time, however, Leander examines how material and semiotic resources are coordinated in the course of interaction. Leander argues that participants use the coordination of multimodal resources to create "identity artifacts" or powerful resources for identity that become associated with individuals. He is concerned with how "artifacts-in-use function to make identity thing-like" (p. 199). Three types of relations are claimed to be important: (a) how semiotic and material resources are brought together to form identity artifacts; (b) how identity artifacts are brought into relation with individuals, and (c) how identity artifacts "point to" or "project" social spaces that extend well beyond them (e.g., a certain tone of voice that points to "the ghetto" as a social space).

Data for this study were drawn from an eleventh-grade classroom in an urban setting. Approximately half of the students were African American and half were European American. The students in this class had a unique school situation in that they took four core academic subjects together as part of their participation in a "school within a school." The activity that Leander (2001) analyzes involves a student discussion of derogatory terms, as part of their discussion of derogatory language in *Huckleberry Finn*. During this interaction, one student, Latanya, an African American female, is positioned as being "ghetto." Leander examines how this positioning cannot be understood by any single social or cultural logic or working of power; the event does not come about, for instance, merely through white oppression. Along with racist positioning, other social spaces are simultaneously created, including "the Black community," and a space of attempted shushing and cueing-in of Latanya. Such spaces are organized through talk, including representations of Latanya's home and family, but also through material objects (e.g., a banner of derogatory terms), through gesture (pointing at Latanya), and through embodied positions (e.g., refusing to face Latanya when she spoke). Leander argues that we must take a more fine-grained approach to observing and understanding the dynamic and relational positionings of bodies that defines insiders and outsiders, especially as these acts of positioning are related to unfolding talk.

Leander (2001) also considers how Latanya contributes to her own negative positioning. Indeed, the entire episode can be considered as an elaborate "participant example" (Wortham, 1994), created on the fly, of what it means to "be ghetto." Yet, even more complex is the way the other students created conditions that invited Latanya to position herself as "ghetto" and then "stepped back" to watch the results and disavow themselves from the scene. Leander analyzes how this type of organizing depends, in part, on a version of the classroom (Hirst, 2004; see the following) in which students and teachers speak abstractly, as if they are not actually located in or sharing any particular space and time. Students who seem more socialized into traditional classroom expectations seem to be able to remove themselves and act as if they are free floating, speaking about their lives apart or together in hypothetical statements. This abstract space of the classroom holds particular challenges for teachers and students who are attempting to engage their real lives with the curriculum; abstract space is, in this sense, an antidote—creating third spaces and new possibilities for pedagogy.

IMPLICATIONS

Whereas we have already begun to describe some implications in reviewing the studies themselves, a number of broad implications for teaching and learning stem from this area of research:

1. Classrooms, and classroom interactions, are not unitary formations, but rather are comprised of multiple social spaces. Conceiving of the classroom as having a unitary "task," with departures being considered "off task," is too simplistic. In these studies, we see a much more complex picture of the classroom as an amalgam of laminated, juxtaposed, and often interpenetrating social spaces. When examining identity and learning, it is more productive to consider the multiple social worlds or spaces of a classroom as a potential resource than as interruptions to a single, unified system.

2. Identities in school are forged through the relationship between highly heterogeneous, everyday cultural resources and traditional academic resources. Identification is not a temporary process that "leads to" learning; rather, learning is continuously tied up in processes of identity that traverse the social worlds of everyday life (including popular culture) and school. Therefore, classroom interactions, such as large group discussions, are as much or more about *whom* they are producing—and *how*—as they are about *what* topic is under discussion.

3. In large and small group interactions, teachers should nurture and give special attention to moments of instability, tran-

sition, or disruption. Such moments are not merely "teach-able moments," but rather index contact zones, "third spaces," or pivots when power relations are being reworked and authoritative school discourses are coming into contact with discourses that are more internally persuasive to the lives of youth.

4. At the micro level of classroom interactions, material resources may be coordinated with talk to form powerful resources for identity work, or identity artifacts. Classroom physical spaces and material objects are not important merely as structures for interaction (e.g., students seated in a circle rather than in rows) but are important as on-the-fly resources for positioning and identity. Changing one's identity possibilities involves changing material and discursive resources.

5. Unstable, heterogeneous openings (e.g., contact zones, third spaces, free spaces) have the potential to provide new openings for identity and learning that cannot be conceived by considering either the curriculum as a static object or the cultural and social worlds of students alone. These potentials are new formations, hybrids. At the same time, such spaces can be recolonized for the reproduction of familiar, asymmetrical categories of identity and power.

Mode II: Anthropologies of Literacy Practices across Space and Time

Research conducted in this mode tends to see spaces as containers to be connected together. Home-school relations are a key area of study here; researchers juxtapose the spaces to compare practices and identities situated in each. Space in this mode is seen as historically shaped and given and as something that influences local practice. Awareness of context and spatial boundaries is critical to this mode of thinking. In current literacy research, this mode has its roots in Heath's (1983) ethnographic study of literacy practices in three distinct neighboring communities. However, we now know much more about what youth in various settings do out of school, as well as how to bridge in- and out-of-school gaps, than we did in 1983. In recent spatial analyses of literacy practices, we have found that it behooves us to look closely at the delineated physical spaces presented in more recent studies, as well as to look at the literacy practices that seem to "go with" such spaces, to learn more about how class-room practices are related to out-of-school identities and how that might matter to classroom teachers.

Out-Of-School Writing and Classroom Practice

All of these studies rely on Gee's (1996) notion of "discourses" with a "D" to understand the "connections among literacy, cul-ture, identity, and power" (Schultz, 2002, p. 360); although we take this into account, our analysis is more concerned with the spatial boundaries represented by each set of findings. In her eth-nography of writing (cf. Basso, 1974), Schultz looked "*across* school and out-of-school settings" (ibid., p. 360). She investi-gated "the relationships between out-of-school writing and [high school] students' participation in classroom practice" (p. 367) and argued from her findings that "writing can bridge these worlds that are too often held separate" (p. 358). For Schultz, in-school and out-of-school literacy practices are very different and very much differentially valued; classrooms and nonschool arenas are distinct social spaces with distinct practices and values. Schultz argues that some literacy practices work *across* both spaces to "conceptualize writing as a thread that crosses school and out-of-school settings" (p. 363), but the spaces themselves are dis-tinct and bounded.

In our reading of Schultz's (2002) study, set in a high school populated with equal thirds African American, Latino and Latina, and Asian American students, we immediately saw the bound-aries. Like many urban schools, "a high fence surrounded the school with a single gate" (p. 364); the school's physical space is clearly demarcated as separate from the surrounding commu-nity. In the same vein, Schultz spent the first year of her study *in* the school and the second year *out* of it, gathering data in the community, in youths' homes. Her three main findings about writing across the in- and out-of-school divide are each illustrated by a single case study. Each finding reinforces the division between home and school spaces in a different way.

First, Schultz (2002) found that, for many students, writing was a private practice done out of school, with no connection to school literacy practices. "Although writing was important to them in their home lives," she notes, "it did not figure into their conceptions of themselves as students" (p. 368). Ellen, an African American girl, kept two diaries, one she labeled as "writing for myself" and the other she called "writing for society" (p. 369). "Ellen and her peers . . . thought of themselves as people who hated to write, forgetting the writing that they did outside the school walls" (p. 370). Ellen's own practices thus contributed to keeping school and home literacy practices separate and unrelated, at least in her mind. Like the African American students in Mahiri and Sablo's (1996) study, who were "writing for their lives," Ellen used her personal journal to "cope with the stresses in her life" (p. 371); she kept the public journal as a record of her life. Both journals were done at home, away from school and teachers, but Schultz argues that they crossed the two spaces, because Ellen wrote about her school life in both her personal and her more public journals.

Schultz (2002) ultimately says that if we enlarge our knowledge of the "capacities of students" (p. 383), widen what we consider as "school literacy practices to include practices that occur in homes, communities, and workplaces" (ibid.), we can bridge the distinct spaces of "in-school" and "out-of-school." Also, teachers might look at student's out-of-school literacy practices to "expand their understandings of their students as writers" (ibid.); the teachers in her study certainly "did not learn enough about students' literacy practices or habits of writing to foster those beyond students' time in school" (p. 384). Schultz's study represents this binary spatial perspective on home and school very clearly and shows, we believe, some of the disconnections between the literacy practices and, indeed, identity work of youth in and out of school. In the next article we review, Rebecca Rogers looks at the "lines of demarcation" between one home and one school, focusing her analytic lens on the Discourses and literacy practices in each space.

Using Critical Discourse Analysis to Explore Funds of Knowledge and Discourses

Rogers's (2003) critical discourse analysis (CDA) of an inner-city African American family's literacy practices both extends and creates problems for Schultz's discussion of home and school literacy practices as distinct, different, and separate. CDA is a complex research method and theory; to summarize briefly, it involves studying interaction and texts of all types with the assumptions that the social world involves relations of power and comprises different "discourses" or sets of belief captured in language (cf. Gee, 1999; Rogers, 2004).

Rogers (2003) uses ethnographic data as well as CDA to analyze in- and out-of-school literacy practices, focusing on "June Treader" and her teenage daughter "Vicky." Rogers's findings about the power differentials between home and school literacies demarcate two distinct spaces that, because of the reproductive capacities of institutionalized discourses, never fully met. June Treader, a working-class woman whom Rogers met in an adult education class, "understood the rules of school," and much of her "struggle was done within the existing discourse of the school" (p. 60). Despite her "assumptions that the literacy work of her daily life—that of family literacy practices—had little value and meaning in the eyes of social institutions" (p. 154), June and her children engaged in what Rogers saw as "schooled literacy" practices (p. 152) at home, and June was an involved, present parent at her daughter's school.

Indeed, Rogers (2003) shows a great deal of "interconnectedness" (p. 63) between the literacy practices of home and school, although these are clearly two distinct physical spaces. Through her analysis, we see how institutional literacy practices evoke "contradictory subjectivities" (p. 125) from June in relation to both literacy and power. Through detailed explorations of home literacy practices, many of which involve filling out forms (WIC paperwork, forms for free and reduced lunch, etc.), Rogers argues that Vicky and June had "learned to see themselves not as literate but as people who had literate failure" (p. 83) because "they identified so closely with the notion of 'schooled literacy'" (ibid.). In other words, they had "internalized the ideology of the school" (p. 154), and both mother and daughter experienced tension between their "personal and public literate lives" (p. 83), tensions that did not go away.

This study both reinforces and complicates a sense of the boundedness of home and school spaces. Rogers (2003) concludes that June Treader may have had the ability to help her children engage in "school literacy" practices at home (i.e., regular book reading, homework time, etc.) and was involved in her children's classrooms, but such practices were not enough to dissolve educational and institutional barriers that conspired to, for instance, place and keep Vicky in self-contained special education classrooms. As with Schultz's (2002) study, home and school are separate, bounded spaces; however, this notion of separate, impermeable spaces is complicated in Rogers's findings because June and Vicky Treader "were proficient with literacy and language and demonstrated considerable knowledge of institutional structures and school organizations" (p. 156). Rogers's analysis of this family's path shows that, even if some practices are shared between the two spaces, institutional discourses still have the power to constrain "individuals' destinies" (p. 156). In the third and final study we review, Elizabeth Moje and colleagues (2004) look more explicitly at how out-of-school funds of knowledge and Discourses may shape students' literacy practices in science classrooms.

Funds of Knowledge, Discourse, and the Creation of "Third Space"

In this third key article, Moje, Ciechanowski, Kramer, Ellis, Carrillo, and Collazo (2004) describe the funds of knowledge and discourses that they found Latino and Latina students drawing on (in and out of high school) in Detroit, Michigan. Citing Moll, Amanti, Neff, and Gonzalez (1992), the authors write that, of course, we need to know about students' funds of knowledge, but "it is also equally important to examine the ways that these funds, or networks and relationships, shape ways of knowing, reading, writing, and talking—what Gee (1996) called Discourses—that youth use or try to learn in secondary schools" (p. 38). By analyzing data collected in two simultaneously conducted studies—an extended ethnographic study and a project-based science curriculum project—their goal is to highlight the ways understanding such funds of knowledge might help educators "construct classroom spaces that can integrate in- and out-of-school literacy practices" (p. 41).

The primary theoretical background of Schultz's study was the ethnography of writing, with an emphasis on literacy practices (Street, 1984) and Discourses. Moje et al. (2004) situate their ethnography of literacy within three different perspectives on third space (Bhabha, 1994), which we can term a *different* or *alternative* space in which knowledges and Discourses from home and school are merged (Moje et al., 2004, p. 41). The first of these definitions of third space is geographic and discursive, using Soja's (1996) understanding of the ways that social space shapes physical space to theorize ways that we might capitalize on students' out-of-school knowledge. From here, they write, "what seem to be oppositional categories can actually work together to generate new knowledges, new Discourses, and new forms of literacy" (p. 42). The second perspective on third space they use is Bhabha's; here, third space is seen through a lens of privilege and postcolonialism, and our attention is focused on the ways that the consciousness of the subordinate is "split" in third spaces and the benefits of the "newness" created there (p. 43). The third and final perspective on space they use is that of Gutiérrez et al. (1995). In this last, third space is "a bridge between community or home-based Discourse to school-based Discourse" (ibid).

The main finding of this study is that students drew on everyday funds of knowledge that *sometimes* connected to the classroom science funds they encountered. "In some cases," they write, "youths' funds reveal the science of everyday life, providing both a bridge to conventional science learning and a site for explicit discussion of the conventions of the texts of different discourse communities. In other cases, students' funds challenge conventional science or provide tools for expanding what counts as knowledge of the natural world" (p. 51). Moje and colleagues summarize and analyze four funds: family, community, peer groups, and popular culture. What is striking about each fund is not the depth of knowledge the researchers describe, but the striking half-matches and, again, jarring disjunctures between "the science of the everyday and the everyday of science" (p. 51).

Moje et al. (2004) suggest several ways to open third spaces "in which scientific findings and experiences are examined in relation to one another—with neither fund [conventional science, or youths' environment and health funds] being privileged, but both being valued (p. 55). In order to address this discrepancy, teachers and students have "to engage with both conventional science funds and everyday funds" (p. 55). Other examples show how youth produce "hybridity" as they draw on peer group funds in the classroom "simply through their simultaneous resistance to and accommodation with their science classroom activities" (p. 57). In each section and subsection, the authors suggest ways to "develop third spaces" based on their findings (p. 60). Their findings on popular culture funds highlight the ways in which "popular culture served as an important fund for the youths' school learning" and how texts, such as episodes of *The Simpsons* and reports on Univision TV, "allowed them to engage with other youth, thus supporting peer funds" (p. 63) in a growing third space.

IMPLICATIONS

We begin with a general implication and then extend into two implications associated with somewhat distinct perspectives.

1. First, we see that secondary school policy needs to change from thinking that school is only about "learning particular content concepts and processes" to "a recognition that secondary school learning is as much about learning to navigate and negotiate the oral and written texts of multiple Discourse and knowledge communities" (Moje et al., 2004, p. 68). Without such a shift, "new knowledges, new Discourses, and new forms of literacy" (p. 42) will not be generated, in- and out-of-school divisions will remain, and "youth whose experiences have not traditionally been valued in schools" will continue to be marginalized (p. 48).

2. When practitioners and researchers see in- and out-of-school spaces as distinct bounded spaces, we must always come to the subject of bridging. From this perspective, if we recognize home literacies and identities and support them in school settings, students have a better chance of success and engagement in school. Our review shows that out-of-school literacy practices are often more engaging and meaningful for youth than classroom literacy practices. Several attempts have been made to link popular culture to school curricula (cf. Dyson, 2003; Morrell, 2002); from this mode of thinking about spaces, it only makes sense to use the practices in which students freely engage out of school to make in-school practices—and content—more relevant and interesting.

3. The notion of third spaces and the hybridization of cultures, resources, and identities, of course, share similar concerns with the previous "bridging" point, but see the traffic across the "bridges" of home and school as always and already active, circulating in multiple directions, and less important for the transfer of goods than as movement and contact. The findings of Moje and her colleagues (2004) urge researchers and teachers to develop third spaces "by engaging students in experiments, discussions, and reading and writing activities that focus on, or at least include, the texts and experiences of many different communities" (p. 65). Rogers's (2003) findings illustrate how institutional discourses obscure potential third spaces; although the Treaders engage in "school literacy" practices at home, the hybridity of these literacy practices is neither noticed nor built on by school personnel. Thus, from one perspective, the classroom is never cut off from the home and other cultures, and, hence, third spaces are always possible, always immanent. From another perspective, educators must educate themselves on the language and literacy practices beyond the classroom in order to recognize the possibilities that heterogeneous classroom worlds offer.

Mode III: Relational Readings of Identities and Social Spaces at Different Scales

In this final mode, we discuss the ways that people's positionings in any given spatial scale are relationally lived. In other words, the classroom is once again conceived as a space or site in relation to other spaces or sites of practice. However, such studies (of which we have found few) look across multiple sets of somewhat bounded spaces to encompass scales of relationships. Appadurai (1999) has theorized that such a "scalar dynamic . . . has to be understood as a complex, overlapping, disjunctive order, which cannot any longer be understood in terms of existing center-periphery models" (p. 221).

Standardized Testing at Multiple Scales of Practice

Anagnostopoulos (2003) has shown the multiple layers of effects that high-stakes testing had on English classrooms in a Chicago high school. In our reading of her work, we see that spatial scales are complexly layered, simultaneous, and often contradictory and that analysis and understanding are not derived by studying first one scale and then another, but instead by moving between and across scales to see complex relationships.

Standardized testing shapes the work of the classroom as it moves forward in time, just as it shapes the kinds of identities that teachers and students take up and the ways in which classroom practices are organized. Analyzing conversations in two classrooms during the teaching of *To Kill a Mockingbird* (Lee, 1960), Anagnostopoulos (2003) found that, because of "district intervention and threats of school closure, . . . talk about the novel's core themes [was seen as] inconsequential or disruptive" (p. 205) to increases in student test scores. Ironically, although the state curricular standards required students to "grapple with the social issues and dilemmas" of the novel, such talk was distinct from (and less valued than) the kinds of "talk that prepared students for the [high-stakes] test" (p. 205). So, we see how classroom discourse was clearly affected by standardized testing; however, Anagnostopoulos also looked at other social spaces, on different scales, to see how students and teachers were positioned by the test.

Students were constructed as "good readers" (p. 191) on many scales or levels—by the state's standards, the test's requirements, and the teachers' pedagogies. In turn, teachers attempted to "maneuver" (p. 207) between standards, tests, and their own ideologies about English teaching. Anagnostopoulos (2003) shows how teachers used the pressures of testing to contain talk about racism and to "cast students who challenged their control over classroom talk and texts as disruptive, and to re-position them as 'academic' readers who uncritically accepted the author's and the teacher's perspectives" (p. 206). However, this analysis across spatial scales allows us to view the problem from multiple perspectives, and we are unable to blame teachers; the test and its rhetoric "exerted power over the teachers" as it "became the authoritative text in the classrooms" (p. 206) and positioned students as "uncritical and minimally skilled" (p. 205).

Appadurai (1999) might term this cultural flow of testing a *scape* or *landscape*; his concepts of the "technoscape" and "ideoscape" suit this mode of thinking. The "technoscape" refers to the way that "technology, both high and low . . . now moves at high speeds across various kinds of previously impervious boundaries" (p. 222). In this sense, standardized tests and the analyses that district personnel and teachers must undertake of them, as well as the ways they enter into and change classroom discourse, are *technologies* that have begun to move across different and new spaces. Similarly, Appadurai's concept of an "ideoscape," a collection of images and conventions that are "directly political" (p. 224), is also related to a scalar perspective on education spaces. For example, the issue of high-stakes testing has become a "political narrative" that involves the question of "what sets of communicative genres are valued in what way" (ibid.).

We believe that spatial work is political work when it moves across relational social spaces because it provides openings at various levels and allows us to study effects across levels. Anagnostopoulos (2003) writes that "the existence of competing visions of reading within policy documents create[d] spaces for maneuver (Ball & Bowe, 1992)" that educators in Chicago could "use to counter the increasingly punitive uses of testing" (p. 207). Teachers were able to use the "spaces for maneuver available within the standards to resist the test's encroachment on their students' learning opportunities" (ibid.); of late, we have seen other researchers and educators conducting scalar analyses as they respond to highly structured reading curricula (cf. Altwerger, 2005). With attention to spaces across scales, we have access to many perspectives and thus many more possible opportunities to create social change through such research.

Barriers to Cultural Contact by Space-Time Organization across Scales

In considering how identities are produced *in* classrooms, while produced *for* classrooms at other scales, Hirst's (2004) work provides important data for second language research and also noteworthy theoretical perspectives for thinking across scales. In this study, Hirst reports on research in Language Other Than English (LOTE) classrooms in Australia—the result of "policies of engagement" between Australia and Asia. What makes Hirst's work distinctive is that she considers how time and space are represented and organized in discourse and material practices at the different scales in which LOTE is a cultural object. In order to theorize how time and space can have different qualities and forms of organization, Hirst draws on Bakhtin's (1981) notion of the chronotope (literally, time-space). Through the study of literature, Bakhtin (1981) demonstrated how settings are not simply given backdrops to the action of characters, but rather express unique qualities of time and space that show us how characters are related to the social worlds around them, how the social world changes, and how characters might change as well. This type of analysis, called chronotopic analysis, has been used outside of literary studies as well, to examine the social world of the classroom (Bloome & Katz, 1997; Leander, 2001). Chronotopic analysis allows us to make distinctions between a given setting (e.g., a classroom) and the ways in which, through talk and other forms of interaction, expectations for identity change in the social world and how the relations between individuals and the social world are created.

In Hirst's (2004) work, a clear example of a dominant chronotope influencing practice in LOTE classrooms is the "time/management chronotope." In this expression of time and space, efficiency is a chief good. Students who study Indonesian in an LOTE classroom are seen as accumulating linguistic capital so that "economic benefits will accrue to the nation's capital" (p. 46). In the time-management chronotope, the problem of LOTE becomes how and where to fit in the subject efficiently so that the most learning can happen in the least amount of time, so that the LOTE teacher can relieve the regular classroom teacher from her duties, and so that the least number of problems happen with the students. Spatially speaking, the teacher in this chronotope represents a kind of container who can be "prepacked, transported in, unloaded, and transported out" (p. 46). The LOTE teacher, in this chronotope, borrows the classroom space of the regular teacher; the material space of the room is thus thought to count little for the meeting of cultures. LOTE lessons are to be packaged in 30-minute increments, commodified, and delivered to many classrooms in many schools. "This bureaucratic rationality structures much of the discourse of schooling, making it difficult to accommodate differences, whether cultural or political, except in certain symbolic ways" (p. 46).

In this study, Hirst (2004) is primarily concerned with the identity of the LOTE teacher and how micro and macro forces constitute his or her identity. In this case, the teacher is a middle-aged Indonesian man (Pak Asheed) who is teaching Indonesian to students in an Australian classroom, all of whom are from middle to low socioeconomic backgrounds. Hirst begins with an account of how, operating behind the scenes at an often subtle level, discourses and accompanying chronotopes, such as the time/management chronotope, position Pak Asheed with little status and mitigate against the legitimacy of the teacher and his lessons. Thus, whereas LOTE classrooms are richly imagined in ways that respond to "third space" desires discussed in the previous sections of this chapter—" . . . an opportunity for two (or more) cultures to come into contact, and potentially into dialogue, enabling new forms of understanding to develop, diverse voices to interanimate, and for dialogic learning to eventuate, with the concomitant construction of hybrid cultural identities" (p. 45)—this imagination is truncated by time/management.

Hirst (2004) analyzes various chronotopes that come into contact with the time/management chronotope and another dominant chronotope of nationalism, including Pak Asheed's attempt to claim the space of the classroom as Indonesian, for instance, by introducing ritual salutations, such as standing and greeting. Some students mock and parody the teacher's salutations, opposing his construction of social space and recreating the classroom as a kind of theater, attempting to make it their own. "Power here is about a struggle and conflict over resources and public spaces—students challenge Pak Asheed's power to claim this space" (p. 58). In the end, the author and reader are left wondering, together, if there is any opportunity for "third spaces" at this site of interaction, any possibility for dialogic interaction and a "new imaginary" (p. 60). A critical challenge to genuine intercultural dialogism that Hirst presents is the dominance of a discourse of neoliberalism: conceptualizing diversity as a "resource to be appropriated" is fundamental to the production and maintenance of "borders for the containment of difference" (p. 61).

IMPLICATIONS

Although work in this area is in particular need of development, early studies still index important implications for policy and pedagogy:

> 1. Educational policies at various levels (national, state, district) are important sites to critique and consider fundamentally contradictory discourses and material practices with respect to teacher and student identity. Desired outcomes, and especially "soft" social goals involving cultural and social diversity that are difficult to measure, may be overwhelmed by contradictory discourses and practices involving the assessment of skills or the management of space and time for efficiency. At the same time, policy contradictions can allow literacy teachers, as political workers, "spaces for maneuver."

2. Teachers' abilities to shape productive learning environments are always mitigated by their own sense of agency and identity in the social spaces in which they are located. Teachers are neither dupes of policy nor free to roam in "counterspaces." Rather, literacy teaching is a practice that must be understood as a practice that functions and struggles across scales of space-time, including national, state, and institutional social spaces.

3. On the ground of literacy education, a valuable tool for administrators and teachers to understand the competing interests struggling over curriculum and pedagogy is to analyze how time and space are represented and practiced in everyday life. What kinds of interests, relations of power, and commitments do these representations and practices hide? Although we often look for obvious signs of interest or ideology, the subtlest—such as space and time—can often hide the greatest consequences.

Concluding Remarks

In certain respects, many of the concepts and implications we advocated in this chapter may appear familiar, and it may even seem that we (and others) are simply cloaking familiar ideas with new, unfamiliar language. To some degree, this perception is accurate. For instance, we might readily invoke Dewey's dialectial titles, such as *The School and Society* (1943/1899), to recall a sense of how tensions and relations between education and the world of the student have been theorized for decades. Dewey certainly seemed to have a sense of the necessary contact between the student's internally persuasive discourses and the school's authoritative discourses. Moreover, within literacy education Dewey's thought has been translated and extended into transactional theory (e.g., Rosenblatt, 1978) concerning the reader's world and the world of the text. Reader-response theory, at its core, is certainly about multiple voices and dialogism.

Hence, given this background, the conversation we are forwarding is a matter of degree. To relations often expressed as binaries (e.g., student-text, student-school), we are pushing for understanding multiples in contact with one another: multivoices, multicultures, multimodalities, multisites of practice, and multiscales. Lefebvre (1991) offers an analogy that is useful to us. If we imagine a house, we see, at first blush, a building parsed into rooms, floors, hall and stairways, etc. The building seems settled and relatively static. Yet, if we might peel back the walls, floors, and ceilings, we notice flows of various types: electricity, gas, electronic data, telephone conversations, water, sewage. The house seems alive, an intersection of various flows. So it is with classrooms. Changing our imagination of the literacy classroom as a site involves peeling back layers from our vision to get at the flows that have been there for some time and yet are constantly changing.

We have considered how literacy classrooms are conceived as important sites for the production of identity, identities caught up in the course of old and new flows. If learning and the change of identity are always related by necessity (Lave & Wenger, 1991), our image of teaching amid such flows becomes much more complex and multifaceted than provided for by current models. Indeed, teaching in the contact zone of cultures and identities—the third space—involves less some superior vision of final destinations and more so the willingness to engage old and new flows.

References

Altwerger, B. (Ed.). (2005). *Reading for profit: How the bottom line leaves kids behind*. Portsmouth, NH: Heinemann.

Anagnostopoulos, D. (2003). Testing and student engagement with literature in urban classrooms: A multi-layered perspective. *Research in the Teaching of English, 38,* 177–212.

Appadurai, A. (1999). Disjuncture and difference in the global cultural economy. In S. During (Ed.), *The cultural studies reader* (2nd ed., pp. 220–32). London: Routledge.

Bakhtin, M. M. (1981). *The dialogic imagination: Four essays* (M. Holquist, Ed., C. Emerson & M. Holquist, Trans.). Austin: University of Texas Press.

Ball, S. J., & Bowe, R. (1992). Subject departments and the "implementation" of national curriculum policy: An overview of the issues. *Journal of Curriculum Studies, 24,* 97–115.

Basso, K. H. (1974). The ethnography of writing. In R. Bauman, & J. Sherzer (Eds.), *Explorations in the ethnography of speaking* (pp. 425–32). New York: Cambridge University Press.

Bhabha, H. K. (1994). *The location of culture.* London: Routledge.

Bloome, D., & Katz, L. (1997). Literacy as social practice and classroom chronotopes. *Reading and Writing Quarterly, 13,* 205–25.

Dewey, J. (1943). *The school and society.* (Rev. ed). Chicago: University of Chicago Press. (Original work published 1899)

Dyson, A. H. (2003). *The brothers and sisters learn to write: Popular literacies in childhood and school cultures.* New York: Teachers College Press.

Fine, M., Weis, L., Centrie, C., & Roberts, R. (2000). Educating beyond the borders of schooling. *Anthropology and Education Quarterly, 31,* 131–51.

Gee, J. P. (1996). *Social linguistics and literacies: Ideology in discourses* (2nd ed.). London: Taylor & Francis.

Gee, J. P. (1999). *An introduction to discourse analysis: Theory and method.* London: Routledge.

Gutiérrez, K., Rymes, B., & Larson, J. (1995). Script, counterscript, and underlife in the classroom: James Brown versus *Brown v. Board of Education. Harvard Educational Review, 65,* 445–71.

Heath, S. B. (1983). *Ways with words: Language, life, and work in communities and classrooms.* Cambridge, UK: Cambridge University Press.

Hirst, E. (2004). Diverse social contexts of a second-language classroom and the construction of identity. In K. M. Leander & M. Sheehy (Eds.), *Spatializing literacy research and practice* (pp. 39–66). New York: Peter Lang.

Jewitt, C. (2006). *Technology, literacy, and learning: A multimodal approach.* New York: Routledge.

Kamberelis, G. (2001). Producing heteroglossic classroom (micro)cultures through hybrid discourse practice. *Linguistics and Education, 12*(1), 85–125.

Lave, J., & Wenger, E. (1991). *Situated learning: Legitimate peripheral participation.* Cambridge, UK: Cambridge University Press.

Leander, K. M. (2001). "This is our freedom bus going home right now": Producing and hybridizing space-time contexts in pedagogical discourse. *Journal of Literacy Research, 33,* 637–79.

Leander, K. M. (2002). Locating Latanya: The situated production of identity artifacts in classroom interaction. *Research in the Teaching of English, 37,* 198–250.

Leander, K. M., & Brown, D. E. (1999). "You understand, but you don't believe it": Tracing the stabilities and instabilities of interaction in a physics classroom through a multidimensional framework. *Cognition and Instruction, 17,* 93–135.

Lee, H. (1960). *To kill a mockingbird.* New York: Warner Books.

Lefebvre, H. (1991). *The production of space* (D. Nicholson-Smith, Trans.). Cambridge, MA: Blackwell.

Mahiri, J., & Sablo, S. (1996). Writing for their lives: The non-school literacy of California's urban African American youth. *Journal of Negro Education, 65*(2), 164–79.

Moje, E. B., Ciechanowski, K. M., Kramer, K., Ellis, L., Carrillo, R., & Collazo, T. (2004). Working toward third space in content area literacy: An examination of everyday funds of knowledge and discourse. *Reading Research Quarterly, 39,* 38–70.

Moll, L. C., Amanti, C., Neff, D., & Gonzalez, N. (1992). Funds of knowledge for teaching: Using a qualitative approach to connect homes and classrooms. *Theory into Practice, 31*(2), 132–41.

Morrell, E. (2002). Toward a critical pedagogy of popular culture: Literacy development among urban youth. *Journal of Adolescent & Adult Literacy, 46,* 72–77.

Rogers, R. (2003). *A critical discourse analysis of family literacy practices: Power in and out of print.* Mahwah, NJ: Erlbaum.

Rogers, R. (Ed.). (2004). *An introduction to critical discourse analysis in education.* Mahwah, NJ: Erlbaum.

Rosenblatt, L. M. (1978). *The reader, the text, the poem: The transactional theory of the literary work.* Carbondale, IL: Southern Illinois University Press.

Rowe, D. W., & Leander, K. M. (2005). Analyzing the production of thirdspace in classroom literacy events. *54th Yearbook of the National Reading Conference*, 318–33. Oak Creek, WI: National Reading Conference.

Schultz, K. (2002). Looking across space and time: Reconceptualizing literacy learning in and out of school. *Research in the Teaching of English, 36,* 356–90.

Sheehy, M. (2002). Illuminating constructivism: Structure, discourse, and subjectivity in a middle school classroom. *Reading Research Quarterly, 37,* 278–308.

Soja, E. W. (1996). *Thirdspace: Journeys to Los Angeles and other real-and-imagined places.* Malden, MA: Blackwell.

Street, B. (1984). *Literacy in theory and practice.* Cambridge, UK: Cambridge University Press.

Wortham, S. (1994). *Acting out participant examples in the classroom.* Philadelphia: John Benjamins.

Wortham, S. (2004). From good student to outcast: The emergence of a classroom identity. *Ethos 32,* 164–87.

CHAPTER EIGHT

Legitimacy, Recognition, and Access to Language and Literacy: English Language Learners at the Secondary School Level

ROBERT T. JIMÉNEZ AND BRAD L. TEAGUE
Vanderbilt University

In this chapter, we identify the academic, linguistic, and social needs of English language learners at the secondary level, as well as the function that these specific needs play in school success. We also discuss many of the major factors that facilitate or impede students' language and literacy learning in English language classrooms. This is important because, in the United States, low levels of literacy have been linked to high dropout rates, especially with regard to linguistic minority students (National Center for Educational Statistics [NCES], 2005).

We contend that a major issue influencing the literacy development of English language learners (ELLs) has to do with the notion of legitimacy. We take this idea of legitimacy from the work of Bourdieu (1991, 1998), who argued that only certain groups and their ways of speaking are granted respect and authority by society. We propose that Bourdieu's ideas about groups and language are relevant to the U.S. context and also that his understanding of legitimacy is a force that shapes the instruction and programs provided to ELLs at the secondary level.

The concept of legitimacy runs through nearly every aspect of social life. For example, we are convinced in part that high dropout rates attributed to secondary ELLs are anchored in the negative portrayals of this population that are found in popular media. During the past year, for instance, multiple crises have occurred around the border between the United States and Mexico. News stories focus on armed vigilante groups searching for illegal immigrants, on deportation hearings for high school graduates reared almost entirely in the United States, and on reports of how ELLs depress local and state test scores. Researchers examine legislation aimed at reforming immigration policies and what to do with undocumented immigrants in the United States (e.g., Reynolds & Gaouette, 2006). To be sure, these are critical issues that affect perceptions of ELL students as legitimate members of U.S. society in general and of secondary schools in particular.

Too often schools fail to recognize ELLs according to their prior cultural experiences, schooling, and literacy learning and, thus, they essentially consign them all to the same broad category of non-English speakers. This generic outlook deprives students of legitimacy as individuals and strips them of their relevant cultural, linguistic, and social capital (Bourdieu, 1998). On the other hand, Peregoy and Boyle (2000) encourage educators to learn as much as possible about individual English learners, arguing that such information "is essential to planning effective literacy instruction" (p. 244). The purpose of this chapter is to offer a glimpse of notions that can form a basis for such effective literacy instruction.

Method

To create this document, first, we relied on our knowledge of literacy, second language acquisition, and bilingual and ELL education; from this knowledge, we generated a list of fifteen key pieces of literature that stimulated our thinking about secondary education and literacy for ELLs. Second, we reviewed all of the issues of the *Journal of Adolescent & Adult Literacy* since 2000 for published research related to these issues. Third, we conducted an electronic search of Educational Resources Information Center (ERIC), using descriptors such as English language learners, secondary education, literacy, second language, English as a second language (ESL), and bilingual. As we reviewed this literature, we included in our list of references additional works, cited by the authors, that we believed to be relevant to our larger purpose, including full-length books and book chapters. We focused primarily on the last seven years of published research and also considered earlier landmark work that directly informed our overall purpose.

Results

We framed our results in three major groups that are most directly involved in the secondary education of ELLs: educators working with secondary students, the students, and their parents. These categories are based on our findings and perceptions that teachers need to know and be able to address specific language and content needs; students must learn about the rules for cultural, social, and linguistic interaction, as well as the content-area expectations of U.S. secondary classrooms; and parents need to be informed about the demands that schooling in the United States places on adolescents and about the roles that they as parents are expected to fulfill.

What the Literature Has to Say to Educators

A number of researchers point out that few teachers receive the necessary professional development to support effectively the literacy learning of adolescent ELLs (Grant & Wong, 2003; Klingner & Vaughn, 2004; Rubinstein-Ávila, 2003/2004). Klingner and Vaughn (2004) argue that this lack of knowledge and experience has consequences for students' ability to learn new information from content-area texts. Other researchers point out that, in general, few secondary teachers have the necessary background to help adolescent students who struggle with literacy (Alvermann & Phelps, 2005). Fu (2004) writes that only 3 percent of the nearly three million practicing public school teachers have taken eight or more credit hours of course work about teaching ELLs. Similarly, Grant and Wong (2003) believe that a powerful impediment to becoming literate for many adolescent ELL students is that many teacher education programs do not "adequately prepare reading specialists to work with language-minority learners . . ." (p. 386). Teacher education programs that do not address these needs are failing both future teachers and their students.

LINGUISTIC NEEDS OF ELL STUDENTS

One way to address effectively the needs of ELL students is to focus on linguistic issues. Harper and de Jong (2004) contend that content-area teachers need to look *at* rather than *through* the language required to participate in secondary education classrooms. At a minimum, looking at necessary language involves identifying what is needed to participate in commonly occurring classroom activities. These authors argue that involvement in classroom discussions requires the ability to question, agree, disagree, interrupt, present an opinion, and ask for clarification or assistance in an appropriate manner (p. 154). Such participation requires knowledge of the "what," "how," and "when" of language. Students need to know, for example, how forming questions differs from forming statements. Furthermore, they must learn that questions invert subject and verb and that it is necessary on occasion to add an auxiliary verb form such as the word *do*. ELLs also need to know how to formulate questions that are relevant to the topics being discussed; that is, they need to understand that their utterances should include content-appropriate information. They also must know that they are expected to express their questions in a manner viewed by other participants as socially and culturally acceptable; otherwise, they run the risk of being excluded from future social interactions.

In addition, students need to be aware of when it is appropriate to ask questions. For example, many teachers accept questions only when they reach certain junctures in the lesson or in their speech. Teachers also typically solicit questions at certain points of their instruction while they present new information. Furthermore, some teachers permit questions throughout their presentations if students follow specific protocols, such as raising their hands and bidding for their teacher's attention. Even then, teachers expect the question to consist of a request for relevant information. These forms and practices are part and parcel of what is deemed legitimate for discussions and other interactions in many U.S. classrooms.

We elaborated on this last example to provide a hint of the complexity involved in what many mainstream educators take for granted. Teachers with a substantial background in teaching ESL recognize the need to make this information explicit to their students; however, it appears that many content-area educators tend to ignore such language issues, given that many or most of their students are native speakers of English and quite familiar with linguistic and social conventions deemed legitimate. Rather than take these conventions for granted, according to Nussbaum (2002), teachers must make clear to their ELL students what the norms are for discourse and other social transactions in their individual classrooms. The ability to orchestrate what we have noted represents a little of what is involved in being recognized as a legitimate speaker. It is this type of literacy proficiency that is necessary to succeed in school, especially in the later grades.

In this vein, García (1999) found in her research with recent immigrant students that students lacked "knowledge of the classroom script" (p. 67). For example, she found that teachers did not understand why these students behaved in ways that seemed highly inappropriate. Specifically, these students were not aware of the politeness protocols of the U.S. classroom, including how to address teachers or when to speak. Jiménez, Smith, and Martínez-León (2003) documented similar interaction patterns in Mexican classrooms. Students in these classrooms felt free to ask questions, interrupt other speakers, and request feedback from teachers throughout a variety of instructional activities. These behaviors were not viewed as rude or inappropriate by most of the teachers in the study who had a Mexican background, suggesting that U.S. teachers without that background could benefit from a more thorough understanding of how schooling functions in other parts of the world. Immigrant students also need explicit instruction on how the rules and expectations in U.S. classrooms differ from those in their countries of origin.

Duff (2001) documented that social studies teachers at the secondary level often required their ELL students to be involved in a variety of activities such as role plays, debates, poster-making, and group presentations. These activities all entail various language, literacy, and interaction skills. However, although the teachers Duff studied were clearly gifted with respect to content knowledge and pedagogical skills, they overlooked the specific language needs required by students to participate in these activities. For this reason, even when the ELL students were encouraged by teachers to participate, they responded with "brief, partially audible responses" (p. 116). In a sense, classroom structures deprived these students of legitimate speaker status (Bourdieu, 1991). For example, being involved in debates may require some knowledge of language used by members of particular groups, such as lawyers and judges. Although such information may be obvious to many middle-class, native speakers of English, it is entirely possible that ELLs and other culturally diverse students find such language unintelligible or, perhaps at the very least, novel.

KNOWLEDGE OF CONTENT

A great deal of the background information useful for making sense of content knowledge in secondary education is highly culturally specific. Townsend and Fu (2001) illustrate the problems that some ELLs experience when they lack knowledge of culturally and discipline-specific abstract concepts, such as *transcendentalism* and *Western expansion*. In a case study of a refugee student, they attributed her failure to succeed in an English literature class to her struggles with complex ideas such as these. As a result, the student was encouraged to enroll in a less rigorous course where she received lower quality instruction, even though she would have preferred to remain in the more challenging class.

O'Byrne (2001) points out that it is not always "lack of familiarity with narrative or expository texts but inability to interact with these texts that prevented the ESL students from having success in the regular English classes" (p. 444). She provides an example of this problem, in which adolescent students simply copied information from literature selections in response to teachers' questions. Teachers viewed these answers as unsupported statements disconnected from the text; they wanted students to explain their answers and to provide examples, although the ELLs had no way of knowing that these specific practices were expected.

In other research, Duff (2001) describes additional difficulties of entering a foreign educational system at the secondary school level. She highlights the "telescoping" nature of curriculum in Canadian schools and how students "have missed earlier social studies courses whose content is studied again in more depth in later grades . . ." (p. 109). Duff also points out that much of the content that ELLs bring with them into English-speaking classrooms, such as Chinese or Mexican history, is not included in official curricula. Bourdieu's (1989) notion of legitimacy is useful here for understanding how some knowledge and information are, or are not, recognized as legitimate academic capital. Although it is probably beyond the ability of U.S. and Canadian educators to restructure curriculum radically, it may be possible to think about ways to use what students have previously studied as bridges to learning mainstream subject-area material. Valdés (2001), for example, describes a teacher who encouraged a student to write in English about an episode from Mexican history, thus providing both the content and the motivation to write in English.

In other research, adolescent immigrant students in Canada expressed views that content contained in the curriculum was "difficult, complex, and advanced" (Gunderson, 2000, p. 700). Part of the reason these students perceived content in this way was that their teachers did not identify specific material to be copied or memorized as homework. In this respect, the students believed that their teachers were failing to perform what they considered to be a teacher's responsibility. The miscommunication was based on a lack of understanding on the part of both teachers and students. Students' parents also had difficulty understanding how schools function in Canada. Fu (2004) likewise notes that teachers need an understanding of how schooling in the United States differs from that in the countries of origin of many ELLs. It can be inferred that beliefs, expectations, and attitudes concerning learning and schooling are culturally shaped and deeply inscribed in what Bourdieu (1989) terms the *habitus,* a part of which is comprised of mental structures through which individuals apprehend the social world (p. 18). The previous examples suggest that the "world perceived as natural" is only natural to insiders who are familiar with the dominant discourse of the secondary education practices in English-speaking North America. Thus, it would seem highly beneficial for teachers to bring what is typically taken for granted in their practices to conscious awareness for ELLs.

NEED FOR COLLABORATION

Researchers encourage content-area teachers and ELL teachers to collaborate for the purpose of teaching relevant language and content in tandem. Such efforts require joint planning between teachers in various fields and also require that ELL specialists begin emphasizing the English knowledge and skills necessary to succeed in the content areas. Ernst-Slavit, Moore, and Maloney (2002) point out that every teacher can expect to work with at least one ELL in the near future, even though content-area teachers seldom think of themselves as language teachers. Similarly, ELL teachers often focus on teaching language alone, with little or no regard for grade-level content. The challenge is to combine these two forms of knowledge so that ELLs have specific linguistic abilities to succeed in subject-area classes.

Harklau's (1999) work also highlights the fact that the failure of ELL and content-area teachers to collaborate frequently results in a situation in which students may receive commendable language instruction in their ELL classes and high quality content instruction in their mainstream classes, but fail to receive integrated instruction that meets both their need to learn discipline-specific language and content simultaneously. O'Byrne (2001) recognizes that typical high school English teachers have a "wealth of tacit knowledge about reading and writing" (p. 448) and that, by collaborating with ELL teachers, they can create the tools needed to build truly multicultural and multilingual classrooms. Unfortunately, failure to develop such collaboration too often marginalizes ELL students and reduces their possibilities for becoming legitimate members of school communities.

What the Literature Tells Us about Students

ELL students often enter schools in the United States eager to learn English (Tse, 2001). Like many members of the general public, students often labor under the misperception that learning another language is simply a matter of exposure to the new language and a desire on their part to work hard at this task. Research, however, paints a more complicated picture. For example, Collier (1987) found that it takes six to eight years for students who enter the United States between the ages of 12 and 15 to develop academic language proficiency in English. Clearly, such proficiency is paradoxically both a prerequisite and the outcome of learning content in English.

Not only are students eager to learn English, they are also often overly confident that they will profit from all-English instruction. ELLs at the secondary level typically want access to the mainstream curriculum because they know that is the only place they will be exposed to high-level content instruction. However, they quickly realize that language barriers in mainstream classes prevent them from learning enough content in a timely manner. As O'Byrne (2001) writes: "First rank, ambitious students from various countries receive Fs on exams and essays. They need help; they ask for help. They want to get ahead" (p. 441).

Indeed, many immigrant students are often determined to achieve results in their studies, believing that, if they work hard, they will succeed. Although such motivation is commendable, many of these students believe specifically that working hard is equivalent to memorizing large amounts of material or tediously copying information. Such an approach rarely achieves the desired result, especially because teachers in U.S. schools often value demonstrations of comprehension, originality, and public participation rather than memorization (Duff, 2001).

Moreover, students often fail to understand how ELL or bilingual instruction can and should facilitate their academic progress. Students typically feel that the time they spend in these programs takes time away from learning the mainstream curriculum. This concern is reasonable if programs designed to provide assistance in learning English are poorly implemented or uncoordinated with the efforts of content-area teachers, which is frequently the case. Still, when ELLs at the secondary level enter mainstream content-area classes without sufficient linguistic abilities, the outcome is often failure; consequently, many of these students drop out of school.

Harklau (1999) notes that ELLs in secondary schools are often placed in low-track mainstream classes after they complete two or three years in an ESL classroom. Nevertheless, opportunities for learning English, as well as subject matter, tend to be very limited within these lower-level classes. In addition, mainstream students in these types of classes are often hostile to ELLs, which, as one might expect, limits yet further the opportunity for them to form meaningful social relationships and to use the new language. Harklau (1999) also notes that the ESL teachers who participated in her study tailored their instruction to the needs of ELLs and provided them with more opportunities to use their English. In contrast, in mainstream classes, ELLs had, on average, only one interaction with the teacher in English per day. In addition, Harklau found that high-track classes provided students with access to the mainstream curriculum but typically did not have the kinds of language support necessary for linguistic minority students to be successful. Valdés (2001) described similar conditions for Latino and Latina students in other U.S. secondary contexts. Clearly, the challenge of providing ELL students with access to content and to the English language is not easily resolved. The literature, however, provides some hopeful possibilities, which we present later in this chapter.

What the Literature Indicates about Parents

Young people have strong desires to belong and to feel as though they are members of school groups. On occasion, however, their academic needs conflict with their home and family responsibilities. In other words, adolescent ELLs are often expected to fulfill significant duties to the family that can conflict with the demands of homework or class projects. For example, Townsend and Fu (2001) describe the responsibilities of their case-study student, Paw, who had to cook dinner for her family every day and fill much of her time with housework. Paw's father emphasized obedience to parents, respect for elders, and helping other members of the family. Additionally, Daisey and José-Kampfner (2002) identify the confusing messages that young Latina women receive at home and in school concerning career, marriage, and motherhood. They argue that students require guidance to develop healthy responses to these mixed messages.

Although it is beyond the purview of educators to interfere in students' home lives, it can be useful to understand how the lives of adolescent ELLs can differ from those of young people from mainstream backgrounds. Educators can provide parents with information about what schools expect from students as well as from parents. Likewise, school personnel can compare and contrast different cultural lifestyles and explain to parents how these differences impact students' experiences in schools. Also, it is important for educators to understand and have accurate information about their students' out-of-school lives. To do so, educators need to listen carefully and respond to various needs expressed by parents, whether these needs involve academics or other issues. Without a doubt, many culturally diverse parents need a better understanding of the language demands of secondary education. They also need explicit evidence that their young people are receiving high quality instruction in language as well as in content areas while they are in ELL classrooms.

Promising Directions

Our review of the literature indicates two areas of promise for improving language and literacy learning opportunities for ELL students in secondary education. The first of these areas involves well-conceptualized, coherent program models. These include programs that are typically based on the special needs of linguistic minority students. The second group of research reports involves high quality, innovative, and focused instruction on topics relevant to success at the secondary level. This work focuses on instructional methods, the use of specific curricular materials, and instruction designed to encourage more involvement with oral language interactions. It also emphasizes the social needs of diverse students. These publications make the case that building meaningful relationships with educators and other adults in school settings may be as important as actual instruction and program models in terms of students' willingness to invest in school completion.

Programmatic Studies

Whitmore and Crowell (2005/2006) tracked down the graduates of a dual-language program ten years after they left it. Specifically, these researchers conducted a three-year ethnographic study of a third-grade bilingual program and then gathered information about students' academic attainment a decade later. Former students described the most important characteristic of the school as "the atypically high level of intellectual expectation for all of the children, regardless of their linguistic, cultural, or socioeconomic backgrounds" (p. 274). They also emphasized that academic work was highly intellectual and authentic and that bilingualism and biliteracy were valued as resources. These researchers (2005/2006) found that 15 of 23 of the students had graduated from high school and that 7 of the students were currently enrolled in a university or community college. They credit whole-language approaches to instruction, along with bilingual education and the building of a community of learners, for these high graduation rates.

Lucas, Henze, and Donato (1990) examined the outcomes of Latino and Latina students at six secondary schools recognized for their effectiveness in working with culturally and linguistically diverse students. These researchers included as exemplary schools those with high average daily attendance, low dropout rates, high numbers of students enrolled in postsecondary schooling, and high standardized test scores. Among the characteristics of these schools that the researchers determined to be responsible for the achievement of language minority students were the following:

◆ Placing value on students' languages and cultures,

◆ Holding high expectations for students, making the education of language minority students a priority,

- ◆ Providing staff with professional development for working with linguistically diverse students, offering a variety of courses and programs,

- ◆ Making available a counseling program with special attention for language minority students, encouraging parents of students to get involved in their children's education, and

- ◆ Empowering ELLs through schooling.

Lucas, Henze, and Donato argue that the combination of these features helped students achieve academic success.

Instructional Approaches

The next category of research that we examined involves more specific instructional approaches. It is important to mention that few studies of this nature have been published. Given the paucity of empirical studies in this area, we think the few that exist are critical starting points for further inquiry.

In one such study, Nussbaum (2002) recognizes that secondary ELLs need to learn how to participate appropriately in oral discussions of academic and social content. He claims that *critical discussions*, that is, discussions of critical topics relevant to students' lives (e.g., immigration), allow them to resolve differences with others as well as to improve their language and content knowledge. Working in two sixth-grade urban classrooms, Nussbaum examined an instructional technique that combined Reciprocal Teaching (Palincsar & Brown, 1984) and a "Transforming Cities" program (a critical social studies curriculum emphasizing urban studies) to promote student discussions. In these classrooms, issues discussed included the treatment of an indigenous population, immigration to the city, and local urban development.

Nussbaum (2002) notes that this critical approach increased the amount of discourse produced by linguistic minority students. He found it especially noteworthy for one male student who gradually began asking questions that involved him in ongoing social interactions, which in turn expanded his linguistic knowledge. These findings suggest that engaging curriculum and explicit instruction on certain linguistic structures (e.g., question formation) can encourage ELLs to participate more actively in grade-level activities.

Similarly, Wolfe (2004) worked with adolescent ELL readers in a large inner-city high school in the Southwest, with the goal of helping them understand abstract literary concepts such as "symbolism" and "theme." The students, mostly immigrants from Mexico, had completed from two to eight years of schooling in the United States. One of their assignments in an advanced ESL course was to read the novel *Bless me, Última*. The teacher validated the contributions of all of the students, even when their comments did not seem relevant to the discussion of the text. For example, while discussing the symbolism of the owl in the novel, one student mentioned that some pet shops in Mexico sell owls.

In addition, whenever possible, the teacher reformulated students' comments to more closely approximate those of scholarly literary analysis. Likewise, the teacher made an effort to connect complex ideas of symbolism and theme to concrete examples. These are important instructional techniques because they involve students in discussion of grade-level literature while providing them with explicit models of how to analyze and process texts.

Valdés (2001) points out how difficult it is to convince many mainstream English teachers to work with ELLs. On a similar note, O'Byrne (2001) notes that many of these teachers never imagined working with ELLs. Thus, one of the significant contributions of Wolfe's (2004) work is that it provides specific guidance for English teachers regarding how to involve linguistic minority students more effectively in learning about literacy concepts.

Conclusions

On the one hand, the literature we reviewed for this chapter makes it clear that ELL teachers focus most of their energy on teaching English. Their efforts at teaching the language, however, too often resemble the approaches taken by foreign language teachers, who are not responsible for their students' academic content learning. The instruction and curricula followed in many ELL classrooms is frequently detached from the concern to support ELLs as they move into the study of literature, mathematics, history, and science. Content-area teachers, on the other hand, concentrate the majority of their attention on subject matter while ignoring the discipline-specific language and literacy requirements for learning within their subject areas. It seems obvious that content-area and ELL teachers at all levels of instruction must begin coordinating their efforts.

One possibility for addressing this problem is to provide opportunities for ELL teachers to teach or observe in the mainstream program and return to the ELL classroom with their newfound understanding of content-area requirements. Another approach is for ELL teachers to establish ongoing discussions with students concerning their language learning needs within the mainstream program. ELL teachers could use this information to design more relevant language learning environments. We believe that such activity would also generate more student and parent support for ELL programs.

In addition to collaboration between teachers, students also need to be involved in making decisions about their schooling, including program placement, curriculum, and class activities. One reason to include students in these decisions is that, better than anyone else, they can express their personal learning goals and desires. They can provide the teachers and other school personnel with firsthand understanding concerning their academic and linguistic needs. Perhaps most important, they can use their own self-assessments to determine where they should be placed with respect to the mainstream curriculum. By engaging in dialogue with students, teachers may avoid the unfortunate tendency to fill the school day of many ELLs with meaningless activities such as those described by Valdés (2001).

Parents need to be informed about what schools expect from them, about how schooling in the new country differs from what they experienced in their native countries, and about what schools expect from students at each grade level. Immigrant parents in particular may find it surprising that educators frequently make assumptions about students' chances for success based on specific parental behaviors. For example, parents who are highly visible in the school setting, especially those who attend parent-teacher conferences, perform volunteer work, and involve themselves with students' homework assignments, lead many teachers to hold higher expectations for their children (Valdés, 1996). Many immigrant parents may also be surprised to find that student involvement in after-school activities is often associated with academic success (Flores-González, 2002). We recommend that parents of ELLs organize themselves for purposes of advocacy, obtaining information about schooling and learning about ways to support their children's efforts in school.

Many of the studies dealing with adolescent second language learners are found in practitioner-oriented journals. Although these reports provide a valuable service to the profession, there is a need for more rigorous research that would provide educators, policymakers, and researchers in the field with more empirically based information.

Bourdieu's (1998) notion of legitimacy serves to guide and anchor efforts to create more effective instructional practices for ELLs in secondary schools. Establishing dialogue among students, teachers, and parents can help create the conditions necessary for ELL students to be seen as legitimate members of the school community and society in general. Dialogue requires negotiation and understanding in place of arbitrary assumptions and decision making. Although there is currently a good deal of anti-immigrant sentiment among the general population, immigration will continue and perhaps even increase in the expanding global economy. We encourage educators, researchers, and policymakers to look at the big picture and to develop better informed approaches to teaching ELL students.

References

Alvermann, D. E., & Phelps, S. F. (2005). *Content reading and literacy: Succeeding in today's diverse classrooms* (4th ed.). Boston: Allyn and Bacon.

Bourdieu, P. (1989). Social space and symbolic power. *Sociological Theory, 7*(1), 14–25.

Bourdieu, P. (1991). *Language and symbolic power* (J. B. Thompson, Ed., G. Raymond & M. Adamson, Trans.). Cambridge, MA: Harvard University Press.

Bourdieu, P. (1998). *Practical reason: On the theory of action.* Stanford, CA: Stanford University Press.

Collier, V. P. (1987). Age and rate of aquisition of second language for academic purposes. *TESOL Quarterly, 21,* 617–41.

Daisey, P., & José-Kampfner, C. (2002). The power of story to expand possible selves for Latina middle school students. *Journal of Adolescent & Adult Literacy, 45,* 578–87.

Duff, P. A. (2001). Language, literacy, content, and (pop) culture: Challenges for ESL students in mainstream courses. *Canadian Modern Language Review, 58,* 103–32.

Ernst-Slavit, G., Moore, M., & Maloney, C. (2002). Changing lives: Teaching English and literature to ESL students. *Journal of Adolescent & Adult Literacy, 46,* 116–28.

Flores-González, N. (2002). *School kids/street kids: Identity development in Latino students.* New York: Teachers College Press.

Fu, D. (2004). Teaching ELL students in regular classrooms at the secondary level. *Voices from the Middle, 11*(4), 8–15.

García, O. (1999). Educating Latino high school students with little formal schooling. In C. J. Faltis & P. M. Wolfe (Eds.), *So much to say: Adolescents, bilingualism, and ESL in the secondary school* (pp. 61–82). New York: Teachers College Press.

Grant, R. A., & Wong, S. D. (2003). Barriers to literacy for language-minority learners: An argument for change in the literacy education profession. *Journal of Adolescent & Adult Literacy, 46,* 386–94.

Gunderson, L. (2000). Voices of the teenage diasporas. *Journal of Adolescent & Adult Literacy, 43,* 692–706.

Harklau, L. (1999). The ESL learning environment in secondary school. In C. J. Faltis & P. M. Wolfe (Eds.), *So much to say: Adolescents, bilingualism, and ESL in the secondary school* (pp. 42–60). New York: Teachers College Press.

Harper, C., & de Jong, E. (2004). Misconceptions about teaching English language learners. *Journal of Adolescent & Adult Literacy, 48,* 152–62.

Jiménez, R. T., Smith, P. H., & Martínez-León, N. (2003). Freedom and form: The language and literacy practices of two Mexican schools. *Reading Research Quarterly, 38,* 488–508.

Klingner, J. K., & Vaughn, S. (2004). Strategies for struggling second-language readers. In T. L. Jetton & J. A. Dole (Eds.), *Adolescent literacy research and practice* (pp. 183–209). New York: Guilford Press.

Lucas, T., Henze, R., & Donato, R. (1990). Promoting the success of Latino language-minority students: An exploratory study of six high schools. *Harvard Educational Review, 60,* 315–40.

National Center for Education Statistics (NCES). (2005). *National Institute of Statistical Sciences/Education Statistics Services Institute Task Force on Graduation, Completion, and Dropout Indicators. Final Report* (NCES Publication No. 2005-105). Washington, DC: Author.

Nussbaum, E. M. (2002). The process of becoming a participant in small-group critical discussions: A case study. *Journal of Adolescent & Adult Literacy, 45,* 488–97.

O'Byrne, B. (2001). Needed: A compass to navigate the multilingual English classroom. *Journal of Adolescent & Adult Literacy, 44,* 440–49.

Palincsar, A. S., & Brown, A. L. (1984). Reciprocal teaching of comprehension-fostering and comprehension-monitoring activities. *Cognition and Instruction, 1,* 117–75.

Peregoy, S. F., & Boyle, O. F. (2000). English learners reading English: What we know, what we need to know. *Theory into Practice, 39,* 237–47.

Reynolds, M., & Gaouette, N. (2006). Senators delay immigration debate to work behind the scenes. *LAtimes.com.* Retrieved June 19, 2007, from http://pqasb.pqarchiver.com/latimes/access/10114 65611.html?dids=1011465611:1011465611&FMT=ABS& FMTS=ABS:FT&type=current&date=Mar+29%2C+2006& author=Maura+Reynolds+and+Nicole+Gaouette&pub=Los+ Angeles+Times&edition= &startpage=A.16&desc=THE+NATION

Rubinstein-Ávila, E. (2003–2004). Conversing with Miguel: An adolescent English language learner struggling with later literacy development. *Journal of Adolescent & Adult Literacy, 47,* 290–301.

Townsend, J. S., & Fu, D. (2001). Paw's story: A Laotian refugee's lonely entry into American literacy. *Journal of Adolescent & Adult Literacy, 45,* 104–14.

Tse, L. (2001). *"Why don't they learn English?" Separating fact from fallacy in the U.S. language debate.* New York: Teachers College Press.

Valdés, G. (1996). *Con respeto: Bridging distances between culturally diverse families and schools: An ethnographic portrait.* New York: Teachers College Press.

Valdés, G. (2001). *Learning and not learning English: Latino students in American schools.* New York: Teachers College Press.

Whitmore, K. F., & Crowell, C. G. (2005–2006). Bilingual education students reflect on their language education: Reinventing a classroom 10 years later. *Journal of Adolescent & Adult Literacy, 49,* 270–85.

Wolfe, P. (2004). "The owl cried": Reading abstract literary concepts with adolescent ESL students. *Journal of Adolescent & Adult Literacy, 47,* 402–13.

Literacy Development of African American Adolescent Males

ALFRED W. TATUM

University of Illinois at Chicago

Corelle's favorite part of English II had been a play we read by August Wilson, *The Piano Lesson*. Every time I taught *The Piano Lesson* since, visions of Corelle have come rushing back through the lovable Boy Willie. In one long monologue, Boy Willie talks about the turning point in his life, the terrifying moment when he confronted the world's opinion of his own uselessness. . . . It is the growing perception of their own uselessness —together with the apparent lawlessness of the world around them— that hurtles boys like Corelle, Larry, Jevon, and Oron (all African American teenage males) toward extinction. . . . But if Corelle is denied his place for too long, he, like Boy Willie, may one day come to believe that the only way to make the world look you in the eye is by pointing a gun at it. (Johnston, 2002, pp. 115–116)

It is extremely disheartening to read reports in research and popular texts about the literacy development of African American adolescent males in the United States. It has become commonplace to chronicle their failures in schools and society. To illustrate the point, I highlight several issues raised in a recent *New York Times* article (Eckholm, 2006). It was reported:

◆ Over the last two decades, the economy did great, but the share of young African American men without jobs climbed.

◆ In 2000, 65 percent of African American male high school dropouts in their twenties were jobless. By 2004, the share had grown to 72 percent of African American male high school dropouts without jobs, compared with 34 percent of white and 19 percent of Latino/Latina dropouts without jobs.

◆ In the inner cities, more than half of all African American men do not finish high school.

◆ By their mid-thirties, six in ten African American men who dropped out of school had spent time in prison.

◆ These negative trends are frequently associated with poor schooling, as studies have shown, and progress has been slight for years.

Academic indicators suggest that conditions need to improve for African American adolescent males in the United States. Using a comprehensive approach developed by the Manhattan Institute to assess dropout rates for a cohort of students who began ninth grade and completed high school four years later, the Education Trust found that only 48 percent of African American males complete high school with their cohort group (Hall, 2005). The Schott Foundation for Public Education reported that much of the problem is concentrated in large cities. Smaller states have the same problem: South Dakota and Maine graduated less than 30 percent of their small number of African American male students on schedule. Thirteen other states graduated only between 30 and 40 percent of African American males with their peer group (Holzman, 2004). Although the problems of these young men are not isolated to reading, there is an urgent need to improve the reading of these young men for their sake and for the sake of society.

An analysis of National Assessment of Educational Progress's long-term trend reading assessments reveals that only 1 in 100 African American seventeen-year-olds can read and gain information from specialized text. An example of specialized text is a science section in a local newspaper (Haycock & Huang, 2001). Many educators feel challenged by the prospect of moving a large percentage of African American males from basic levels of reading achievement to proficient and advanced levels.

As an African American, I have stared down the barrel of a gun five times in less than four decades at the hands of other African American males, three times before turning sixteen. Thus, I have firsthand experience of one of the adaptive behaviors, i.e., crime, used by many of these young men who succumb to the weight of adverse conditions in schools and society. Many of these young men are caught between wandering in the *wilderness* and searching for the *promise,* political and social metaphors in American society (Asante, 2003). The *wilderness* represents something difficult, perhaps unknown: a place where one does not know what to expect. On the other hand, the *promise* is the expectation that something good is going to happen.

The following conversation between two African American teenagers captured in *Our America: Life and Death on the South Side of Chicago* (Jones & Newman, 1997) illustrates the struggle between the wilderness and the promise:

> Man, why ain't you been to school (promise)
>
> GEORGE: School ain't shit (wilderness)
>
> How you gonna be something if you don't go to school? (promise)
>
> You ain't learning shit now, so why? Why? (wilderness)
>
> You ain't learning shit out here. I bet I'm gonna see your ass twenty-five years from now begging for a quarter so you could get a drink! (promise)
>
> I ain't gonna be alive in ten years because I'll be selling my drugs and they're gonna pop my ass. No one's gonna be alive in twenty more years. (wilderness)
>
> I'm gonna be alive! I know I am! (promise)
>
> Your ass ain't gonna be alive in ten years! (wilderness)

Asante describes an eternal optimism about what could happen if national will existed to create a constructive human transformation of African American males shaken by the *wilderness* experience.

Meaningful reading and writing opportunities in classroom environments with high-quality literacy teaching can lead to a constructive human transformation of the African American adolescent male. Yet, all too often, African American adolescent males find themselves in classrooms with curricular and pedagogical misalignments between literacy instruction and their needs. If attending a low-performing high school, these young men likely experience little challenge in reading assignments. The contrasting lesson provided at the Educational Trust National Conference in 2005 offers a startling glimpse between two ninth-grade lessons connected to the same text (see Table 9.1).

In "Too Cool for School," a chapter reflecting his school experience on the west side of Chicago, Cose (2002) writes:

> It came to me as I was sitting at my desk trying to keep myself interested as the teacher led the class, one listless word at a time, through the book I had read the first day of school, a book (and not a particularly interesting one) she would end up taking the entire semester to slow-walk us through. (p. 69)

TABLE 9.1. Two Ninth-Grade Assignments

The Odyssey High-Level Assignment	*The Odyssey* Low-Level Assignment
Comparison/Contrast Paper between Homer's Epic Poem, *The Odyssey*, and the Movie *O Brother, Where Art Thou?* By nature, human beings compare and contrast all of the elements of their world. Why? In the juxtaposition of two different things, one can learn more about each individual thing as well as something about the universal nature of the things being compared. For this 2–3 page paper, ask yourself the following questions: What larger ideas do you see working in *The Odyssey* and in *O Brother, Where Art Thou?* Do both works treat these issues in the same way? What do the similarities and differences between the works reveal about the underlying nature of the larger idea? Your thesis should take a position on the "larger idea" and then break that larger idea into smaller but related ideas, i.e., components of the larger idea.	Divide class into three groups. Group 1 designs a brochure entitled "Odyssey Cruises." The students listen to the story and write down all of the places that Odysseus visited in his adventures and list the cost to travel from place to place. Group 2 draws pictures of each adventure. Group 3 takes the names of the characters and the gods and goddesses in the story and then designs a crossword puzzle.

In analyzing his experience and characterizing the teaching as a slow walk through, Cose concluded that teachers deemed African American males as unteachable or incapable of keeping up if the class proceeded at a normal pace. Similar to Cose's experiences, African American adolescent males often encounter literacy instruction that is misplaced and mispaced. Take the following description from a lesson I observed in a Baltimore middle school delivered to a class with African American boys who struggled with reading:

> As a prereading activity, new vocabulary was being introduced. The teacher held a bell he would use to control the pace of the lesson and told the students to get ready. He called out the word *Agatha*. The students repeated the word. The process was repeated with the words *Demarco, Adeline, Emilia*, and *pumpernickel*. Then the students took turns reading aloud. The teacher corrected every miscue: "No, that's not *coastal*, that's *castle*." He then had the students respond aloud to the assessment questions at the end of the text. They provided wrong answers for a majority of the questions. For each incorrect response, the teacher provided the correct answer, but did not explain why that response was better than the others.

The students were reading from decontextualized text and were not provided with any explicit strategy instruction. This lesson can be described as deadening. It is not clear why this lesson was selected to address the literacy needs of African American males living in an urban environment and struggling with reading. It is not clear how this lesson helped students use skills and strategies independently. It is not clear what conceptualization of literacy instruction governed the lesson. Was it designed to help the young men become functionally literate? Was it designed to empower the young men? It makes sense to ask the following questions: Out of all of the reading materials in the world, why was this reading selection chosen for those young African American adolescent males? What is being undertreated with this type of lesson? How can these young men perceive schooling and its potential to help them navigate mainstream society if these types of lessons persist? Misplaced and mispaced instruction, fueled by low expectations, lead many of these young men to resist and reject the instruction they receive in schools. More damaging, however, this misalignment contributes to high dropout rates and low college enrollment rates. Low-quality instruction that is disconnected from the larger reality these young men face leaves them underprepared to perform academically, notably in the areas of reading and writing.

In this chapter, I bring attention to the need to reconceptualize the role of literacy instruction for African American males in high school. Literacy instruction for these young men must be audited to determine whether it is planned to reverse the negative life outcome trajectory experienced by a large percentage of these young men. Literacy instruction must be audited to determine whether it helps them decide what they want to do with the rest of their lives. The aims of reading and writing instruction are broader than measuring achievement in school.

If we accept the premise that literacy instruction should be aligned to address academic, cultural, emotional, and social trajectories of African American adolescent males, we must ask at minimum two questions: Why do we select the reading materials we do for African American males? Why do we select the writing topics we do for African American males? To help answer these questions, I provide a brief description of related research.

Who Is the African American Male?

Almost one hundred years ago, James Weldon Johnson (1912/ 1990) offered a narrative titled *The Autobiography of an Ex-Colored Man*. He describes the anguish of an eleven-year-old who finds out that he is a colored boy. Although he is studious and plays the piano well, the young boy, who could pass for white, loses years of reassurance after being confident for most of his life. Finding out he was a colored boy was one of the tragedies of his life. He describes the psychological impact in the following manner:

> From that time I looked out through other eyes, my thoughts were colored, my words dictated, my actions limited by one dominating, all-prevailing idea which constantly increased in force

and weight until I finally realized in it a great, tangible fact. And this is the dwarfing, warping, distorting influence which operates upon each colored man in the United States. He is forced to take his outlook on all things, not from the viewpoint of a citizen, or a man, nor even a human being, but from the viewpoint of a colored man . . . through the narrow neck of one funnel. (p. 9)

There can be little doubt that the fact of blackness remains a hallmark of the identities for the more than four million African American males enrolled in grades K–12 in the United States. This is a residual effect of living in a country whose wealth, to a large extent, was constructed on race-based slavery, followed by a full century of *de jure* segregation and discrimination in every major aspect of a black citizen's social, economic, and political existence (Gates, 2004).

Hogue (2003) discusses the African American as being constituted within an unequal white or black binary system:

In this binary system, which is reinforced by the cultural, social, political, and economic institutions and apparatuses of the United States and Western Civilization, the African American is represented only in terms of his experience of racism. To be represented as a victim of racial oppression is to be defined exclusively and negatively by someone else's discourse. For the African American, racial oppression/victimization becomes the site of a beginning of an origin, and the events of African American history and culture are defined in terms of the beginning. In short, the African American is represented as a passive object of a White middle class that is the maker of history. As a consequence, other African American representations, identities, and experiences that do not fit into this White/Black binary are ignored. (p. 13)

African American males born in the late 1980s and 1990s are now enrolled in middle schools and high schools throughout the nation. Many of these young men are discouraged by the outcomes of the civil rights era, in large part because the reverse of events in those years catapulted many communities into an economic downturn. This happened around the same time the onslaught of drugs, drug trafficking, and drug-related violence further debilitated their communities. Despite the passage of the civil rights laws that gave African Americans access to better jobs, housing, and education and despite the rise of a large African American middle class, young African American males today still experience race-based and class-based tensions.

The late 1980s also marked the explosion of the West Coast hip-hop scene, which ushered in the commercial success of gangster rap. This was followed by an attack on the philosophy of the juvenile justice system. As media images of juvenile crime became more graphic, the criminalization of African American males was heightened. In California, for example, sweeping changes in the juvenile justice system connected to Proposition 21 led it to become the state with the nation's biggest prison population and corrections system. Politicians gained political capital by becoming tough on youth crime and espousing tougher crime laws.

Tougher crime laws cemented the image of the African American male as the young superpredator, a new species of criminal. The 1980s and 1990s have been characterized as punishment decades. Watkins (2005) writes, ". . . the triple bind of race, class, and youth made life a real challenge. . . . To be young, Black, or Latino, and poor in California was almost a crime itself during the punishment decade" (p. 179).

Schools were not inoculated against these images and descriptors.

African American males are also failing in suburban communities. Abigail and Stephen Thernstrom (2003) illuminate the quality of instruction received by African American students in one suburban community that they believe is endemic in many suburban communities:

> The student body of Cedarbrook Middle School in a Philadelphia suburb is one-third Black, two-thirds White. The town has a very low poverty rate, good schools, and long-established Black middle class. . . . The class in which the teacher was explaining that the 2 in 21 stands for 20 . . . was 100 percent Black. A few Black students were taking accelerated English, but no Whites were sitting in the English class that was learning to identify verbs. (p. 1)

Next, I turn to characteristics of effective literacy teaching for these young men in America's classrooms.

Effectively Teaching the African American Adolescent Male

Four bodies of research figure prominently in identifying literacy practices that are effective with African American adolescent males: research-based reading and writing practices, research on African American males in schools, research on adolescent literacy, and research on boys and reading. Over the past ten years, the education of African American males has been the focus of several texts, including *Educating African American Males* (Fashola, 2005), *African American Males in School and Society* (Polite & Davis, 1999), *Bad Boys: Public Schools in the Making of Black Masculinity* (Ferguson, 2000), and *Teaching Reading to Black Adolescent Males* (Tatum, 2005). Several other texts have focused on reading and boys. Prominent among them are *To Be a Boy, To Be a Reader* (Brozo, 2002); *Boys, Literacies and Schooling* (Rowan, Knobel, Bigum, & Lankshear, 2002); and *Reading Don't Fix No Chevys* (Smith & Wilhelm, 2002). During the same period, there has been a call to rethink and reconceptualize adolescent literacy (Alvermann, Hinchman, Moore, Phelps, & Waff, 2006; Jetton & Dole, 2004; Moore, Bean, Birdyshaw, & Rycik, 1999). Addressing the literacy development of African American adolescent males requires competencies in each of these areas. Following are suggestions from recent research.

Research-Based Reading and Writing Practice for Adolescents

Teaching reading strategies figures prominently for improving adolescents' reading comprehension. When strategies are modeled, many students come to realize that comprehension depends on a combination of their own personal effort and strategy use in searching for understanding (Borkowski, 1992). They benefit when teachers model, talk aloud, or make their thinking public (Pressley & Afflerbach, 1995). Students also benefit when teachers gradually reduce their support and help them assume independent control of the strategies they have been learning. Providing clear indications about correctness, repeating correct responses, being encouraging, rehearsing correct information by both speaking and underlining it, and reminding students about important information to learn have positive effects (Winne, Graham, & Prock, 1993). This can potentially cause students to self-regulate strategy use and to use the strategies, particularly if they are informed of the benefits and provided with evidence of the contributions of the strategies that lead to improved performance on comprehension-related tasks.

Instruction for adolescents should include explicit strategy instruction. Adolescent students benefit when teachers move them toward using comprehension strategies independently and help them understand the value of the strategies. They also benefit when they are given opportunities to use their strategy knowledge and receive corrective feedback and reinforcement about their strategy use.

Research on African American Males in Schools

African American adolescent males are more likely than other students to be in classrooms staffed by inexperienced teachers. Many underprepared teachers are assigned to disadvantaged schools with a large percentage of African American students and where working conditions are not attractive and turnover rates are highest (Darling-Hammond, 1998).

A closer look at the "good teaching" of African American students (Foster, 1997; Hollins, 1996; Irvine, 1991; Ladson-Billings, 1995) has led to a distinctive educational philosophy and pedagogy, along with insights into the aspects of the teachers' behaviors that are considered effective. The "good teachers" of African Americans who emerge from these studies may be described as follows: They are concerned individuals who command respect, are respectful of pupils, and who, although caring, are strict in requiring all students to meet high academic and behavioral standards. They are concerned not only with the students' cognitive development but also with their affective, social, and emotional development. They use a culturally responsive approach to literacy teaching.

Ladson-Billings (1992), in her rich description of culturally responsive teaching, added the design of a culturally responsive approach to literacy teaching that aims to guide students toward academic success and cultural competence; nurture their consciousness, which allows them to critique societal norms; and use the students' culture as a vehicle for learning. Activities based on the norms of the students' community are incorporated into the classroom, cooperation is emphasized over competition, and learning is structured as a social activity. Culturally responsive teachers also legitimate African American culture and make it a frame of reference.

Although much of what I have described refers to teaching practices, it is also necessary to give attention to curriculum, which has been a defining feature of black education (Watkins, 2001a). Curricular domains are sites for learning that allow students to enter important cultural traditions of knowing and doing that have planned shapes and structure (Applebee, 1996). Curricular, pedagogical, and evaluative activities in day-to-day life in schools play a significant role in preserving, if not generating, inequalities (Apple, 1990).

Many African American students are denied opportunities within the curriculum to engage in academically rigorous tasks that push them to levels of maximum competency (Darling-Hammond, 1997). Literacy educators may not be aware of the curriculum orientations of African Americans and the formation of these orientations (Watkins, 1993, 2001b). They also may not understand how curriculum orientations stifle or postpone academic growth, rendering students powerless. As a result, these educators can become inadvertent accomplices to poor educational practices for students of color.

Bringing attention to curriculum orientations figures prominently when supporting teachers to advance the literacies of African Americans students. Murrell (2002) argues that the failure to interrogate harmful instructional and curricular practices critically will continue to harm African American children. The selection of curriculum materials or the designation of curriculum materials by teachers and school districts has been connected to an ideological concept of the role of literacy in the lives of African American students (Watkins, 1993). Many curriculum orientations for African Americans have not been designed to empower them, often ignoring cultural definitions of race and class that have been constituted as historical and social constructs. Unless teachers begin to understand schools as part of a wider dominant culture, the experiences of many students will be marginalized and the students will not be able to draw on these experiences to gain control of their lives (Giroux, 1988).

African American adolescent males, like other students, benefit from a literacy curriculum that makes them functional and critical within the school environment (Sylvester, 1994). Such a curriculum includes creating opportunities for repeated, meaningful application of academic skills, authentic opportunities for discussion, and opportunities for students to imagine themselves in new roles. Students should be able to question and analyze their realities in the context of the curriculum and discuss strategies for overcoming academic and societal barriers so that they do not view their social, academic, and economic realities as unalterable.

Research on Adolescent Literacy

A renewed focus on adolescent literacy has succeeded in highlighting the literacy needs of older students. However, the roles that literacy plays in the lives of adolescents and the functions of literacy for these students are still in the process of being defined. For example, certain "binaries" exist between the literate lives of adolescents in school and their out-of-school literacy (Alvermann, 1998). School-sanctioned literacy, in many cases, does not match with adolescents' tastes; this mismatch is possibly the most marked for poor and reluctant readers (Worthy, Moorman, & Turner, 1999). Such binaries lead many adolescents to approach school-sanctioned literacy with little enthusiasm (Hynds, 1989).

Many adolescents live complex lives and are interested in being viewed as coming to their work in schools with existing knowledge, skills, and plans for the future. Many are also eager to participate in literate practices that are suited to the ways in which they view their day-to-day lives. They draw on multiple, overlapping, and interactive bodies of knowledge to make sense of their school subjects. For example, Obidah (1998) described four overlapping bodies of literacy. She examined African American adolescents' use of their *literate currency*—the multiple and interactive forms of literacy that have significant impact on the encounters between the teacher and students in the course of everyday schooling. She identified *popular culture literacy, peer literacy, school literacy,* and *home/community literacy* as sources that students use to negotiate their experiences and draw information from in order to respond to the knowledge taught in schools. Students' literacies are an important force that can disrupt or perpetuate how they act, interact, and understand their literate experiences (Moore & Cunningham, 1998). Adolescents begin to assert their agency, that is, individual decision making (to do or not to do) as they interpret the multiple social, cultural, and linguistic variables that envelop them in and out of school. How they shape and are shaped by the literacies in their lives as they take cues from past and current literate experiences to make sense of new literate activities may depend on how others in their lives listen and respond to them (Mosenthal, 1998). The ways in which these students see themselves as readers and writers influence their point of view about a particular class and how they interact with the teacher (Rex, 2001).

The Commission on Adolescent Literacy of the International Reading Association (Moore et al., 1999) identified general principles for helping adolescent readers:

◆ Provide adolescents with access to a wide variety of reading materials that they can and want to read,

◆ Provide instruction that builds their skill and desire to read,

◆ Take into account the complexities of individual adolescent readers, respect their differences, and respond to their characteristics,

◆ Use assessments that show their strengths as well as their needs and that will help them best grow as readers, and

◆ Model and provide explicit strategy instruction in reading comprehension and study strategies across the curriculum.

Until the broader conceptualization of what it means to teach adolescents reaches the classroom teacher, a large percentage of African American adolescent males may well continue to experience reading materials and practices that cause them to dislike school literacy activities, as well as unmotivating skills instruction that detracts from the time these students spend reading and writing.

Research on Boys and Reading

Recent texts on boys and reading focus on acknowledging boys' masculine identities during literacy instruction. Brozo (2002) suggested using literature with traditional male archetypes as an entry point into literacy for boys. Other authors suggest making the reading curriculum more appealing to boys who may view reading as a passive, female activity (Maynard, 2002). Boys may reject reading as a way of separating themselves from all that is female and establishing themselves as males. "If the masculine self is oppositional to the literate self, then it must seem to many boys that literacy is relatively unimportant and irrelevant" (Gilbert & Gilbert, 1998). Teachers can benefit by becoming "gender aware" in their teaching practices (Maynard, 2002).

Gender awareness and emphases on masculinity have led to several recommendations for engaging boys with reading:

- ◆ Use male-oriented texts with male characters versus female-oriented texts.

- ◆ Use texts that engage boys emotionally with characters and issues they care about, as well as texts that mark their identity.

- ◆ Expose boys to more nonfiction that involves "finding out" information.

- ◆ Use texts that legitimize the male experience and support boys' views of themselves.

Smith and Wilhelm (2002) found that, although boys believed in the importance of school literacy in theory, they often rejected and resisted it in practice because it was not related to their immediate interests and needs. The boys wanted to get information about real events and situations. The boys also liked texts that could be easily exported into conversations and that provided multiple perspectives. They found that all of the young men with whom they worked were passionate about activities in which they experienced flow (Csikszentmihalyi, 1990). Four conditions of the flow experience include a feeling of control, an appropriate level of challenge, clear goals and feedback, and a focus on the immediate. Unfortunately, most of the young men did not experience flow in their literature activities in school and therefore saw schooling as superficial.

Rethinking the Role of Literacy Instruction for African American Adolescent Males

Too often, African American adolescent males experience an imbalance between an out-of-school literacy overload and an in-school literacy underload (Tatum, 2006). As a result, they lack appropriate literacy experiences inside of school to help critique, understand, and navigate life outside of school. Life outcome indicators, as discussed throughout this chapter, make it increasingly apparent that literacy is more than just reading and writing for African American adolescent males. Much of what they experience or fail to experience in school shapes their life outcome trajectories. Literacy instruction for these young men is about being responsive to multiple literacy needs and shaping a trajectory that leads to positive life outcomes.

Addressing the literacy development of these young men requires multiple competencies, including knowledge about the African American male, the role of public policy and its impact on the image of the African American adolescent male, and research on literacy instruction. A productive starting point for planning literacy instruction for African American adolescent males is recognizing that it is not just about their literacy development; it is about their lives.

References

Alvermann, D. E. (1998). Imagining the possibilities. In D. E. Alvermann, K. A. Hinchman, D. W. Moore, S. F. Phelps, & D. R. Waff (Eds.), *Reconceptualizing the literacies in adolescents' lives* (pp. 353–72). Mahwah, NJ: Erlbaum.

Alvermann, D. E., Hinchman, K. A., Moore, D. W., Phelps, S. F., & Waff, D. R. (Eds.). (2006). *Reconceptualizing the literacies in adolescents' lives* (2nd ed.). Mahwah, NJ: Erlbaum.

Apple, M. W. (1990). *Ideology and curriculum* (2nd ed.). New York: Routledge.

Applebee, A. N. (1996). *Curriculum as conversation: Transforming traditions of teaching and learning.* Chicago: University of Chicago Press.

Asante, M. K. (2003). *Erasing racism: The survival of the American nation.* Amherst, NY: Prometheus Books.

Borkowski, J. G. (1992). Metacognitive theory: A framework for teaching literacy, writing, and math skills. *Journal of Learning Disabilities, 25,* 253–57.

Brozo, W. G. (2002). *To be a boy, to be a reader: Engaging teen and preteen boys in active literacy.* Newark, DE: International Reading Association.

Cose, E. (2002). *The envy of the world: On being a black man in America.* New York: Washington Square Press.

Csikszentmihalyi, M. (1990). *Flow: The psychology of optimal experience.* New York: Harper & Row.

Darling-Hammond, L. (1997) *The right to learn: A blueprint for creating schools that work.* San Francisco: Jossey-Bass.

Darling-Hammond, L. (1998). New standards, old inequalities: The current challenge for African-American education. In L. A. Daniels (Ed.), *The state of black America 1998* (pp. 109–71). New York: National Urban League.

Eckholm, E. (2006, March 20). Plight deepens for black men, studies warn. *New York Times,* pp. A1.

Fashola, O. S. (Ed.). (2005). *Educating African American males: Voices from the field.* Thousand Oaks, CA: Corwin Press.

Ferguson, A. (2000). *Bad boys: Public schools in the making of black masculinity.* Ann Arbor: University of Michigan Press.

Foster, M. (Ed.). (1997). *Black teachers on teaching.* New York: New Press.

Gates, H. L., Jr. (2004). *America behind the color line: Dialogues with African Americans.* New York: Warner Books.

Gilbert, R., & Gilbert, P. (1998). *Masculinity goes to school.* New York: Routledge.

Giroux, H. A. (1988). Literacy and the pedagogy of voice and political empowerment. *Educational Theory, 38,* 61–75.

Hall, D. (2005). *Getting honest about grad rates: How states play the numbers and students lose.* Washington, DC: The Education Trust.

Haycock, K., & Huang, S. (2001) Are today's high school graduates ready? *Thinking K–16, 5*(1), 3–17.

Hogue, W. L. (2003). *The African American male, writing, and difference: A polycentric approach to African American literature, criticism, and history.* Albany: State University of New York Press.

Hollins, E. R. (1996). *Culture in school learning: Revealing the deep meaning.* Mahwah, NJ: Erlbaum.

Holzman, M. (2004). *Public education and black male students: A state report card.* Cambridge, MA: Schott Foundation for Public Education.

Hynds, S. (1989). Bringing life to literature and literature to life: Social constructs and contexts of four adolescent readers. *Research in the Teaching of English, 23,* 30–61.

Irvine, J. J. (1991). *Black students and school failure: Policies, practices, and prescriptions.* Westport, CT: Praeger.

Jetton, T. L., & Dole, J. A. (Eds.). (2004). *Adolescent literacy research and practice.* New York: Guilford Press.

Johnson, J. W. (1990). *The autobiography of an ex-colored man* (W. L. Andrews, Ed.). New York: Penguin Books. (Original work published in 1912)

Johnston, M. (2002). *In the deep heart's core.* New York: Grove Press.

Jones, L., & Newman, L. (with Isay, D.). (1997). *Our America: Life and death on the south side of Chicago.* New York: Washington Square Press.

Ladson-Billings, G. (1992). Reading between the lines and beyond the pages: A culturally relevant approach to literacy teaching. *Theory into Practice, 31,* 312–20.

Ladson-Billings, G. (1995). Toward a theory of culturally relevant pedagogy. *American Educational Research Journal, 32,* 465–91.

Maynard, T. (2002). *Boys and literacy: Exploring the issues.* New York: Routledge.

Moore, D. W., Bean, T. W., Birdyshaw, D., & Rycik, J. A. (1999). Adolescent literacy: A position statement. *Journal of Adolescent & Adult Literacy, 43,* 97–112.

Moore, D. W., & Cunningham, J. W. (1998). Agency and adolescent literacy. In D. E. Alvermann, K. A. Hinchman, D. W. Moore, S. F. Phelps, & D. R. Waff (Eds.), *Reconceptualizing the literacies in adolescents' lives* (pp. 283–302). Mahwah, NJ: Erlbaum.

Mosenthal, P. B. (1998). Reframing the problems of adolescence and adolescent literacy: A dilemma-management perspective. In D. E. Alvermann, K. A. Hinchman, D. W. Moore, S. F. Phelps, & D. R. Waff (Eds.), *Reconceptualizing the literacies in adolescents' lives* (pp. 325–52). Mahwah, NJ: Erlbaum.

Murrell, P. (2002). *African-centered pedagogy: Developing schools of achievement for African American children.* New York: Teachers College Press.

Obidah, J. E. (1998). Black-Mystory: Literate currency in everyday schooling. In D. E. Alvermann, K, A. Hinchman, D. W. Moore, S. F. Phelps, & D. R. Waff (Eds.), *Reconceptualizing the literacies in adolescents' lives* (pp. 51–71). Mahwah, NJ: Erlbaum.

Polite, V. C., & Davis, J. E. (Eds.). (1999). *African American males in school and society: Practices and policies for effective education.* New York: Teachers College Press.

Pressley, M., & Afflerbach, P. (1995). *Verbal protocols of reading: The nature of constructively responsive reading.* Hillsdale, NJ: Erlbaum.

Rex, L. A. (2001) The remaking of a high school reader. *Reading Research Quarterly, 36,* 288–314.

Rowan, L., Knobel, M., Bigum, C., & Lankshear, C. (2002). *Boys, literacies and schooling: The dangerous territories of gender-based literacy reform.* Philadelphia, PA: Open University Press.

Smith. M. W., & Wilhelm, J. D. (2002). *"Reading don't fix no Chevys": Literacy in the lives of young men.* Portsmouth, NH: Heinemann.

Sylvester, P. S. (1994). Elementary school curricula and urban transformation. *Harvard Educational Review, 64,* 309–31.

Tatum, A. W. (2005). *Teaching reading to black adolescent males: Closing the achievement gap.* Portland, ME: Stenhouse.

Tatum, A. W. (2006). Adolescents' multiple identities and teacher professional development. In D. E. Alvermann, K. A. Hinchman, D. W. Moore, S. F. Phelps, & D. R. Waff (Eds.), *Reconceptualizing the literacies in adolescents' lives* (2nd ed., pp. 65–79). Mahwah, NJ: Erlbaum.

Thernstrom, A., & Thernstrom, S. (2003). *No excuses: Closing the racial gap in learning.* New York: Simon & Schuster.

Watkins, S. C. (2005). *Hip hop matters: Politics, pop culture, and the struggle for the soul of a movement.* Boston: Beacon Press.

Watkins, W. H. (1993). Black curriculum orientations: A preliminary inquiry. *Harvard Educational Review, 63,* 321–38.

Watkins, W. H. (2001a). Blacks and curriculum: From accommodation to contestation and beyond. In W. H. Watkins, J. H. Lewis, & V. Chou (Eds.), *Race and education: The roles of history and society in educating African American students* (pp. 40–65). Boston: Allyn and Bacon.

Watkins, W. H. (2001b). *The white architects of black education: Ideology and power in America, 1865–1954.* New York: Teachers College Press.

Winne, P. H., Graham, L., & Prock, L. (1993). A model of poor readers' text-based inferencing: Effects of explanatory feedback. *Reading Research Quarterly, 28,* 53–66.

Worthy, J., Moorman, M., & Turner, M. (1999). What Johnny likes to read is hard to find in school. *Reading Research Quarterly, 34,* 12–27.

From Contexts to Contextualizing and Recontextualizing: The Work of Teaching

JAMES S. DAMICO, GERALD CAMPANO, AND JEROME C. HARSTE
Indiana University

Imagine yourself as a high school teacher in the following class-room:

> Several boys, sitting in the back of the class, draw pictures of lowrider art; two African American girls seated at opposite ends of the room use their eyes and shoulders to communicate silently with each other; two boys use cellular phones to share photos they took of their neighborhoods; and a Hmong refugee girl writes a narrative of her experiences, using her emergent English skills to convey the power of her story.

If you are studying this classroom from the perspective of a teacher, a researcher, or a teacher-researcher, this description provides an initial, simplified sketch of the "context." And there are, of course, many ways of viewing, interpreting, and making sense of what is happening in this context. "Context" is frequently taken as a given, bounded, and often relatively static aspect of reality in many monographs or studies. However, in this chapter, we argue that this interpretive and sense-making work is dynamic and ongoing and that participants—teachers and students in class-rooms as well as researchers studying what happens in class-rooms—are always engaged, consciously or not, in the socially contested processes of defining how classroom events and experiences are to be understood.

Brian Street (1993) argues that culture should not be viewed as a noun, as static or reified, but, more productively, as a verb, as practices that people *do* rather than things that people *have*. We make a similar case, placing emphasis on the contextualizing work that educators *do* with adolescent youth. Rather than view teachers as technicians dutifully carrying out externally imposed definitions of context (e.g., what curriculum and instruction should look like, what counts as student learning, etc.), we see teachers as contextualizers and, perhaps more important, as recontextualizers—as context creators, shapers, and transformers. We believe this stance is especially significant today. The literacy field has developed complex understandings about the diverse cultural and linguistic resources and knowledge that children and youth bring to school, the varied ways that people can read and be literate, and the primacy of "the social" in learning—all of which signal the import of a perspective of literacy as social practices (Luke & Freebody, 1997). In spite of this movement toward complexity, educational policy in secondary school has been moving toward contextualizing curriculum and instruction in narrow and reductive ways, taking its cue from "scientifically based research" at the elementary level. In this climate, it is all the more important for secondary educators to work against these constraints by contextualizing or recontextualizing what should count as meaningful literacy practices in their classrooms.

Looking Back to Frame Where We Are

In the previous edition of this book, the chapter about "contexts" discussed reading in secondary schools in terms of three contexts: linguistic, situational, and cultural (Smith, Carey, & Harste, 1982). The *linguistic context* was defined as the written text and everything that appears visually on the page. The *situational context* was defined as the setting in which a reading event occurs, including the individuals involved, the location, expectations, and other factors impinging on the immediate event. The *cultural context* was defined as the social and political matrix in which the reading event occurs. The metaphor of an ever expanding circle was offered to encourage thinking about what teachers might do to support secondary students in their reading: what linguistic features of text they might highlight, what situational factors they needed to consider, and what cultural or political factors were important in order to engage students more fully with comprehending text.

When that chapter was published in 1982, the literacy field was working within a framework of certain conceptual understandings. The impact of cognitive psychology had taken hold, bringing an emphasis on comprehension such that meaning-making was seen as central to the reading process and, more generally, to the language learning process. Strong readers and language learners were found to monitor consistently for meaning. Ken Goodman had shown that young proficient readers use several cueing systems simultaneously and that similar conditions operate in early language learning. Schema theory helped us see reading as a process through which readers actively construct and revise schema—networks of associations or organizational units—to make sense of new information. This coincided with a rediscovery of Rosenblatt's work and interest in Reader Response Theory and transactional perspectives. Although reading comprehension and, more generally, working with texts had become better understood as a transaction between a text and a reader, researchers in 1982 were just beginning to investigate seriously the role of social context(s) in the meaning-making process.

Much has happened in the past twenty-five years. Literacy theorists and practitioners have advanced our understandings of how readers engage with texts and how teachers engage students to work with texts. The contemporary landscape of reading has been reconfigured with conceptual markers: literacy events (Heath, 1983), funds of knowledge (Moll, 1994), Discourse and discourse (Gee, 1996), reading as a social process involving situated practices (Barton, Hamilton, & Ivanič, 2000; Bloome, 1985; Luke & Freebody, 1997; Street, 1995), culturally relevant instruction (Gay, 2000; Ladson-Billings, 1994, 2001; Nieto, 2002), multiliteracies and designs (New London Group, 2000), and new literacies (Lankshear & Knobel, 2003; Leu & Kinzer, 2000). All of these markers have helped engender a reframing of the field from *secondary reading* to *adolescent literacy* or *adolescent literacies* (Alvermann, Hinchman, Moore, Phelps, & Waff, 1998). Here we consider this reframing, using the three contexts from the 1982 chapter—linguistic, situational, cultural—to frame the conceptual advances in the field and to consider implications for classroom practice. We conclude with a set of principles that secondary school educators can employ to guide their work with adolescent youth.

Cultural Context(s): Seeing Students as Cultural Beings and Workers

During the past few decades, the broader context of education has been indelibly shaped by sociocultural perspectives of literacy and learning. Employing a sociocultural approach in her ethnography, *Ways with Words*, Heath (1983) demonstrated how language and culture are inextricably linked and that what constitutes literacy differs across communities. She also identified the mismatches between literacy practices of a working-class African American community and a working-class white community with the literacy practices in the schools. Like Freire and Macedo (1987), who argued that one reads the *world* in order to understand the *word*, Heath helped lead a shift in viewing reading as, first and foremost, a social and cultural practice. Luke and Freebody (1997) describe this as a movement from psychological to sociological models of reading. As a result of this shift, literacy is "more usefully understood as existing in the relations between people, within groups and communities, rather than as a set of properties residing in individuals" (Barton & Hamilton, 2000, p. 8).

Building on the seminal work of Heath, literacy researchers using sociocultural perspectives have extended understandings of literacy, moving from an *autonomous model,* which views literacy as sets of neutral, universal and isolated skills, to an *ideological model,* which views literacy as highly contextualized, culturally informed social practices (Street, 2003). The ideological model also carries with it the understanding that students bring to school rich and sophisticated knowledge and cultural resources (Gay, 2000; Ladson-Billings, 1994, 2001; Nieto, 2002). An ideological model also foregrounds that literacy is political and suffused with issues of power, thus focusing attention on how larger systems of meaning operate in society (Finn, 1999) and how these meanings shape the formation of identities and practices in classrooms.

Returning to the vignette that opens this chapter, we can see how teachers' choices matter in contextualizing the cultural and social identities of students. Should the students' lowrider art be viewed as unequivocally "not school"? Is it merely a hobby, a leisure activity? Or, as Peter Cowan suggests (2004), is it a legitimate form of visual literacy and a medium to convey meaning that is deeply rooted in community and history, as meaningful intellectual work that could also launch and sustain deeper historical and cultural inquiry? Is the Hmong student's refugee narrative an example of ill-formed "broken" English? Or are her words inflected with cultural values as she draws on her experiences to grapple with intense ethical and political issues? Would the two boys sharing photos on cell phones be viewed as playing inappropriately with gadgets? Or could their photos be understood as a clever method to capture components of their cultural and home lives? Do the young women's nonverbal communication or silence reflect reticence and intellectual disengagement? Or, as Stephanie Carter (2001) suggests, could the paralinguistic interaction be a sophisticated way of forging group solidarity in the midst of an official, Eurocentric curriculum?

Different answers to these questions chart different pedagogical pathways and learning opportunities for students. A view of literacy that valorizes conventional definitions of literacy as working solely with print-based texts and that divorces culture from literacy positions students in the opening vignette as engaged in behaviors or tasks that are fundamentally unrelated to literacy. In contrast, a view of literacy as socially situated practices begins with a stance that values the potential cultural richness of lowrider art, an English language learner's written texts, photographs taken and stored on a new technology, and a culturally and historically situated critique of Eurocentric curricula. These practices can be viewed as fundamentally literate—integrally bound with the identities, experiences, and cultures of youth—and, as a result, as sites for potentially meaningful literacy work in classrooms.

Situational Context(s): Seeing Students as Complex Literate Beings

A working definition of literacy in this chapter includes the understanding that children and youth engage in varied and complex literacy practices in a range of settings. Consequently, how educators contextualize the place(s) where literacy learning occurs is of central importance. Using a framework of *multiliteracies,* The New London Group (2000) outlines a new environment of literacy pedagogy, one that acknowledges the dynamic qualities of people's working lives (emphasis on productive diversity), civic lives (emphasis on civic pluralism), and personal lives (emphasis on "multilayered lifeworlds"). Reflecting the changing ways we work, live, and communicate (Cope & Kalantzis, 2000), the idea of multiliteracies, or multiple literacies, expands the definition of literacy to include "multiple modes and technologies" (Anstey, 2002). Additionally, this multiliteracies approach has generated a range of insights into the complex literate lives that students lead, as researchers have documented the everyday literacy activities and practices of children and youth in their homes and communities (Barton, Hamilton, & Ivanič, 2000; Hull & Schultz, 2002; Mahiri, 2004). These examples include studies of the writing practices of two Mexican college students (Guerra & Farr, 2002); the home literacy practices of a young refugee girl from Cambodia (Skilton-Sylvester, 2002); the reading practices of a Hong Kong immigrant with Japanese, Chinese, and American comic books (Lam, 2004); and the ways that food service workers use literacy (Mirabelli, 2004). Included as well are studies grounded in new media and technologies, including those that document the learning affordances of first-person shooter games (Gee, 2003), adolescents' use of instant messaging (Jacobs, 2004; Lewis & Fabbos, 2005), and creation of digital stories (Hull, 2003; Hull & Nelson, 2005).

These studies of children and youth's literacy practices enlarge our understanding of what counts as situational context, helping us, for example, appreciate the complex literacy practices and learning (i.e., students reading, interpreting, and producing a range of texts) that take place in settings outside of school. These practices have implications for how educators might negotiate the roles that diverse home and community literacy practices of students could play in classrooms. The opening vignette helps us consider how teachers negotiate the boundaries between out-of-school and in-school literacies. Will drawings of lowrider culture, or other practices with distinctive cultural iconography, be dismissed because they do not fall within the bounds of traditional scholastic writing? Or will these drawings be viewed as rich resources of intellectually curious students and as integral to a substantive interdisciplinary curriculum? Will new technologies, such as cell phones, be uniformly barred entry into classrooms? Or will the curricular possibilities of cell phones—including their ability to document images easily (and spontaneously)—be tapped into? Will the young women's eye and shoulder movements (and other nonverbal communication practices) be ignored, viewed as irrelevant to reading and writing print-based texts? Or might their nonverbal practices actually be viewed as literary responses, representative of a sophisticated blending of personal, textual, and historical response?

Linguistic Context(s): Seeing Students as Readers and Writers of Diverse Texts

In the 1982 chapter, the linguistic context was defined as the written text and everything that appears visually on the page. Our understanding of what constitutes a text has certainly evolved since this time. The first major shift seemingly occurred when the traditional high school reading curriculum became expanded. With roots in 1960s activism, educators over the past several decades began to question the ethnocentrism of English education and to expose students to more literature by women and minority authors. The idea of inclusiveness certainly met resistance. But perhaps the more radical proposition was the fundamental challenge to the ontological status of the canon, which began to lose a little bit of its aura. It was no longer a given that the texts students were reading represented the pinnacle of human literary achievement or that a particular tradition could be universalized adequately to represent the experiences of all peoples. For many, the idea of a set and transcendent canon became replaced by an interest in the *process* of canon formation, a process some argued was invariably political and value-laden (Banks, 1993).

Once the canon became demystified, it was not too much of a leap for reading researchers and educators to question the privileged role that books themselves play in the literacy curriculum. Undoubtedly influenced by the more general *linguistic turn* in philosophy, with its insight that language plays a central role in constructing (and imprisoning) people in *reality*, educators began to think about how texts other than traditional books could serve important pedagogical purposes. "Great authors" did not have a monopoly on worthy texts. In fact, adolescents in particular seemed to be especially innovative in marshaling a host of semiotic resources to create meaning, and they helped us understand a variety of ways students could author and respond to experience. This multiliteracies perspective reflected a move from psychological to sociological models of reading, which shifted the "classroom focus to the particular texts, discourses, and practices to which students have access and to the different kinds of social activities and cultural action that instruction can shape, encourage and yield" (Luke & Freebody, 1997, p. 208). Thus, in theory if not broadly in classroom practice, the traditional English book became decentered in at least two ways. First, the notion of text was expanded to include items such as images, drawings, photos, and graffiti (Conquergood, 1997), the latest multimodal technologies, and discourse writ large (Foucault, 1980; Gee, 1996). Second, the text itself became perhaps less important than the social practices which surrounded it, including the ways in which teachers created opportunities for students to draw on their own cultural resources to transact with both the *word* and the *world* (Freire & Macedo, 1987).

Returning to our vignette, we can now begin to see the various ways teachers might contextualize or recontextualize what counts as a text and the ways students can engage with texts. A traditionalist may not even consider the boys' drawings of lowrider art as anything more than doodling. However, a sociocultural and multicultural perspective helps us understand how the students' lowrider art is a type of textual production that includes iconography dating back to pre-Columbian Mesoamerica. Furthermore, the students might not be merely drawing, but also participating in a sophisticated form of visual literacy (i.e., reading and writing texts) that is intimately tied to youth culture and identity (Cowan, 2004). If framed in this manner, a teacher might make different pedagogical moves than dismissing the boys' work as nonschool or even oppositional behavior.

Examining the student's refugee narrative, a teacher could focus primarily on the degree to which the text did not conform to an institutional model, such as the five-paragraph essay, and be concerned solely with the work the child would need to do in order to master requisite English language conventions. However, the child's writing might also be understood as having a certain unique integrity as hybridized genre that combines a specific form of cultural storytelling and memory work with academic writing. When we look at the two boys sharing photos on cell phones, it is easy to see that a teacher could dismiss and disallow this apparent nonschool technology. Alternatively, the boys could be understood as using a new technology in the potential service of significant academic work, such as comparing and contrasting visual texts of their neighborhoods. Finally, the notion that the young women's silence is a text that might be understood as it relates to power, positioning, and cultural solidarity perhaps pushes our understanding of what constitutes a text the furthest.

Implications for Classrooms: A Set of Guidelines

In the preceding sections we used the opening vignette to highlight what could be considered ends on a contextualizing continuum as we attempted to accentuate the fundamentally different ways educators can contextualize literacy practices in particular settings—from acultural perspectives that see out-of-school literacies as disconnected and irrelevant to more culturally and linguistically sensitive perspectives. We now offer the following set of guidelines to characterize the kind of contextualizing work that secondary school educators can enact with students in their classrooms.

◆ Value students for who they are, including their families, their languages, and their literacies; acknowledge the cultural and linguistic resources and knowledge that students bring into the classroom.

◆ Open up space in the classroom for teachers and students to choose, study, and talk about topics of personal and social importance.

◆ Broaden students' understanding of what it means to be literate and of alternate ways of knowing and being in the world.

◆ Help students find, cultivate, and interrogate their voices through the use of conversation, collaboration, and multiple literacies (reading, writing, art, drama, movement, music, etc.).

◆ Support students in interrogating multiple viewpoints, taking responsibility to inquire, being reflective, and becoming more consciously aware of the systems of meaning that operate in texts (of all kinds) to position them and to endow them with identities they may or may not wish to take on.

◆ Invite studies of the relationship between literacy and power, including how language and other literacies are used to construct identities, represent events, and position groups of people.

◆ Engage students in a variety of literacies for a variety of purposes, all of which are important to the lives that students are now living and the lives they wish to live in the future.

Concluding Thoughts

In an educational era of standardization, testing ubiquity, and top-down reforms, the work of teaching is, to a large degree, being contextualized by those who are not in classrooms. Teachers we work with in Indiana speak to this issue, describing the loss of their curricular and instructional agency with comments such as, "There is no time to do anything but what we're told. It's become all about evaluation and measurement." In fact, teachers working in poor or historically disenfranchised communities, especially urban areas, are the most likely to feel constrained by bureaucratic mandates, inadequate resources, overcrowded classrooms, and a persistent lack of time for personal and collaborative reflection.

We believe that external contextualizing forces present perhaps the gravest danger for teachers, especially in light of what we have come to know about the sophisticated literacy practices of adolescents. Under present policy circumstances, it is especially difficult to remain attentive to students' cultural recourses, be mindful of situational dynamics, or think creatively about how students might transact with a variety of complex texts.

In this chapter, we have chosen to emphasize new or multiple literacies in out-of-school settings, rather than focus on examples from secondary school classrooms, to maintain a broad lens on the necessity of taking agency when it comes to contextualizing and recontextualizing what counts as literacy learning. As educators, we are involved in the process of constantly reading and rereading our classrooms; how we read has important implications for the spaces we create—and do not create—for our students to take full advantage of schooling.

Note

1. Lowrider art includes drawings that feature distinctive Mexican American and Latino and Latina iconography, such as Aztec pyramids, figures from Aztec and Mayan mythology, and lowrider cars. Lowriders are customized cars that are often low to the ground, with skinny tires and custom wheels; they often feature elaborate paint schemes of Mexican American icons (Cowan, 2004).

References

Alvermann, D. E., Hinchman, K. A., Moore, D. W., Phelps, S. F., & Waff, D. R. (Eds.). (1998). *Reconceptualizing the literacies in adolescents' lives*. Mahwah, NJ: Erlbaum.

Anstey, M. (2002). "It's not all black and white": Postmodern picture books and new literacies. *Journal of Adolescent & Adult Literacy, 45*, 444–57.

Banks, J. A. (1993). The canon debate, knowledge construction, and multicultural education. *Educational Researcher, 22*(5), 4–14.

Barton, D., & Hamilton, M. (2000). Literacy practices. In D. Barton, M. Hamilton, & R. Ivanič (Eds.), *Situated literacies: Reading and writing in context* (pp. 7–15). London: Routledge.

Barton, D., Hamilton, M., & Ivanič, R. (Eds.). (2000). *Situated literacies: Reading and writing in context.* London: Routledge.

Bloome, D. (1985). Reading as a social process. *Language Arts, 62,* 134–42.

Carter, S. (2001). *The possibilities of silence: African-American female cultural identity and secondary English classrooms.* Unpublished doctoral dissertation, Vanderbilt University, Nashville, Tennessee.

Conquergood, D. (1997). Street literacy. In J. Flood, S. B. Heath, & D. Lapp (Eds.), *Handbook of research on teaching literacy through the communicative and visual arts.* (pp. 354–75). New York: Simon & Schuster Macmillan.

Cope, B., & Kalantzis, M. (Eds.). (2000). *Multiliteracies: Literacy learning and the design of social futures.* London: Routledge.

Cowan, P. (2004). Devils or angels: Literacy and discourse in lowrider culture. In J. Mahiri (Ed.), *What they don't learn in school: Literacy in the lives of urban youth* (pp. 47–74). New York: Peter Lang.

Finn, P. J. (1999). *Literacy with an attitude: Educating working-class children in their own self-interest.* Albany: State University of New York Press.

Foucault, M. (1980). *Power/knowledge: Selected interviews and other writings, 1972–1977* (C. Gordon, Ed.). New York: Pantheon Books.

Freire, P., & Macedo, D. (1987). *Literacy: Reading the word and the world.* South Hadley, MA: Bergin & Garvey.

Gay, G. (2000). *Culturally responsive teaching: Theory, research, and practice.* New York: Teachers College Press.

Gee, J. P. (1996). *Social linguistics and literacies: Ideology in discourses* (2nd ed.). London: Taylor & Francis.

Gee, J. P. (2003). *What video games have to teach us about learning and literacy.* New York: Palgrave Macmillan.

Guerra, J. C., & Farr, M. (2002). Writing on the margins: The spiritual and autobiographical discourse of two Mexicanas in Chicago. In

G. Hull & K. Schultz (Eds.), *School's out! Bridging out-of-school literacies with classroom practice* (pp. 96–123). New York: Teachers College Press.

Heath, S. B. (1983). *Ways with words: Language, life, and work in communities and classrooms.* Cambridge, UK: Cambridge University Press.

Hull, G., & Schultz, K. (Eds.). (2002). *School's out! Bridging out-of-school literacies with classroom practice.* New York: Teachers College Press.

Hull, G. A. (2003). Youth culture and digital media: New literacies for new times. *Research in the Teaching of English, 38,* 229–33.

Hull, G. A., & Nelson, M. E. (2005). Locating the semiotic power of multimodality. *Written Communication, 22,* 224–61.

Jacobs, G. E. (2004). Complicating contexts: Issues of methodology in researching the language and literacies of instant messaging. *Reading Research Quarterly, 39,* 394–406.

Ladson-Billings, G. (1994). *The dreamkeepers: Successful teachers of African American children.* San Francisco: Jossey-Bass.

Ladson-Billings, G. (2001). *Crossing over to Canaan: The journey of new teachers in diverse classrooms.* San Francisco: Jossey-Bass.

Lam, W. S. E. (2004). Border discourses and identities in transnational youth culture. In J. Mahiri (Ed.), *What they don't learn in school: Literacy in the lives of urban youth* (pp. 79–98). New York: Peter Lang.

Lankshear, C., & Knobel, M. (2003). *New literacies: Changing knowledge and classroom learning.* Buckingham, UK: Open University Press.

Leu, D. J., Jr., & Kinzer, C. K. (2000). The convergence of literacy instruction with networked technologies for information and communication. *Reading Research Quarterly, 35,* 108–27.

Lewis, C., & Fabos, B. (2005). Instant messaging, literacies, and social identities. *Reading Research Quarterly, 40,* 470–501.

Luke, A., & Freebody, P. (1997). The social practices of reading. In S. Muspratt, A. Luke, & P. Freebody (Eds.), *Constructing critical literacies: Teaching and learning textual practice* (pp. 185–226). Cresskill, NJ: Hampton Press.

Mahiri, J. (Ed.). (2004). *What they don't learn in school: Literacy in the lives of urban youth.* New York: Peter Lang.

Mirabelli, T. (2004). Learning to serve: The language and literacy of food service workers. In J. Mahiri (Ed.), *What they don't learn in school: Literacy in the lives of urban youth* (pp. 143–62). New York: Peter Lang.

Moll, L. C. (1994). Literacy research in community and classrooms: A sociocultural approach. In R. B. Ruddell, M. R. Ruddell, & H. Singer (Eds.), *Theoretical models and processes of reading* (4th ed., pp. 179–207). Newark: DE: International Reading Association.

New London Group. (2000). A pedagogy of multiliteracies designing social futures. In B. Cope & M. Kalantzis (Eds.), *Multiliteracies: Literacy learning and the design of social futures* (pp. 9–37). London: Routledge.

Nieto, S. (2002). *Language, culture, and teaching: Critical perspectives for a new century.* Mahwah, NJ: Erlbaum.

Skilton-Sylvester, E. (2002). Literate at home but not at school: A Cambodian girl's journey from playwright to struggling writer. In G. Hull & K. Schultz (Eds.), *School's out! Bridging out-of-school literacies with classroom practice* (pp. 61–90). New York: Teachers College Press.

Smith, S. L., Carey, R. F., & Harste, J. C. (1982). The contexts of reading. In A. Berger & H. A. Robinson (Eds.), *Secondary school reading: What research reveals for classroom practice* (pp. 21–37). Urbana, IL: National Council of Teachers of English, National Conference on Research in English, and ERIC Clearinghouse on Reading and Communication Skills.

Street, B. (2003). What's "new" in new literacy studies? Critical approaches to literacy in theory and practice. *Current Issues in Comparative Education, 5,* 77–91.

Street, B. V. (1993). Culture is a verb: Anthropological aspects of language and cultural processes. In D. Graddol, L. Thompson, & M. Byram (Eds.), *Language and culture: Papers from the annual meeting of the British Association of Applied Linguistics held at Trevelyan College, University of Durham, September 1991* (pp. 23–43). Clevedon, UK: British Association for Applied Linguistics in association with Multilingual Matters.

Street, B. V. (1995). *Social literacies: Critical approaches to literacy in development, ethnography and education.* London: Longman.

Adopting Reader and Writer Stances in Understanding and Producing Texts

RICHARD BEACH AND DAVID G. O'BRIEN
University of Minnesota

In this chapter, we explore the reciprocal relationship between reading and writing instruction and how each can improve the other. In doing so, we reach beyond the familiar curriculum framework that artificially separates reading, writing, speaking, listening, and viewing to explore how reading and writing may be integrated by engaging students in practices involved in better understanding and producing texts.

Defining Reading and Writing in Terms of Strategies

One approach to thinking about integrating reading and writing instruction has been to define them as shared processes —the notion that both can be tapped and enhanced with similar strategies. These strategies include predicting, connecting to background knowledge, comprehension monitoring, identifying cues to text structure, summarizing key points, questioning, understanding vocabulary, and critical reading.

Many national research and policy reports, professional materials for teachers, and published literacy programs use the terms *skills* and *strategies* interchangeably. This is not our view; a distinction between skills and strategies has important implications for what we should teach and what students should know and know how to do to become proficient readers and writers. *Skills* are things readers and writers do automatically, without thinking about them, whereas *strategies* are thoughtful plans (Duffy, 2003). When most secondary students read critically with comprehension, they initiate a whole range of skills tied to the efficient, automatic, and confident use of what they know about language, how language works, and how text features impact comprehension (Paris, Wasik, & Turner, 1991). Readers who don't possess these kinds of skills may lack strategies or thoughtful plans for reading; for example, struggling readers may not have an established metacognitive way to help themselves read for understanding and solve problems when they have difficulty understanding a text. Strategy instruction helps, but sometimes readers need to develop both skills and strategies through practice— they need enough time to hone skills and strategies.

Strategy instruction has become a popular approach in reading instruction because it serves to address the high level of interest in teaching reading to improve test scores and for schools to avoid being labeled as failing (Ivey & Fisher, 2005). The term *strategies* has become a broad, generic collection of instructional activities, instructional frameworks, and students' approaches to understanding texts. More important, the term *strategies* has become synonymous with a list of isolated, decontextualized quick fixes—summarizing, predicting, applying prior knowledge, mapping connections, etc., that, if employed in the classroom, are assumed to raise scores on reading tests. This leads to teaching strategies as a set of isolated activities without considering how reading engages students in purposeful activities within larger social contexts (Duffy, 2003). For example, too often, students are constructing concept maps or other graphic organizers for comprehending texts in a vacuum, without any sense of how what they learn from their reading helps them construct knowledge that enhances an understanding of the world.

The value of teaching strategies emanates from cognitively grounded research on reading comprehension processes and instruction (Duke & Pearson, 2002) and over 20 years of work on explicit instruction and teacher explanation (Duffy, 2003; Duke & Pearson, 2002; Williams, 2002). Research shows that being strategic is a characteristic that separates expert from nonexpert readers (Paris, Wasik, & Turner, 1991; Pressley, 2002). Furthermore, reports that synthesize reading research indicate that explicit instruction in comprehension strategies by teachers who are well prepared can increase students' use of the strategies, which positively impacts their reading (e.g., RAND Reading Study Group [RRSG], 2002). As well, the National Reading Panel (National Institute of Child Health and Human Development, 2000), whose report has influenced policy more than other reports, concluded that explicit instruction in comprehension strategies is beneficial because students often learn to use the strategies on their own, which may also motivate them to read. The Panel recommended that teachers learn how to teach multiple strategies appropriate for the "natural" settings in which students read. However, the Panel also concluded that there is a lack of substantial evidence showing a definite positive effect of teaching strategies in various content areas.

In addition, the Reading Next report (Biancarosa & Snow, 2004), a follow-up to the Reading First initiatives targeting adolescents rather than primary-grade learners, recommended that both reading and writing instruction be grounded in authentic contexts in which students use reading and writing. Furthermore, both *The International Reading Association Position Statement on Adolescent Literacy* (Moore, Bean, Birdyshaw, & Rycik, 1999) and the *NCTE Position Statement on Reading* (1999) recommended that teachers provide students with texts and activities that engage them in purposeful activities, as opposed to teaching decontextualized strategies.

Similarly, during the 1980s and 1990s, the strong emphasis in writing instruction on teaching composition resulted in a focus on teaching what was sometimes referred to as the skills or strategies of prewriting, drafting, revising, and editing. This approach too often led to treating components of writing as isolated entities without consideration of larger social contexts driving composition. Thus, many students perceived that there was little purpose for their writing. As with traditional reading instruction, students employed strategies but rarely were engaged in the writing process, which is often fostered by a sense of social purposes.

In comparison, recent projects have been developed that address writing in authentic ways and with social dimensions. For example, the National Writing Project report, *Because Writing*

Matters: Improving Student Writing in Our Schools (National Writing Project & Nagin, 2006), posits that writing instruction needs to engage students in critical thinking, problem solving, analysis, and imagination. Similarly, the NCTE Writing Initiative (2003) focuses on the need to provide schoolwide and community support for writing as a tool for engaging in critical thinking and learning in all subject-matter areas. To be sure, recent reading and writing research and instruction have been evolving toward more meaningful ways for students to design, produce, and interpret texts.

From Strategy Instruction to Engagement in Purposeful Classroom Activities

These various reports highlight the need to shift from focusing on teaching strategies to helping students become strategic readers and writers in authentic contexts. Teachers have become increasingly effective in teaching strategies, even when they perceive that students are not engaged by this strategy instruction (Duffy, 2003). However necessary these strategies might seem, we think there is a different way to look at reading and writing.

We prefer the concept of *practices*—general cultural ways of using literacy within purposeful activities (Barton, 1994; Beach, 2000). This concept highlights fostering persistent engagement in the use of practices in an activity over time (Ivey & Fisher, 2005; Simpson, Stahl, & Francis, 2004). Our view of *activity* draws on sociocultural Activity Theory to focus on how activities are designed to achieve some outcome or objective (Engeström, 1987; Lewis, Enciso, & Moje, 2006; Roth & Lee, 2007).

For example, engaging in a fund-raising campaign is an activity designed to raise funds for a school, organization, or cause. Given the objective of a fund-raising campaign, to raise money, participants employ the literacy practices associated with developing promotional ads, targeted mailings, phone calls to donors, etc. If participants perceive this outcome or objective as worth pursuing because it serves some larger social good or fosters a sense of community, they may be engaged in literacy. Thus, in planning instruction, teachers need to devise activities that have some purposeful, engaging outcome or objective in which students collaboratively employ literacy practices in ways that may give them a sense of agency.

In acquiring literacy *practices*, students may also learn to be *strategic* in their use of reading and writing practices—knowing how to use appropriate language, frame a convincing argument, draw on relevant knowledge and experience, define related beliefs and attitudes, and formulate a sense of purpose (Fitzgerald & Shanahan, 2000; Shanahan, 2006). Readers and writers in an activity draw on the same knowledge of language use, content, experience, beliefs, and attitudes in reading and writing texts; writers use reading to acquire content knowledge and expand their knowledge through writing (Shanahan, 2006). They also apply their metacognitive knowledge about language and text conventions from reading texts, knowledge that transfers to reflecting on and revising their texts (Beach & Friedrich, 2006).

Readers and writers are also continually aware of how their use of these practices is shaped by participation in social contexts. Thinking about context requires that students move between identifying problems or issues through reading and writing to framing issues in ways that can be understood by their audiences. Bereiter and Scardamalia (1987) describe this process as moving between a context-problem space and a rhetorical-problem space, which requires students to consider audiences' beliefs, knowledge, and needs. In writing for peers, for example, students may include references to their peers' knowledge of popular youth culture to build on their audiences' prior knowledge.

Students also frame questions or issues that contextualize their understanding and construction of texts based on purposes for reading and writing within social contexts or activities (Beach & Myers, 2001). Students are therefore not simply reading textual material, but also reading the social context to construct or write that context as a question or issue. For example, in participating in an activity of tutoring elementary students using children's literature, middle school students may frame their reading of children's literature with the following question: How can I use these books to engage my students in reading? This question then frames the high school students' responses to children's literature within the larger activity of promoting their tutees' engagement with reading, a purpose that itself engages the middle school students. The more students are engaged with achieving the purpose or objective of their activity, the more motivated they are to read or write texts associated with achieving that purpose or objective (Gee, 1996; Guthrie, 2004; Wilhelm, Baker, & Dube, 2001).

It is therefore the classroom activity itself associated with reading and writing that becomes critical in engaging students. One reason that struggling readers fail to engage in literacy practices in school is because they perceive little purpose or value in reading for the sake of acquiring skills or strategies designed to help them pass a test, as opposed to reading something to engage in a purposeful activity (Alvermann, 2002b; Jetton & Dole, 2004; Strickland & Alvermann, 2004; Wigfield, 2004). Struggling readers also perceive the disparity between their low level of engagement in instructional reading materials and their high level of engagement in IM'ing, online chat rooms, or on MySpace/Facebook in which their reading is part of some larger social activity (Alvermann, 2002a; Lankshear & Knobel, 2003; Lewis & Fabos, 2005; Kamil, Intrator, & Kim, 2000).

In addition, struggling readers often have difficulty inferring the author's "main point" or the gist of texts found in multiple-choice tests, inferences based solely on assumptions about the author's purpose intuited from the text itself without any sense of the larger social context shaping the author's purpose. In contrast, when struggling readers create their own texts within an activity, they are learning how their texts serve to convey their intended meanings, given an activity's larger social purpose.

All of this suggests that the role of the teacher is therefore to create activities in which students understand and produce texts to achieve some larger social purpose. This can include simulations or drama activities, for example, mock elections in which candidates are running for student council based on their positions on issues facing students in their school. Other students can adopt the roles of campaign managers, teachers, administrators, business owners, student voters, etc. They may send written or online memos to each other formulating their positions, seeking voters' support, or networking; audiences may reply to the memos by agreeing with or challenging their contentions. The activity ends with the student voters casting their votes for the candidates.

In this mock-election scenario, students' reading and writing of memos are shaped by their engagement with the larger purpose of winning the election by using effective campaign tactics. As they read the memos, they infer writers' underlying political agendas and personas so that they can craft an appropriate reply or determine whether they were persuaded by the memos to vote for a candidate. As they write, they know that they need to identify issues in ways that appeal to their peers and gain their allegiance or support.

Through participation in a mock election, students gain confidence in the use of these practices. They learn to contextualize the meaning of language in texts with the larger emerging consensus regarding candidates' positions on issues—the ability to read not only texts, but also the beliefs and opinions of others.

Adopting Reader and Writer Stances in Understanding and Producing Texts

In employing the kinds of practices described in the previous section of this chapter, students shift between reader and writer stances as they work to understand and produce texts. In adopting a reader stance for understanding a text, students infer not only ideas conveyed by the text's writer, but also the writer's beliefs, persona, and agendas within a larger social context. For example, in a classroom mock election, a student voter receives a memo from the candidate and interprets the meaning of the memo not only as it relates to the candidate's stance on certain issues, but also how he or she will respond as a writer who is being positioned by the candidate to respond in a certain way. In writing a reply to such a memo, for example, a student voter may adopt a skeptical stance. Indeed, moving between these reader and writer stances involves the ability to perceive oneself as more than a reader of texts, as someone who can also assume an active role in responding to texts.

This active stance as a writer is fostered by many students' participation in the online world of blogs, wikis, and MySpace.

Although students in the past used the Web primarily as a passive information source from a reader stance alone, they can now use it to share their writing actively on networking sites with a worldwide audience through participation on the "read/write Web" (Richardson, 2006, p. 1). At the same time, given the differences between the conventions of digital and printed text, students need to draw on their experience reading online digital texts to know how to write digital texts. Learning to select appropriate buttons or icons, navigate hypertextual links, use images to understand words, or discern the norms of netiquette in a particular site from a reader stance transfers to knowing how to create digital texts from a writer stance.

Reading and writing digital texts requires a different set of practices than the left-to-right, linear processing of print. In the textual migration from the page to the screen (Kress, 2003), students learn to scan the screen for visual cues, icons, location on the page, and functions to determine what item to click on, based on what is considered most relevant to the information they are seeking. This requires that they have some sense of the importance of certain cues over others, based on what is most relevant to achieving their purposes for reading (Kress, 2003). Given the possibility of students wandering aimlessly from site to site, it is important that they clarify their purposes from a reading stance while searching the Web. A study of students' navigation of hypertext cites the example of two students reading the same official Lance Armstrong site to write about the topic of the influence of lifestyle on health (McNabb [with Thurber, Dibuz, McDermott, & Lee], 2005). In this study, the student who kept in mind the purpose for the search was successful in navigating several online sources. The other student, who focused more on personal rather than academic purposes, gained little information from online sources. This suggests that, in formulating assignments, teachers need to help students clarify their purposes for searches within the context of their activity, while at the same time allowing students to formulate their own purposes. If students are clicking on links in a random order without a clear sense of purpose, teachers can model selection of appropriate links and categories. Given optional links to follow, students also need to be able to predict which links will provide relevant information. To help students reflect on reasons for making these predictions, Coiro (2005) recommends using a screen-capture program to capture the site's pages associated with a search and then printing out the results to share with students, along with questions focusing their attention on the site's features and links to make inferences about its topics, purposes, creators, and audiences. To help students learn to preview a page, she has students focus on the page title, menu choices, potential pathways for links, interactive features, information about the creator and date of the site, and site maps—all of which lead to decisions regarding further exploration.

The print-based reading instruction students receive in schools may also work against their ability to read digital texts. Reading digital texts involves reading for relevance of information by clicking through hypertexts, as opposed to the linear, left-to-right conventions involved in the processing of print texts (Kress, 2003). Students who are taught that they should infer a central gist or "main point" around which a text coheres or to write texts that are organized around their "thesis statement" may experience difficulties when they read or write digital hypertexts based on multiple, divergent links that do not cohere around a central organizing point.

In a study of her college students' responses to a wiki created by herself and a colleague about Georgia O'Keefe, Dobson (2005) compared her students' experiences reading the wiki to their experiences constructing their own wikis. Some of her students noted that they had difficulty reading the wiki texts because they thought they were missing certain meanings by following some links as opposed to others. In contrast to their difficulty in reading the wiki, students expressed more positive reactions to writing wikis, because they gained pleasure in creating their own multiple paths and playing off each other's writing. Dobson's research suggests that students need assistance in learning to read digital texts based on the different set of reading conventions that are associated with reading digital texts. Learning these ways of reading digital texts, given certain purposes for reading, may then transfer to learning to write digital texts within purposeful activities.

Middle School Students' Adoption of Reader and Writer Stances

We illustrate students' uses of these reader and writer stances related to having a sense of purpose with data from an ongoing project (O'Brien, Beach, & Scharber, 2007) in which we are studying "struggling" middle school readers. The two-year class, which started in seventh grade and continued into students' eighth-grade year, was designed to help students pass high-stakes tests that they ultimately need to graduate. As with many struggling readers, these students are not highly engaged with in-school literacy learning because they often perceive little value in reading or writing in school. In some cases, they experience high levels of engagement with out-of-school literacy.

The curriculum for this class consists of participation in a formal reading program; reading young adult novels (sustained silent reading and teacher read-alouds); writing activities such as writing stories, comic books, wikis, and poetry; journal responses to their reading; and sharing of story writing, poetry, and PowerPoint presentations about topics such as favorite games or young adult novels. For example, students created a fictional town similar to that of Lake Wobegon, populated it with characters, and created stories about the characters, an activity similar to that developed by Roessing (2004). Students also published their writing on the school district's Moodle site, creating an alternative sense of a larger public audience. These practices, which were relatively engaging for most of the students, were integral to participating in inquiry projects, media productions, and in collaboratively producing other written products. They also involved constant shifts in both reader and writer stances. In one of the activities, students created a comic book using ComicLife software that provided them with templates for creating blocks, characters, and dialogue bubbles. In participating in this activity, students read a sheet of directions on how to use the software and also read other comics. In addition, they read their peers' comic productions. In doing so, they were reading for a larger purpose within an activity: learning to design comics to impress their peers. In another activity, students used stories they created to develop a radio broadcast modeled after Garrison Keillor's

Prairie Home Companion. To do so, they also used software to create sound effects to accompany their stories.

Students were engaged in these activities, adopting both reader and writer stances when called for, because the activities allowed them not only to display competence through uses of digital tools, but also to share knowledge with peers within a collaborative community. This, in turn, enhanced their sense of the value of the practices employed in that classroom. Students' engagement in these activities suggests that rather than building a "remedial" classroom community around a focus on correcting deficit skills, building on students' positive engagement in activities serves to enhance their positive attitudes toward being in such a community and acquiring reading and writing practices (O'Brien, 2001; O'Brien, Springs, & Stith, 2001).

Helping Students Shift between Reader and Writer Stances during Activities

Through participation in activities such as those described earlier in this chapter, students learned to shift between reader and writer stances by understanding and producing texts. As *readers*, they considered how they are being positioned by a text to acquire certain ideas or to adopt certain beliefs. As *writers*, they considered how their readers would respond to the ways in which they were being positioned. We now turn to some suggestions for how to help students learn to use particular practices to shift between reader and writer stances during activities.

Applying Prior Knowledge

In reading and writing texts, students apply requisite prior knowledge to a text, knowledge acquired through their participation in an activity. In reading and writing their stories about their fictional town, the middle school students in our study were continually focusing on whether, given assumptions about their prior knowledge, audiences would understand the descriptions of students' town.

In adopting a writer's stance, students must therefore consider whether or not their reader knows about a certain topic, concept, or idea. If they assume that a reader may not be familiar with a topic, concept, or idea, they may provide *new* information within the text or through hypertext as a link. Students therefore need to adopt what they assume to be their reader's stance to reflect on whether their text provides the necessary information.

To help writers learn to reflect on their audience or reader's prior knowledge leading to decisions about what topics, concepts, or ideas need hypertext links, teachers can model questions such as the following by doing a think-aloud with a hypertext projected on a screen:

As a reader	As a writer
◆ What do I now know about this topic, concept, or idea? ◆ What do I need to know more about to better understand this topic, concept, or idea? ◆ What am I most interested in knowing more about? ◆ How can I find the information I need to better understand this topic, concept, or idea?	◆ What may my readers already know about this topic, concept, or idea? ◆ If my readers may not have knowledge of this topic, concept, or idea, what do they need to know to better understand this topic, concept, or idea? ◆ In writing a digital text, what links can I use to provide my readers with relevant information?

Contextualizing Events and Actions

Another important practice involved in adopting reader and writer stances involves contextualizing events and actions portrayed in texts as social contexts or worlds (Beach & Myers, 2001). For example, in interpreting short stories or novels, readers explain characters' actions in light of the situation or context in which they act, as well as the purpose for their actions. McMahon (2002) formulated the following questions about context shaping a character's actions:

ACT: "What does the character do?"

SITUATION: "How does the character understand the situation in which he acts?"

AGENT: What is the character's moral character?" "How does the character understand himself as the agent in this act?"

PURPOSE: "What does the character intend—aim to gain or accomplish—by this act?"

ATTITUDE: "With what attitude or feeling does the character perform this act?" (p. 3)

By contextualizing events and character acts in a story, students perceive consistent patterns in characters' acts that suggest that these characters have adopted a certain agenda or plan. From these patterns, they can also infer that these characters are conforming to or resisting the norms operating in a social world.

Returning to our earlier example, in reading a text such as a memo in a mock election, students contextualize text in light of people's actions and identities in an activity. For example, as a voter, Jill receives a memo from the Chamber of Commerce asking her to support a candidate because he had promised to lower corporate taxes, something the Chamber argued would stop companies from "fleeing the state." Jill contextualizes this memo as reflecting a larger business agenda of attempting to reduce corporate taxes, something she believes adversely influences the state's revenues and ability to support health care and education.

By contextualizing these larger agendas, students can then identify writers' or characters' voices as reflecting certain attitudes or ideological positions. They do so by asking, "Who is speaking here?" This is a question in which the "who" represents different stances associated with alternative perspectives on a topic or issue.

To contextualize texts, students can pose the following questions:

As a reader	As a writer
◆ How are social contexts or worlds shaping the characters' or people's actions in text worlds?	◆ What is the social context or world in which I am writing a text?

◆ What are the characters' or authors' allegiances to beliefs and attitudes operating in these contexts or worlds? ◆ Who is speaking here? What persona or voices are being adopted in this text? ◆ How is the social context or world in which I am reading a text influencing my interpretation of that text?	◆ How does this social context or world shape my writing of this text?

Employing Genre Features

Another set of practices related to adopting reader and writer stances has to do with students employing genre features in reading and writing texts (Pappas & Pettegrew, 1998). In reading a story, students draw on their knowledge of narrative genres to make intertextual connections to other texts with similar storylines, character types, themes, topics, issues, or perspectives. They also apply knowledge of genre to attend to certain text features—titles, first and last sentences, opening scenes, etc. Furthermore, they draw on knowledge of storyline and narratives to make predictions related to story outcomes and resolutions.

Similarly, in switching to a writer stance, students draw on genre knowledge in constructing narratives. For instance, Weih (2005) found that students who listened to and analyzed Native American folktales used features of those folktales in writing their own narratives. Analysis of the students' stories indicated that they had acquired knowledge of features of the folktale genre, which they employed in their writings.

In our study, we found that students drew extensively on their genre knowledge of narratives that operated in video games to write stories. For example, one student, Dayvar, created a comic book, entitled "Die," derived from his experience playing video action games. His comic book portrayed two "good guy" heroes teaming up to defeat their enemy, an idea he derived from playing these games. He also acquired problem-solving strategies from his game playing, so his story characters were continually identifying challenges and systematically determining how to address these challenges. Therefore, his genre knowledge of narrative development, acquired in "reading" games, transferred to his construction of comic book stories.

Students also acquired knowledge of nonfiction and expository text genres from essays, reports, math problems, lab reports, and so forth, and made associations with texts in various subject areas. By applying knowledge of these genres to their reading, students attend to cues signaling the use of certain rhetorical strategies (Pappas & Pettegrew, 1998).

In reading expository texts, students also learn to attend to cues signaling organizational or argumentative structures, for example, "in contrast" or "on the other hand" to signal use of comparison or contrast. And, in adopting a reader stance, students learn to attend to how figurative language—metaphors, similes, or personification—is used to enhance understanding of concepts or experiences (Smith, 1994). Metaphors or similes help readers move from the familiar to the unfamiliar, by providing them with a familiar concept to relate to something that is unknown.

Genres can also be seen as mediating social activity as situated action or "typified rhetorical strategies" (Bawarshi, 2003; Coe, Lingard, & Teslenko, 2002). For example, in the genre of the political stump speech, speakers typically attempt to gain audience sympathy or identification by listing problems and portraying themselves as effectively addressing these problems. Readers therefore draw on the knowledge of how the stump speech functions socially to establish a relationship between a candidate and the audience. They also judge the effectiveness of using certain social genres in achieving the outcome of an activity—in this case, whether or not the stump speech encourages them to vote for a candidate.

Students also use knowledge of social genres to construct their sense of their audiences' beliefs, knowledge, and needs. They use this information to frame their positions or arguments in ways that might influence their audiences. Teachers can help students learn to construct audience-strategy relationships by having them write for actual audiences about actual issues. For example, one middle school teacher, knowing that her school board was considering closing her school, had her middle school students write a letter to the school board arguing against the shutdown (Sheehy, 2003). In collaboratively drafting their letter, the students grappled with how to convince the school board of the value of their community school, reading the political context of their audience as adults who might not take their letter seriously unless it was bolstered by evidence. As a result of collaboration and data collection, they were able to craft a single letter that one student read aloud at a school board meeting. The school board was so impressed by the students' statement that they decided not to close the school. From this experience, students acquired knowledge of how to employ social genres to influence change. Understanding how to construct this letter required students to assess how their writing might achieve their larger purpose. To help students infer genres, teachers might ask students to address the following questions:

As a reader	As a writer
◆ How is this text organized in a way to help me understand its meaning?	◆ How can I use cues and organize my text to help my readers understand my text?
◆ What cues are being used to signal how I should read this text?	◆ What kind of activity am I engaged in and what is the object or outcome driving this activity?
◆ What kinds of social genres are being employed by the writer?	◆ What social genres can I use that best achieve this object or outcome?
◆ What are the roles, agendas, purposes, and larger objects associated with the use of this social genre?	◆ What roles, language, images, or links do I need to employ in using this social genre to achieve my object or outcome?

Rereading and Revising Texts

Students also learn to shift between reader and writer stances through rereading and revising texts. By rereading texts, particularly texts such as difficult poems (Blau, 2003), students learn to adopt alternative perspectives with each reading, often moving to more complex interpretations. They recognize that their initial reading of a text often generates only partial understanding. With each rereading, students formulate new, alternative interpretations that can be used to alter previous interpretations (Petrosky, 2005). After creating a paper trail of written responses on various aspects of a text, students can return to their initial responses to share with peers what they learned from rereading the text from different perspectives.

Learning to revise their interpretations as readers transfers to students revising their writing. To revise their texts, students recognize that their drafts do not always convey their desired meanings to their audiences and thus need revision. They are more likely to recognize the inadequacy of their drafts by adopting the perspectives of different audiences who may need, among other things, more information or more clearly defined arguments.

Teachers can foster this transfer between rereading and revising texts by having students work in pairs to engage in think-aloud rereadings of a short poem. In doing so, students adopt different perspectives—reading the poem from the perspective of an adult—their parent, principal, coach, grandparent, etc.—or someone whose race, class, or gender differs from their own. For example, two male students may ask themselves, "If we read this poem from the perspective of a female, how might it be different?" After each rereading, students reflect on what new interpretations they acquired from that reading and how the adoption of a different perspective influenced their perspectives.

Then, students might write a poem, revising the poem several times by considering the perspectives of audiences who may respond to it in different ways. For example, they may ask themselves, "How would my coach respond to this poem?" After each revision, students reflect on how the revision altered the meaning of the poem and how adoption of different perspectives resulted in different meanings. In this activity, learning to adopt different rereadings from a reader stance transfers to revising texts from a writer stance.

Students are more likely to revise drafts if they are receiving teacher or peer feedback in conferences or online feedback sessions related to issues of understanding drafts. To provide effective peer feedback, students need to be trained in ways of responding to drafts, training that builds on adopting a reader stance (Beach & Friedrich, 2006; Ferris, 2003). Given students' propensity to avoid specific feedback or to provide only vague judgmental comments, students need to be trained to provide specific, "reader-based" feedback (Elbow, 1973). Rather than judging a draft or telling a writer what revisions to make, in giving "reader-based" feedback, peers describe their experiences of being engaged, involved, and intrigued by specific aspects of a draft. As well, they might cite instances where they were confused, lost, or puzzled, or created expectations for navigating a text, descriptions that the writer could use to judge the draft and to entertain optional revisions. To train students to provide "reader-based" feedback, teachers can employ "think-aloud" activities (Pressley & Afflerbach, 1995; Wilhelm, 2001) with short texts to assist students in describing their specific thoughts while reading a text.

Unfortunately, students may reject their peers' feedback because they do not always appreciate that readers may have difficulty with their writing. Furthermore, students can become stuck in the writer stance and perceive little value in peer feedback. Training in peer feedback should therefore encourage writers to listen and be open to peers' comments by recognizing the need to adopt a reader stance. As writers, students need to able to sort through the feedback they receive to determine what changes, if any, they need to make in the draft. In conferences, they can rehearse some of these changes to elicit further feedback from their peers as to whether these changes improve the draft. From engaging in peer feedback as readers, students learn to self-assess their writing.

To help students give feedback, self-assess, and revise, teachers can ask their students to respond to the following questions:

As a reader giving peer feedback	As a writer receiving the feedback
◆ What specific things in a text engage, involve, confuse, intrigue, puzzle, or create expectations for me? ◆ What do I perceive to be the writer's intentions or purposes shaping the writing? ◆ Does the draft fulfill those intentions or purposes?	◆ Based on the readers' descriptions, what are some problems in my draft? What revisions do I need to make to address those problems? ◆ What are my intentions or purposes for specific parts of my draft? What revisions do I need to make to fulfill those intentions or purposes?

Grappling with Text Accessibility and Interactivity

As readers of texts, students experience wide variability in the ease of reading a text based on the quality of editing or formatting. Aspects of formatting include word choice, syntax, forecasts, summaries, layout, font sizes, illustrations, subheads, or use of white space. Texts that are easy to read provide readers with cues to reduce reader uncertainty by creating expectations for where a text is going (Smith, 1994). Previewing the direction of a text by the use of subheadings or cues embedded in text structure such as "in contrast . . ." helps readers predict or anticipate subsequent information. Similarly, students may experience difficulty with websites or blogs with too much text information, too many different font sizes, unfamiliar location of buttons or links, disorienting use of background or font color, or misuse of banners or columns.

Accessibility is also influenced by the students' level of engagement or willingness to interact with a text and their perceptions of the writer creating the text. For example, in reading PowerPoint presentations, students perceive presentations with pictures and graphs, bullets presented line-by-line, use of popular media sounds and images, and color backgrounds as particularly engaging (Apperson, Laws, & Scepansky, 2006). At the same time, although PowerPoint presentations can be designed to be engaging, they can also position audiences as passive receptacles of knowledge, reifying a transmission mode of learning (Tufte,

2006). This suggests again the need to embed the understanding and producing of texts within a larger, purposeful activity in which students are using texts to engage their audiences in participating in an activity in an interactive manner.

To engage audiences in an interactive mode in presenting texts such as PowerPoint presentations, students can shift to a reader stance and consider how to involve their audiences through hyperlinked bullet points, questions, discussion, brainstorming, freewriting, peer sharing, or even game-like activities. In creating a PowerPoint presentation on homelessness, for example, a student might include a series of questions and activities in which a peer audience imagines creating a government agency to address such issues.

In designing websites that address their audience's need for relevant information, students can switch to a reader stance to infer potential audience purposes or needs for reading their site. They format their site by placing salient information, buttons, or links on the initial page so that audiences can readily spot the information they are seeking. And, in writing blogs, they can invite reader participation through soliciting their comments and by the use of links to other websites and blogs.

To assist students in fostering readability and interactivity, teachers might ask students to address the following questions:

As a reader	As a writer
◆ How much do I know or believe about the topic of this text, and what does the writer do to provide useful prior knowledge or discussion of relevant beliefs?	◆ What prior knowledge or beliefs do my audiences need to help them understand my topic or relevant beliefs about this topic?
◆ What features of this text make it easy or hard to read?	◆ What text or design features do I use to help guide readers through my text?
◆ Do I know where my writer is taking me in this text and what cues are being used to signal where I should go?	◆ How do I engage readers through interactive activities within my text?

◆ How engaged am I with this text in terms of participation in an activity? What interactive features are being used to engage me?	

Conclusions

Extensive research into typical reading and writing strategies shows that teachers are knowledgeable about particular strategies and instructional routines to get at reading and writing processes. However, much of this work has been framed by cognitive and linguistic models that tend to look at reading and writing processes as sets of technical skills and strategies to be learned in structured, routine approaches that do not engage students. In this chapter, we make the case that reading and writing strategies are better conceptualized as sets of practices that students engage in as part of larger social and cultural contexts and purposeful activities. By participating in such activities, students acquire various practices involved with switching between reader and writer stances. The extent to which students are willing to acquire these practices depends on whether students perceive themselves acquiring new ways of thinking about or experiencing the world. Thus, the teacher's role is to create purposeful activities that lead to reading and writing texts with socially situated purpose.

References

Academic Excellence Is Focus of NCTE Writing Initiative. (2003, September). *Council Chronicle*. Retrieved April 8, 2006, from http://www.ncte.org/pubs/chron/highlights/110669.htm?source=gs

Alvermann, D. E. (Ed.). (2002a). *Adolescents and literacies in a digital world*. New York: Peter Lang.

Alvermann, D. E. (2002b). Effective literacy instruction for adolescents. *Journal of Literacy Research, 34*, 189–208.

Apperson, J. M., Laws, E. L, & Scepansky, J. A. (2006). The impact of presentation graphics on students' experience in the classroom. *Computers and Education, 47,* 116–26.

Barton, D. (1994). *Literacy: An introduction to the ecology of written language.* Cambridge, MA: Blackwell.

Bawarshi, A. (2003). *Genre and the invention of the writer: Reconsidering the place of invention in composition.* Logan: Utah State University Press.

Beach, R. (2000). Reading and responding to literature at the level of activity. *Journal of Literacy Research, 32,* 237–51.

Beach, R., & Friedrich, T. (2006). Response to writing. In C. A. MacArthur, S. Graham, & J. Fitzgerald (Eds.), *Handbook of writing research* (pp. 222–34). New York: Guilford Press.

Beach, R., & Myers, J. (2001). *Inquiry-based English instruction: Engaging students in life and literature.* New York: Teachers College Press.

Bereiter, C., & Scardamalia, M. (1987). *The psychology of written composition.* Hillsdale, NJ: Erlbaum.

Biancarosa, G., & Snow, C. E. (2004). *Reading next—A vision for action and research in middle and high school literacy: A report to Carnegie Corporation of New York.* Washington, DC: Alliance for Excellent Education.

Blau, S. D. (2003). *The literature workshop: Teaching texts and their readers.* Portsmouth, NH: Boynton/Cook.

Coe, R. M., Lingard, L., & Teslenko, T. (Eds.). (2002). *The rhetoric and ideology of genre: Strategies for stability and change.* Cresskill, NJ: Hampton Press.

Coiro, J. (2005). Making sense of online text. *Educational Leadership, 63*(2), 30–35.

Dobson, T. (2005). *In medias res: Usability and the digital artifact.* Paper presented at the meeting of the National Reading Conference, Miami.

Duffy, G. G. (2003). *Explaining reading: A resource for teaching concepts, skills, and strategies.* New York: Guilford Press.

Duke, N. K., & Pearson, P. D. (2002). Effective practices for developing reading comprehension. In A. E. Farstrup & S. J. Samuels (Eds.),

What research has to say about reading instruction (3rd ed., pp. 205–42). Newark, DE: International Reading Association.

Elbow, P. (1973). *Writing without teachers.* New York: Oxford University Press.

Engeström, Y. (1987*). Learning by expanding: An activity-theoretical approach to developmental research.* Helsinki, Finland: Orienta-Konsultit Oy.

Ferris, D. R. (2003). *Response to student writing: Implications for second language students.* Mahwah, NJ: Erlbaum.

Fitzgerald, J., & Shanahan, T. (2000). Reading and writing relations and their development. *Educational Psychologist, 35,* 39–50.

Gee, J. P. (1996). *Social linguistics and literacies: Ideology in discourses* (2nd ed.). London: Taylor & Francis.

Guthrie, J. T. (2004). Teaching for literacy engagement. *Journal of Literacy Research, 36,* 1–29.

Ivey, G., & Fisher, D. (2005). Learning from what doesn't work. *Educational Leadership, 63*(2), 8–14.

Jetton, T. L., & Dole, J. A. (Eds.). (2004). *Adolescent literacy research and practice.* New York: Guilford Press.

Kamil, M. L., Intrator, S. M., & Kim, H. S. (2000). The effects of other technologies on literacy and literacy learning. In M. L. Kamil, P. B. Mosenthal, P. D. Pearson, & R. Barr (Eds.), *Handbook of reading research* (Vol. 3, pp. 771–88). Mahwah, NJ: Erlbaum.

Kress, G. (2003). *Literacy in the new media age.* London: Routledge.

Lankshear, C., & Knobel, M. (2003). *New literacies: Changing knowledge and classroom learning.* Buckingham, UK: Open University Press.

Lewis, C., Enciso, P. E., & Moje, E. B. (Eds.). (2006). *Reframing sociocultural research on literacy: Identity, agency, and power.* Mahwah, NJ: Erlbaum.

Lewis, C., & Fabos, B. (2005). Instant messaging, literacies, and social identity. *Reading Research Quarterly, 40,* 470–501.

McMahon, R. (2002). *Thinking about literature: New ideas for high school teachers.* Portsmouth, NH: Boynton/Cook.

McNabb, M. L. (with Thurber, B. B., Dibuz, B., McDermott, P. A., & Lee, C. A.). (2005). *Literacy learning in networked classrooms: Using the Internet with middle-level students.* Newark, DE: International Reading Association.

Moore, D. W., Bean, T. W., Birdyshaw, D., & Rycik, J. A. (1999). *Adolescent literacy: A position statement for the Commission on Adolescent Literacy of the International Reading Association.* Newark, DE: International Reading Association.

National Council of Teachers of English. (1999). *NCTE position statement on reading.* Retrieved April 5, 2006, from http://www.ncte.org/about/over/positions/category/read/107666.htm?source=gs

National Institute of Child Health and Human Development (NICHD). (2000). *Report of the National Reading Panel: Teaching children to read: An evidence-based assessment of the scientific research literature on reading and its implications for reading instruction* (NIH Publication No. 00-4769). Washington, DC: U.S. Government Printing Office.

National Writing Project, & Nagin, C. (2006). *Because writing matters: Improving student writing in our schools* (Rev. and updated ed.). San Francisco: Jossey-Bass.

O'Brien, D. (2001, June). "At-risk" adolescents: Redefining competence through the multiliteracies of intermediality, visual arts, and representation. *Reading Online, 4*(11). Retrieved April 26, 2005, from http://www.readingonline.org/newliteracies/lit_index.asp?HREF=/newliteracies/obrien/index.html

O'Brien, D., Beach, R., & Scharber, C. (2007). "Struggling" middle schoolers: Engagement and literate competence in a reading writing intervention class. *Reading Psychology, 28,* 51–73.

O'Brien, D., Springs, R., & Stith, D. (2001). Engaging at-risk students: Literacy learning in a high school literacy lab. In E. B. Moje & D. G. O'Brien (Eds.), *Constructions of literacy: Studies of teaching and learning in and out of secondary schools* (pp. 105–23). Mahwah, NJ: Erlbaum.

Pappas, C. C., & Pettegrew, B. S. (1998). The role of genre in the psycholinguistic guessing game of reading. *Language Arts, 75,* 36–44.

Paris, S. G., Wasik, B. A., & Turner, J. C. (1991). The development of strategic readers. In R. Barr, M. L. Kamil, P. B. Mosenthal, & P. D. Pearson (Eds.), *Handbook of reading research* (Vol. 2, pp. 609–40). New York: Longman.

Petrosky, A. (2005). *The reading difficult text example.* Unpublished report, University of Pittsburgh.

Pressley, M. (2002). *Reading instruction that works: The case for balanced teaching* (2nd ed.). New York: Guilford Press.

Pressley, M., & Afflerbach, P. (1995). *Verbal protocols of reading: The nature of constructively responsive reading.* Hillsdale, NJ: Erlbaum.

RAND Reading Study Group [RRSG] (2002). *Reading for understanding: Toward an R&D program in reading comprehension.* Santa Monica, CA: Rand. Retrieved September 3, 2006, from http://www. rand.org/multi/achievementforall/reading/readreport.html

Richardson, W. (2006). *Blogs, wikis, podcasts, and other powerful Web tools for classrooms.* Thousand Oaks, CA: Corwin Press.

Roessing, L. (2004). Building a community of stories and writers: Lake Wobegon comes to the classroom. *The Quarterly, 26*(4). Retrieved September 3, 2006, from http://www.writingproject.org/cs/nwpp/ print/nwpr/2147

Roth, M.-W., & Lee, Y.-J. (2007). "Vygotsky's neglected legacy": Cultural-historical activity theory. *Review of Educational Research, 77*(2), 186–232.

Shanahan, T. (2006). Relations among oral language, reading, and writing development. In C. A. MacArthur, S. Graham, & J. Fitzgerald (Eds.), *Handbook of writing research* (pp. 171–83). New York: Guilford Press.

Sheehy, M. (2003). The social life of an essay: Standardizing forces in writing. *Written Communication, 20,* 333–85.

Simpson, M. L., Stahl, N. A., & Francis, M. A. (2004). Reading and learning strategies: Recommendations for the 21st century. *Journal of Developmental Education, 28,* 2–32.

Smith, F. (1994). *Understanding reading: A psycholinguistic analysis of reading and learning to read* (5th ed.). Hillsdale, NJ: Erlbaum.

Strickland, D. S., & Alvermann, D. E. (2004). Learning and teaching literacy in grades 4–12: Issues and challenges. In D. S. Strickland & D. E. Alvermann (Eds.), *Bridging the literacy achievement gap, grades 4–12* (pp. 1–13). New York: Teachers College Press.

Tufte, E. R. (2006). *The cognitive style of PowerPoint: Pitching out corrupts within* (2nd ed.). Cheshire, CT: Graphics Press.

Weih, T. G. (2005). The genre of traditional literature influences student writing. *Reading Horizons, 46,* 77–91.

Wigfield, A. (2004). Motivation for reading during the early adolescent years. In D. S. Strickland & D. E. Alvermann (Eds.), *Bridging the literacy achievement gap, grades 4–12* (pp. 56–69). New York: Teachers College Press.

Wilhelm, J. D. (2001). *Improving comprehension with think-aloud strategies.* New York: Scholastic Professional Books.

Wilhelm, J. D., Baker, T. N., & Dube, J. (2001). *Strategic reading: Guiding students to lifelong literacy, 6–12.* Portsmouth, NH: Boynton/Cook.

Williams, J. P. (2002). Reading comprehension strategies and teacher preparation. In A. E. Farstrup & S. J. Samuels (Eds.), *What research has to say about reading instruction* (3rd ed., pp. 243–60). Newark, DE: International Reading Association.

Using Scaffolding in Teaching Core Literature

JEANNINE D. RICHISON AND ANITA HERNÁNDEZ
California Polytechnic State University

MARCIA CARTER
San Luis Obispo [California] County Office of Education

Jeannine Richison: During the summer of my son's tenth birthday, he and I took a memorable trip to Europe. He had already shown considerable interest in history, art, and architecture, and I was anticipating rich shared experiences while visiting great architectural monuments, especially in Italy. On our first morning in Venice, we poured over the guidebooks at breakfast and then set out by water taxi to the beautiful Piazza San Marco. What better place to start than the imposing Byzantine church, the Basilica San Marco? To my dismay, as we reached our destination, I saw that the Basilica was covered with an intricate networking of pipes, boards, and clamps, the telltale sign of restoration of the thirteenth-century façade of mosaics and carved marble archways. Pushing my disappointment aside, I turned to my son to assure him we would still be able to visit the interior. His response to the turn of events was completely unexpected. He was absorbed in the intricacies of the scaffolding and full of wonder about how the structure would look up close. He envied the workers whose task it was to clean and restore the artwork.

Similarly, secondary school English teachers approach the great monuments of literature on a daily basis. We know the legacy of words that awaits readers, and we seek answers to how to scaffold to enable our students to get an up close view of what, to them, may be an ambiguous text. As teachers, it is our job to create a framework of understanding relevant to the ideas in core texts both by mining students' comparative background experiences and by creating appropriate academic background if it does not already exist.

What Is Scaffolding?

Education researchers and theorists generally refer to what people already know about a subject as "background knowledge," what cognitive psychologists refer to as an element of cognition, a *schema* (plural: *schemata* or *schemas*) (Anderson & Pearson, 1984; Rumelhart, 1980). These elements of cognition or background knowledge are independent, active, and continuous. Schemata are knowledge structures but also active processes in the construction of knowledge, giving meaning to new experiences as well as structuring cognition in a meaningful way (Johnson, 1987). Mining and creating background knowledge in preparation for the reading of a core text uses students' schemata as knowledge structures (prior experience) and as an active process that helps students categorize the new information and understand it in relation to preexisting knowledge. Learning involves expanding existing information and creating a vast repertoire of schemata that assist in the comprehension of new information (Smith, Carey, & Harste, 1982). What we already know profoundly impacts our comprehension of new material. Scaffolding refers to both the curricular materials and methodological process of accessing and creating background knowledge that generates student interest in and comprehension of literature.

Why Use Scaffolding?

Numerous studies confirm the value of background knowledge in learning new information relevant to a content area (Dochy, Segers, & Buehl, 1999; Schiefele & Krapp, 1996; Tamir, 1996). Marzano (2004) reported the average correlation between background information and academic achievement to be .66. By increasing background knowledge by one standard deviation, a student's academic test results may be expected to increase by twenty-five percentile points. Lack of academic background knowledge results in a decrease of academic performance to a similar degree (Marzano, 2004).

Students Who Lack Reading Proficiency: Native Speakers of English

In addition to the benefits of creating academic background knowledge for all students' success, scaffolding provides a solution to how teachers may assist student populations who have special classroom needs. One group is students who are not proficient readers. The National Assessment Governing Board has established three achievement levels or performance standards designating what students should know and be able to do on individual state-standardized assessments: "*Basic* denotes partial mastery of the knowledge and skills . . . at a given grade; *proficient* represents solid academic performance[—]students reaching this level have demonstrated competency over challenging subject matter; and *advanced* signifies superior performance" (NCES, 2005, p. 2). Students performing below *proficient* are germane to this analysis because the federal government has established the 2013–2014 academic year as the goal year for all students in U.S. public schools to perform at *proficient* or *advanced* levels. According to the reading results of *The Nation's Report Card on Reading*, an average of 27.5 percent of our nation's eighth graders are below *basic* and 43.82 percent perform at *basic*. If these data are correct, nearly three-quarters of our nation's students could benefit from increased academic background knowledge in order to become more proficient readers and to meet federal standards (NCES, 2005, p.16).

Advanced literacy tends to be developed in the high school years. The process is analogous to the rite of passage that kindergartners and first graders move through as they learn the alphabet or "break the code" in the first stages of reading (Christie, 2002). Abstraction characterizes most of the textbooks and other reading material that high school students encounter. Abstract language is found, for example, in generalizations, definitions, embedded clauses in sentences, and argumentation with evidence

(Christie, 2002; Scarcella, 2002; Schleppegrell, 2004). Such abstract language presents a difficulty that many students are unable to overcome without intervention. Furthermore, students are expected to be able to analyze and interpret texts, extract meanings, recognize errors, and write concise compositions using grammatical devices. Without knowledge of how to do these tasks, many students stop trying.

Students Who Lack Reading Proficiency: English Language Learners

The second group of students who have a difficult time accessing grade-level texts are the vast majority of English language learners (ELLs), who in the 2003–2004 school year accounted for approximately 5 million of the 49 million students enrolled nationwide (National Clearinghouse for English Language Acquisition & Language Instruction Educational Programs [NCELA], 2005). Of the 5 million, 47 percent were enrolled in grades 6 to 12 (Capps, Fix, Murray, Ost, Passel, & Herwantoro, 2005). Some teachers who work with ELLs regard it as a joyful as well as a challenging experience. The joy comes from seeing how much new knowledge ELLs acquire. The challenging aspect comes from working with ELLs who hit a plateau and do not make the progress that their teachers hope for.

Research reveals the challenges that high school teachers face in working effectively with ELLs and the challenges that ELLs face in their classrooms (August & Hakuta, 1997; Christie, 2002; Harklau, 1994; Scarcella, 2002; Schleppegrell, 2004; Valdés, 2001; Valdés & Sanders, 1999; Walqui, 2000). For example, when teaching ELLs, high school teachers face at least two challenges. These students have varying degrees of skill in speaking, reading, writing, and listening, yet some schools expect ELLs at the beginning and intermediate stages to acquire competency in both the English language and the subject matter content by being immersed in English-only mainstream classes—a practice that requires considerable scaffolding for ELLs.

A high school teacher may have ELLs who range in their command of the English language from newcomers with little or no English to writers of sophisticated prose. Some of these students may have been in the United States since kindergarten or first grade but still have not achieved advanced levels of reading and writing. These individuals are sometimes referred to as ESL lifers (Wong Fillmore & Snow, 2000).

Competence in a second language depends on several factors, including age, length of time in U.S. schools, motivation to learn, the amount of access to English, and quality of instruction. Although thirteen-year-old students, because of their greater cognitive abilities, may initially acquire a second language faster than five-year-olds, the former tend to retain accents and ungrammatical structures more than the latter (August & Hakuta, 1997; Bialystok & Hakuta, 1994; Oyama, 1976; Snow, 2000). Furthermore, if students are proficient in their first language, they tend to acquire mastery over English faster than students who have a lower proficiency in their first language (Cummins, 1981). This type of background—that is, their first language—provides the "frame" on which students may develop second language skills as well as academic skills. Thus, those students who have a grade-level command of literacy skills and study skills in their primary language are in an excellent position to acquire a second language and move quickly into mainstream classes. These are the success cases that many teachers and administrators like to highlight. However, the reality is that the vast majority of ELLs have limited literacy skills in their first language, which means that even their first language skills do not readily match the literacy demands of their high school teachers (Freeman & Freeman [with Mercuri], 2002; Valdés, 2001). Providing these students with easier-to-understand text, which reinforces the skills they already have, and increasing the difficulty of text used in support of the core text, both in content and in format, enhances their understanding of the core text and adds to their store of academic background knowledge. This type of scaffolding can be accomplished in mainstream classrooms without compromising the academic needs of the other learners, including those who are already proficient and those in need of expanded opportunities.

Challenges That ELLs Face in High School Classrooms

ELLs must learn not only to speak English, but also to process rapid explanations given by their teachers on any given topic and to take notes simultaneously (Valdés, 2001). In response to promoting high academic expectations for ELLs, Teachers of English to Speakers of Other Languages (TESOL, 1997/ 2006) defined three goals in language competence for these students:

1. They must use English to communicate in social settings.

2. They must use English to achieve academically in all content areas.

3. They must use English in culturally appropriate ways.

Teachers of English as a second language (ESL) assist students in all three ways, whereas content-specific teachers focus primarily on the second goal, by teaching students to write high-level compositions such as science lab reports, mathematical solutions to problems, or historical essays.

On average, it takes three to five years to acquire a level of oral language that is comparable to that of native speakers and four to seven years to acquire a level of academic language that allows for mastery of academic content on the high school level (August & Hakuta, 1997). How much English a given group of students acquire depends on the amount of access they have to English. In an ideal situation, ELLs would enroll in ESL classes and also be offered opportunities throughout the school day to interact with fluent speakers of the language on various types of academic and nonacademic topics (Valdés, 2001). By scaffolding core literature through the use of appropriate processes and materials, English teachers offer students multiple levels of access to what otherwise would be inaccessible text. In addition, a number of resources exist to help high school teachers specifically to use the TESOL standards in their classrooms (e.g., Agor, 2000; Irujo, 2000; Snow, 2000).

Mastering content to succeed in school requires students to build intricate and multiple networks of knowledge in mathematics, the sciences, the social sciences, the humanities, and the arts.

In other words, they must learn facts, ideas, skills, and strategies within each of the content areas. They are also expected to display their knowledge using connected discourse to explain concepts, make hypotheses, predict events, infer details, report information, and arrange sequences. Furthermore, students are expected to process classroom language on the spot. However, for ELLs at the beginning and intermediate levels of proficiency, comprehending complex language interactions such as rhetorical questions or expert explanations may be extremely difficult (August & Hakuta, 1997). Content-area teachers, along with those teaching English, would benefit their students by incorporating scaffolding processes and materials into their curriculum as well.

Access to Mainstream Curricula through Scaffolding Processes

Even among ESL classes, there are more or less efficient ways to teach ELLs. For example, Valdés (2001) found that ESL classes organized to teach grammatical structures and vocabulary without any reference to academic content were less successful in helping students master English than ESL classes that taught both English and subject matter content.

Mrs. Samuels (not her real name), who taught both mainstream English and advanced ESL, wove content into her ESL classes. When, for example, she taught "Casey at the Bat," she informed the students about how the game is played and how it is regarded as one of the nation's greatest pastimes. Mrs. Samuels understood that literacy occurs within a cultural as well as a linguistic context, and she helped orient her students to the cultural background of the game of baseball. When she taught *Tom Sawyer*, she discussed the historical background of the novel and instructed students in the linguistic context by focusing on confusing lexical items (e.g., *ferry* versus *fairy*). For writing assignments, Mrs. Samuels often had the students compose essays or stories about their own real experiences. One of her assignments helped students understand verb tense by requiring them to compare their wishes today with their wishes ten years earlier and what they expected their wishes would be ten years from now. Teachers like Mrs. Samuels are cognizant of the literacy demands that mainstream secondary classrooms make on all students, including ELLs.

ELLs need various types of scaffolds in order to access the mainstream curriculum (August & Hakuta, 1997; Bruner, 1983; Walqui, 2000). The ideal is to scaffold in the students' zone of proximal development—that is, the area between their own development and their development when they are assisted by a more capable peer or adult (Vygotsky, 1978). This is the area where students develop new skills and new knowledge.

Teachers can incorporate instructional scaffolds into their teaching as they work with ELLs, in particular those who have intermediate level fluency, in either shelter classes or mainstream content classes:

1. *Modeling:* Students observe the learning being demonstrated or taught by the teacher (Walqui, 2000).

2. *Bridging:* Students become involved because their own personal experience is being used as part of the learning activity (Walqui, 2000).

3. *Schema Building:* Students experience learning that has interconnected concepts within a subject or with other subjects (Walqui, 2000).

4. *Contextualization:* Students experience learning through visual, auditory, or kinesthetic senses (Walqui, 2000).

5. *Metacognitive Development:* Students learn skills to better comprehend text and to write well-structured compositions (Walqui, 2000).

6. *Text Representation:* Students apply their new knowledge, preferably in a new genre or medium (Walqui, 2000).

7. *Verbal Scaffolding:* Students hear their teacher or fellow students elucidate a difficult concept (Bruner, 1983).

Teachers scaffold students' oral language during group discussions by guiding their exploratory talk as they appropriate new concepts into their existing language repertoire. They also raise students' critical understanding of new and old concepts so that they do not flounder in misunderstandings (Maloch, 2002). The instructional scaffolds for ELLs who have achieved an intermediate level of English proficiency allow teachers to choose from the most appropriate instructional scaffold or to bundle together a set of scaffolds, depending on the curricular needs of their ELLs. The scaffolds are meant to assist students in gaining access to the curriculum. As students develop their knowledge base, the scaffolds are removed and replaced by new scaffolds for other curricular demands. The students are expected to participate actively, rather than remain passive and have their content and language knowledge become stagnant.

Scaffolding Using Materials

Although lack of funding presents problems for schools in providing direct academic experiences in the form of field trips or other real-life experiences, virtual experiences are readily available through reading, lectures, films, and other sources. Because background knowledge is stored in both linguistic and nonlinguistic forms, the use of visual and auditory stimuli to enhance already existing schemata or to help shape new experiences is valuable, in combination with reading, in increasing academic information. Creating theme sets linked to a core text may combine print sources that enhance access of the core text for all students. These sets may begin with children's picture books and move through chapter books, books classified as adolescent literature, nonliterary text, and selections from multiple genres and media (Richison, Hernández, & Carter, 2006). Using children's picture books and graphic novels to scaffold a text adds to the visual imagery already present in a student's schemata. The introduction of many thematically linked pieces of text from a variety of genres presents the opportunity for all students to participate in the act of visualization (Richison, Hernández, & Carter, 2002).

Researchers have also shown that the use of visual imagery while reading helps students monitor their comprehension (Wilhelm, 1997). Visualizing scenes and characters from a text is a key difference between proficient and developing readers. Concrete visualization provided by picture books, cartoons, film, photographs, and graphic novels supports insufficient reading strategies of poor readers and provides a scaffold to more reflective response when working with more sophisticated text with similar ideas (Richison, Hernández, & Carter, 2002). Opportunities to read and reflect on multiple texts in preparation for the core text build students' academic background experiences with regard to the enduring understandings of the core text, most of which have their philosophical roots in other disciplines, thus supporting academic content areas as well as English.

In addition to the value of scaffolding a core text with visual and conceptual background experiences to increase student performance, exposure to relevant vocabulary may be introduced in prereading experiences. If students are motivated to read the assigned text and they try to read it but find that the language is too dense or conceptually abstract, they often withdraw from the task. Providing background language experiences, with conceptually manageable texts, sets students up for success with ambiguous texts. Traditional vocabulary work, consisting of identification of uncommon words, looking up the definition, and perhaps using the word in a sentence, may improve the chances of student success, but the linguistic context of the literature may not be enough to represent meaning to students with little background on which to draw. Vocabulary encountered in high interest and usually shorter contexts and used in meaningful inquiry about substantial topics carries over to the more difficult text and assists in meaning-making. Words are simply labels for packets of information (Marzano, 2004). If students can recognize the packet and visualize its content, its vocabulary label brings with it the packet's preexisting meaning when the word is encountered in a new context.

Assuming that language takes on meaning in a situational context (Smith, Carey, & Harste, 1982), we must recognize that literature cannot be studied in isolation. The reader, the text, and the "poem" created in their interaction present the richest opportunity for research on literature study (Rosenblatt, 1978). Teachers generally view satisfactory reading comprehension through the lens of two variables: *meaning maintenance*—or the ability to recall plot detail, character components, and information presented in class lectures—and *meaning generation*—the ability to question or apply meaning from the text to some outside construct or experience (Smith, Carey, & Harste, 1982). Meaning maintenance adds little value to a person's education or quality of life. Meaning generation, on the other hand, stimulates critical thinking and application skills that carry over into other areas of thought and life. Scaffolding experiences with an intertextual approach allow students the opportunity to make text-to-self, text-to-text, and text-to-world connections (Tovani, 2000) that enhance embodied schemata and provide the active processes that build new schemata in an organized and meaningful way. Activities before, during, and after reading that stimulate inquiry and meaning generation and use multiple means of self-expression, such as writing, speaking, and performing, provide means for new meaning to be locked into memory.

Scaffolding: What Does This Mean for Teachers?

Scaffolding and building access to ideas for all learners in the mainstream English classroom does not have to be an imposing task. For example, it is sometimes difficult for students to visualize the concept of the writer's point of view. Words alone may not provide insight into what point of view means in a novel or short story, especially for students whose first language is not English. However, a wordless picture book intended for young readers displays the concept quite well. Istvan Banyai's (1995) *Zoom* begins with a small picture of a rooster. The next page pulls back from the view of the rooster to the larger setting where we see that it is a *picture* of a rooster in a room. The next page pulls even further back to a view of the house containing the room in which the picture of the rooster is displayed. There are no words in this book, only points of view from smaller to larger settings. After using this picture book, students have an idea of what point of view might mean in literature. For a book taking the general view back to the specific, teachers might try using Steve Jenkins's (1995) *Looking Down*, where there are several examples useful to understanding point of view. Children's books often illustrate issues and terms that are difficult to comprehend in careful detail and with simplicity. These simple books with important concepts fit well within sets illustrating larger issues, such as theme. However, it is best to use these children's books as part of a larger, theme-based set of texts, anchored by a core text.

One such core text, *Their Eyes Were Watching God* by Zora Neale Hurston (1978), is an example of a novel that is frequently used for the secondary classroom. This novel tells the story of Janie Mae Crawford, a beautiful, fair-skinned, seventeen-year-old African American girl living in rural Florida in the early twentieth century. Janie's life story includes three marriages, leading to a mature insight into life, living, and being independent. This novel could serve as the core text that includes other books on the theme of overcoming differences, such as Jacqueline Woodson's (2001) *The Other Side*. Intended for ages five and up, this children's story has two girls, one black and one white, who gradually get to know each other as they sit on a fence that divides their town. *Child of the Owl*, Lawrence Yep's (1990) novel for ages twelve and up, features a twelve-year-old girl who knows little about her Chinese heritage until she is sent to live with her grandmother in San Francisco, where she begins to comprehend what her family background means to her. A novel directed toward maturing teens addresses the issues of being born out of wedlock as well as suffering child abuse: *Bastard Out of Carolina*, by Dorothy Allison (1993), is narrated by Ruth Ann Boatright and set in the 1950s. Ruth Ann is born to an unmarried fifteen-year-old. Ruth Ann's birth certificate is stamped ILLEGITIMATE in big letters. Overcoming the stigma officially placed on her makes Ruth Ann triumphant in her decision to find her own way. This small set contains two books that are framed for very young students but are useful as a set on the themes of coming of age or overcoming adversity. Using theme sets to scaffold literature for diverse learners is one of the best practices for today's classrooms. Another best practice is the use of activities that provide further exploration of the big ideas in the texts.

Working with Theme Sets

In 2001, the Association for Supervision and Curriculum Development published a Mid-Continent Research for Education and Learning meta-analysis of over 1,200 previously conducted studies. The resulting document, *Classroom Instruction That Works* (Marzano, Pickering, & Pollock, 2001), features nine effective teaching strategies:

1. Identifying similarities and differences

2. Summarizing and note taking

3. Reinforcing effort and providing recognition

4. Homework and practice

5. Nonlinguistic representations

6. Cooperative learning

7. Setting objectives and providing feedback

8. Generating and testing hypotheses

9. Cues, questions, and advance organizers

Using the first strategy listed, for example, a teacher might ask students to read two essays displaying differing views on the same topic and to compare the two viewpoints in preparation for a class discussion. To begin, students fold their papers in half and draw a line down the middle of the paper, designating one side for Article 1 and the other side for Article 2. As they read, students note the arguments presented by the two authors and create a statement to be used for the discussion. That statement, the product of a higher-level thinking assignment, prepares them to defend or qualify a comparison, a task often performed in English classes.

This comparison assignment uses four of the strategies listed: identifying similarities and differences, summarizing and note taking, generating and testing hypotheses, and advance organizers. If the classroom includes students with second language needs, the teacher could plan to scaffold the task so that all of the students can access the material. The teacher may also use a modeling technique when making the original assignment. One such technique is the use of a think-aloud reading strategy. After making the assignment, the teacher models the initial note taking of one viewpoint for each article, talking about what he or she is reading and thinking while going through the articles. Then, when writing the two opposing viewpoints on the divided paper, the teacher again models the possible statement using just this one comparison point. Thus, the teacher purposefully makes this difficult assignment accessible to all of the students, not just those who are native speakers.

Other Suggested Activities

TEN CRITICAL WORDS

Select and define ten of the most important words from the text that students are assigned to read. Ask them to find each of the words as they are reading and explain the reason that particular word has significance for the chapter (or short story or other text). When all of the students are finished with the list of ten, ask them to work in groups of four to share their statements of significance. They select the most explanatory definition within a whole class discussion. Scaffolding strategies used include metacognitive development, verbal scaffolding, and schema building, as well as similarities and differences, cooperative learning, generating hypotheses, summarizing, and note taking (Marzano, Pickering, & Pollock, 2001).

TRACKING POSTER

Much like a beacon of light focused on a scene in the dark night, a tracking poster uses images to support a theme, to illustrate a character's traits, to follow a motif or a specific character, or to highlight the character's movement within the novel. To assign the tracking poster on theme, for example, students "spotlight" the theme stated in words in the middle of the poster. To support that theme, students surround the theme statement with images illustrating events in the novel, characters' actions, and other supporting information. Teachers may also require the use of quotations from the text and qualify how many and what type of quotations may be used based on the purpose of the assignment. Students should be prepared to explain their poster to the class. Scaffolding strategies used include schema building, contextualization, and text representation (Bruner, 1983; Walqui, 2000), as well as advance organizers, summarizing, and note taking (Marzano, Pickering, & Pollock, 2001).

CANNIBAL ISLAND

Students receive a written description of a large jungle island in the Pacific peopled by cannibals. They pair up and collaborate to place certain characters from the novel on that island. To ensure survival of all of the marooned characters, the students are to specify and explain what traits each of the characters has that enable the entire group to survive. Scaffolding strategies include text representation and verbal scaffolding (Bruner, 1983; Walqui, 2000) as well as cooperative learning and generating and testing hypotheses (Marzano, Pickering, & Pollock, 2001).

ART SMART

Using such websites as http://witcombe.sbc.edu/ARTHLinks.html, students use the setting in the novel as a time frame to find and display art copies of the novel's time period. The same activity could be carried out with music. Scaffolding strategies include contextualization (Bruner, 1983; Walqui, 2000) as well as the use of nonlinguistic representations (Marzano, Pickering, & Pollock, 2001).

Conclusion

Students with diverse needs and skills populate classrooms, but teaching in this environment does not have to be an overwhelming series of tasks, especially if the teacher plans carefully and with an eye to using the most effective strategies to access the curriculum. Research has shown that scaffolding processes and materials provide just such access. Skillful teaching directed toward all of the students, not just those who can easily access the curriculum, is good teaching—expected by every stakeholder in an educated society.

References

Agor, B. (Ed.). (2000). *Integrating the ESL standards into classroom practice: Grades 9–12*. Alexandria, VA: Teachers of English to Speakers of Other Languages.

Allison, D. (1993). *Bastard out of Carolina*. New York: Plume.

Anderson, R. C., & Pearson, P. D. (1984). A schema-theoretic view of basic processes in reading comprehension. In P. D. Pearson, R. Barr, M. L. Kamil, & P. Mosenthal (Eds.), *Handbook of reading research* (pp. 255–91). New York: Longman.

August, D., & Hakuta, K. (Eds.). (1997). *Improving schooling for language-minority children: A research agenda*. Washington, DC: National Academy Press.

Banyai, I. (1995). *Zoom*. New York: Viking.

Bialystok, E. & Hakuta, K. (1994). *In other words: The science and psychology of second language acquisition*. New York: Basic Books.

Bruner, J. (with Watson, R.). (1983). *Child's talk*. New York: Norton.

Capps, R., Fix, M., Murray, J., Ost, J., Passel, J. S., & Herwantoro, S. (2005). *The new demography of America's schools: Immigration and the No Child Left Behind Act*. Washington, DC: The Urban Institute.

Christie, F. (2002). The development of abstraction in adolescence in subject English. In M. J. Schleppegrell & M. C. Colombi (Eds.), *Developing advanced literacy in first and second languages: Meaning with power* (pp. 45–100). Mahwah, NJ: Erlbaum.

Cummins, J. (1981). The role of primary language development in promoting educational success for language minority students. In *Schooling and language minority students: A theoretical framework* (pp. 3–50). Los Angeles: Evaluation, Dissemination, and Assessment Center.

Dochy, F., Segers, M., & Buehl, M. M. (1999). The relation between assessment practices and outcomes of studies: The case of research on prior knowledge. *Review of Educational Research, 69*, 145–86.

Freeman, Y. S., & Freeman, D. E. (with Mercuri, S.). (2002). *Closing the achievement gap: How to reach limited-formal schooling and long-term English learners*. Portsmouth, NH: Heinemann.

Harklau, L. (1994). Tracking and linguistic minority students: Consequences of ability grouping for second language learners. *Linguistics and Education, 6*, 217–44.

Hurston, Z. N. (1978). *Their eyes were watching God*. Urbana: University of Illinois Press.

Irujo, S. (Ed.). (2000). *Integrating the ESL standards into classroom practice: Grades 6–8*. Alexandria, VA: Teachers of English to Speakers of Other Languages.

Johnson, M. (1987). *The body in the mind: The bodily basis of meaning, imagination, and reason*. Chicago: University of Chicago Press.

Maloch, B. (2002). Scaffolding student talk: One teacher's role in literature discussion groups. *Reading Research Quarterly, 37*, 94–112.

Marzano, R. J. (2004). *Building background knowledge for academic achievement: Research on what works in schools*. Alexandria, VA: Association for Supervision and Curriculum Development.

Marzano, R. J., Pickering, D. J., & Pollock, J. E. (2001). *Classroom instruction that works: Research-based strategies for increasing student achievement*. Alexandria, VA: Association for Supervision and Curriculum Development.

National Center for Education Statistics (NCES). (2005). *The nation's report card: Reading 2005*. Retrieved September 3, 2006, from: http://nces.ed.gov/nationsreportcard/pdf/main2005/2006451.pdf

National Clearinghouse for English Language Acquisition & Language Instruction Educational Programs (NCELA). (2005). *The growing numbers of limited English proficient students: 1993/94–2003/04*. Retrieved September 3, 2006, from http://www.ncela.gwu.edu/policy/states/reports/statedata/2003LEP/GrowingLEP_0304_Dec05.pdf

Oyama, S. (1976). A sensitive period for the acquisition of a nonnative phonological system. *Journal of Psycholinguistic Research, 5*, 261–83.

Richison, J. D., Hernández, A. C., & Carter, M. J. (2002). Blending multiple genres in theme baskets. *English Journal 92*(2), 76–81.

Richison, J. D., Hernández, A. C., & Carter, M. J. (2006). *Theme-sets for secondary students: How to scaffold core literature.* Portsmouth, NH: Heinemann.

Rosenblatt, L. M. (1978). *The reader, the text, the poem: The transactional theory of the literary work.* Carbondale: Southern Illinois University Press.

Rumelhart, D. E. (1980). Schemata: The building blocks of cognition. In R. J. Spiro, B. C. Bruce, & W. F. Brewer (Eds.), *Theoretical issues in reading comprehension: Perspectives from cognitive psychology, linguistics, artificial intelligence, and education* (pp. 33–58). Hillsdale, NJ: Erlbaum.

Scarcella, R. (2002). Some key factors affecting English learners' development of advanced literacy. In M. J. Schleppegrell & M. C. Colombi (Eds.), *Developing advanced literacy in first and second languages: Meaning with power* (pp. 209–25). Mahwah, NJ: Erlbaum.

Schiefele, U., & Krapp, A. (1996). Topics of interest and free recall of expository text. *Learning and Individual Differences, 8*(2), 141–60.

Schleppegrell, M. J. (2004). *The language of schooling: A functional linguistics perspective.* Mahwah, NJ: Erlbaum.

Snow, M. A. (Ed.). (2000). *Implementing the ESL standards for pre-K–12 students through teacher education.* Alexandria, VA: Teachers of English to Speakers of Other Languages.

Smith, S. L., Carey, R. F., & Harste, J. C. (1982). The contexts of reading. In A. Berger & H. A. Robinson (Eds.), *Secondary school reading: What research reveals for classroom practice* (pp. 21–37). Urbana, IL: National Council of Teachers of English, National Conference on Research in English, and ERIC Clearinghouse on Reading and Communication Skills.

Tamir, P. (1996). Science assessment. In M. Birenbaum & F. J. R. C. Dochy (Eds.), *Alternatives in assessment of achievements, learning processes, and prior knowledge* (pp. 93–129). Boston: Kluwer Academic.

Teachers of English to Speakers of Other Languages (TESOL). (2006). *PreK–12 English Language Proficiency Standards.* Alexandria, VA: Author.

Tovani, C. (2000). *I read it, but I don't get it: Comprehension strategies for adolescent readers.* Portland, ME: Stenhouse.

Valdés, G. (2001). *Learning and not learning English: Latino students in American schools.* New York: Teachers College Press.

Valdés, G., & Sanders, P. A. (1999). Latino ESL students and the development of writing abilities. In C. R. Cooper & L. Odell (Eds.), *Evaluating writing: The role of teachers' knowledge about text, learning, and culture* (pp. 249–78). Urbana, IL: National Council of Teachers of English.

Vygotsky, L. (1978). *Mind in society: The development of higher psychological processes.* Cambridge, MA: Harvard University Press.

Walqui, A. (2000). *Access and engagement: Program design and instructional approaches for immigrant students in secondary school.* Washington, DC: Center for Applied Linguistics.

Wilhelm, J. D. (1997). *You gotta BE the book: Teaching engaged and reflective reading with adolescents.* New York: Teachers College Press & Urbana, IL: National Council of Teachers of English.

Wong Fillmore, L., & Snow, C. (2000). *What teachers need to know about language. Special Report.* Clearinghouse on Languages and Linguistics. Washington, DC: Center for Applied Linguistics.

Woodson, J. (2001). *The other side* (E. B. Lewis, Illustrator). New York: G. P. Putnam's Sons.

Yep, L. (1990). *Child of the owl.* New York: HarperTrophy.

CHAPTER THIRTEEN

Federal and State Literacy Mandates for Secondary Schools: Responding to Unintended Consequences

JILL LEWIS
New Jersey City University

GARY MOORMAN
Appalachian State University

O ver the last fifty years, public schools in the United States have been dramatically successful in providing education for all students, including minorities, English language learners (ELLs), students living in poverty, and students with special needs. Currently, the No Child Left Behind Act (NCLB, 2001) and the Individuals with Disabilities Education Act (IDEA, 2004) are having profound effects on virtually every student and educator in the United States. As their implementation has proceeded, serious educational policy issues have risen. The broad question that we address in this chapter is as follows: Can Congress ratify and enforce legislation that positively impacts education outcomes at the state and local levels?

Although federal attention to education is not new, the standard of high-level universal literacy is. Therefore, we begin this chapter by framing literacy, federal legislation, and educational policy in a historical perspective to show the evolution and expansion of literacy instruction. We then provide an overview of recent legislation and examine the intended as well as unintended consequences of NCLB. Finally, we address the question, "When unforeseen negative outcomes result from federal education legislation, how can groups and individuals advocate to mitigate these outcomes?"

Historical Perspective

The invention of writing systems ranks among the highest achievements of human culture. Writing systems first emerged in Western culture sometime before 3000 BC as communities moved from hunter–gatherer tribes into socially stratified and politically complex societies (Diamond, 1999). These systems were valuable because they made transmission and storage of information easier and more efficient. Writing gave permanence to law, history, religion, and science, allowing each discipline to develop in systematic ways. Knowledge could be transported, reorganized, and revised, making communication more accurate, precise, and persuasive. Because knowledge brings power, the ability to use writing systems brings power to literate societies and individuals. Hence, from the beginning, literacy has been inherently political.

In the United States, the goal of widespread literacy began in colonial times and reflected a Judeo-Christian religious emphasis. The General Court of Massachusetts passed one of the first public education laws in 1647. It begins, "It being one chief point of that old deluder, Satan, to keep men from the knowledge of the Scriptures . . ." and concludes, "It is therefore ordered that every township in this jurisdiction, after the Lord hath increased them to the number of fifty householders, shall then forthwith appoint one within their town to teach all such children as shall resort to him to write and read" (as cited in Smith, 1965, p. 13). Jefferson later argued for public schools that would develop a "natural aristocracy" (Shannon, 2001, p. 12). By today's standards, Jefferson's plan for schooling was limited: free education for "all" did not include many groups, such as blacks or Native Americans. His three-year plan focused on reading, writing, history, and mathematics. It is clear that the notion of literacy, neither on the part of the early colonists nor the Founding Fathers, included the universality and the high standards currently taken for granted.

By the beginning of the twentieth century, the Industrial Revolution, which began decades earlier, created a large demand for a literate workforce. Attacks on the effectiveness of U.S. schools, particularly in the area of reading, became increasingly political (Allington, 2002). Critics of education argued for the implementation of an efficiency model that blended science and business, in the belief that applying the business principles of Carnegie, Vanderbilt, and Rockefeller would work in educational settings (Shannon, 2001). An assembly line model of education came into wide practice. Basal readers were introduced that gave teachers explicit scripts to follow in their instruction. Textbooks and teachers' manuals were designed to standardize the curriculum and provide teachers with the "science" of instruction.

Over the course of the twentieth century, people in the United States gradually adopted the belief that all children can and should learn to read and write and that being literate means far more than the ability to decode basic text. Both of these perceptions fueled the political debates concerning how to best achieve the country's literacy goals and who should determine whether these goals are being achieved. Since its founding, local control has been a hallmark of the U.S. educational system. However, during recent years, the federal government has assumed a larger role in identifying literacy issues, crafting legislation to address these issues, and, for at least a while, increasing support for literacy initiatives. Tied to this support are a growing number of federal regulations that limit local control of education, as we describe in the next section of this chapter.

Recent Federal Education Legislation and Reauthorizations

President Lyndon Johnson signed the Elementary and Secondary Education Act (ESEA) into law on April 11, 1965. The purpose of this legislation was to bridge the education gap between rich and poor and to meet the special needs of educationally deprived children by putting considerable federal dollars into education. ESEA was a significant departure from business as usual. Harold

Howe II, the U.S. Commissioner of Education from 1965 to 1968, told *Education Week* in a 1999 interview that ESEA was the federal government's "first really direct reach into [all] school districts in the United States" (Robelen, 2005, p. 1). For the first time, local schools were accountable to Washington and subject to its one-size-fits-all mandates.

Laws that are due to expire must come up for reauthorization, which may result in changes to the laws themselves, as well as to some of the regulations for implementation. Numerous changes have occurred in ESEA since 1965. Title I funding formulas have been modified to respond to the misuse of federal money by schools. Since the late 1980s, much of the focus has shifted to finding ways for the federal government to hold states and districts accountable for showing better academic results. This shift resulted from the persistence of achievement gaps for poor and minority children that had led to the initial legislation.

During the Reagan administration many federal school programs were consolidated and cuts were made in spending for education. The 1988 reauthorization of ESEA was particularly significant:

> It began to focus on educational outcomes, including demands for testing and accountability. That emphasis grew more focused and intensive under President Clinton with the 1994 re-authorization of the ESEA and the Goals 2000: Educate America Act. These were the first federal education laws that required states to develop systems of standards and aligned assessments. (Robelen, 2005, p. 1)

The most sweeping reform of federal education policy since the enactment of ESEA was its reauthorization in 2002. The NCLB was signed into law by President George W. Bush on January 8, 2002. Its exacting federal requirements pose both fiscal and educational challenges at state and local levels. Although the impact of NCLB is felt the most at the elementary level, this legislation will doubtless have considerable impact on secondary schools. According to the U.S. Department of Education (USDOE),

> As states and communities implement *NCLB* and achievement gaps are eradicated in the early grades, we can expect that many

more young people will enter high school well prepared to master a rigorous curriculum. But our nation cannot afford to wait. True to its name, *NCLB* recognizes that change also is needed to help today's high school students catch up quickly and master both basic and advanced academic skills. (USDOE, 2004, n.p.)

The most invasive requirement of NCLB for secondary schools is the establishment of annual achievement objectives for all students. States are required to set a baseline to measure progress toward the goal of ensuring that all students are proficient in reading and math by the 2013–2014 school year (USDOE, 2004). Adolescents take the statewide assessment in grade 8 and again between grades 10–12, with most states giving the assessment in grade 11. The definition of proficiency and the design or identification of tests that are aligned with state standards and content are also the responsibility of the states. Incremental targets for Adequate Yearly Progress (AYP) must be set that indicate minimum levels of increased student performance (Linn, Baker, & Betebenner, 2002). All groups of students, including low-income students, students from racial and ethnic groups, students with disabilities, and students with limited English language proficiency, are expected to meet AYP standards. At least 95 percent of students in each of these groups must be tested.

Schools that fail to meet AYP goals are designated as "schools in need of improvement" and face escalating negative consequences. Schools failing to achieve AYP for two years must notify parents of a two-year improvement plan, use at least 10 percent of their Title I funds for professional development, and provide public school choice for all students. If they are identified (or misidentified) as failing for a third year, they must also provide supplemental services to students, such as private tutoring. After four years, the local school district must do at least one of the following: replace staff, implement a new curriculum, extend the school year or day, appoint an outside expert, or restructure internal organization. If the school does not meet AYP for five consecutive years, it must prepare a plan and make arrangements for restructuring. Any school labeled as failing for six consecutive years must reopen as a public charter school, replace all or most of the school staff related to the failure or enter into a contract with a private management company, turn school operations over to the state, and undertake major reforms and restructuring (USDOE, 2002).

Secondary schools are to be held accountable in other ways as well. Graduation rates are to be monitored and considered part of the AYP objectives. High schools that receive Title I funds must hire only "Highly Qualified Teachers" (HQT) in core academic areas (English, reading or language arts, mathematics, science, foreign languages, civics, economics, arts, history, and geography). A HQT must have full certification, a bachelors degree, and demonstrated competence in subject matter and pedagogy (National Education Association [NEA], Teacher and Paraprofessional Quality; 'No Child Left Behind' Act/ESEA, n.d.). Beginning in 2007–2008, all states must administer science assessments once during grades 9–12. As of this writing, NCLB is undergoing reauthorization. The Aspen Institute's Commission on No Child Left Behind, as well as other groups, have held hearings in which many individual and organizational stakeholders have provided written and oral testimony. These include repeated requests for revision to the AYP requirements, especially for ELLs; use of greater flexibility in assessment, with a call for a "growth model" to determine student achievement; and more funding to meet the testing mandates. The International Reading Association (IRA) has also called for inclusion of expertise in teaching reading in the definition of the HQT.

A second federal education bill that has been through a series of reauthorizations modifying regulations and the role of the federal government in local education issues is the IDEA. This is actually a reauthorization of the 1975 Education for All Handicapped Children Act (EAHCA). EAHCA provided guarantees for students with identifiable disabilities, including nondiscriminatory testing, evaluation, and placement; the right to due process; education in the least restrictive environment; and a free and appropriate education. This legislation also established the right of special needs children to an Individualized Education Plan (IEP), which was to include relevant instructional goals and objectives, appropriate length of school year, the criteria to be used in evaluation and measurement, and the most appropriate educational placement. At this point, advocates for special education were trying to provide the right to an education for children who had been excluded from the educational system (Werts, Tompkins, & Culatta, 2007).

In 1990, EAHCA, amended and renamed IDEA, layered additional changes on special education mandates. A major change was the use of person-first language; for example, disabled student was replaced by student with disability (Mock, 2007). Significant changes involved the inclusion of students with low-incidence disabilities (e.g., autism), mandated implementation of transition plans, and required extension of services to children as young as three years of age. In 1997, IDEA was again reauthorized, providing for the inclusion of special needs students in districtwide and statewide assessments, measurable goals and objectives, and proactive behavior plans.

In 2004, IDEA was reauthorized again. The major impact of this legislation is to align IDEA with NCLB, specifically in regard to assessment. When the 1997 IDEA mandated that students with disabilities be included in assessments, many students were given accommodations to level the playing field by removing barriers resulting from a disability, such as having texts in Braille for the blind. But NCLB dramatically increases both the frequency and importance of assessments. Furthermore, NCLB stipulates that 95 percent of all students must participate in district and state assessments that offer no accommodations, and most students with disabilities take the tests unassisted. The federal government thus determined the extent to which local districts could provide possibly needed special assistance to its special education population.

The Question of Unfunded Mandates

State and local education officials have bristled at criticisms from the federal government and from policymakers and taxpayers that public schools have ignored their accountability for student achievement. They have countered that federal funding for education is typically a mere 7 percent or less of a state's total spending on education and that NCLB imposes additional burdens on already cash-strapped state and local budgets. In their view, NCLB is an unfunded mandate wherein one governmental entity requires, but does not pay for, the enactment of policies by another governmental entity. The U.S. General Accounting Office's (GAO) study of May 2004 examined whether the Unfunded Mandates Reform Act of 1995 (UMRA) was being violated in several federal initiatives. It "was enacted to address concerns expressed by state and local governments about federal statutes and regulations that require these non-federal parties to expend resources to achieve legislative goals without being provided federal funding to cover the costs" (GAO, 2004). The GAO is clear that it would be incorrect to label NCLB an unfunded mandate. Technically, states can refuse to participate in the program. According to the report,

> The No Child Left Behind Act is a well-known example that has intergovernmental implications, but was not identified as a Federal mandate under UMRA. No Child Left Behind provides Federal grants for a host of education programs, requires states to design and implement standards and assessments, and provides financial penalties for states that fail to achieve certain standards over 2 consecutive years. (GAO, 2004, n.p.)

Although legally NCLB may not be an unfunded mandate, many believe it is an underfunded one. On January 8, 2004, high-ranking Democratic members of Congress wrote the Secretary of U.S. Department of Education, "Last year alone, the Act was underfunded by $7.5 billion. Underfunding by such a drastic amount undermines not only successful implementation, but the very spirit of the law" (Kennedy et al., 2004, n.p.). Since that time, the federal budget for education has continued to be severely cut. In 2006, Congress could not agree on the FY2007 Education budget; in February 2007, it passed a Continuing Resolution that merely retained education funding at the 2006 levels, with specific education appropriations being made at the department level.

Unintended Consequences

We should assume that any federal law that imposes requirements on local school districts is intended to be in the best interests of children and our country's future. Because those who draft the legislation are convinced of the reasonableness of a law, sometimes they cannot critically analyze its possible outcomes beyond intended positive goals. But when the federal or state government enacts education legislation that blankets all students and schools, all stakeholders must consider the outcomes of that legislation, including possible unintended consequences that may cause harm. In this section, we focus only on NCLB and its unintended consequences because NCLB in particular has created problems for local districts and schools.

Opinions on the impact of NCLB vary greatly. On one extreme are those who say the act is a political imposition that excludes educational stakeholders and experts. An opinion poll released in December 2003 found that nearly half of school principals and superintendents view NCLB federal legislation as politically motivated or aimed at undermining public schools (Farkas, Johnson, & Duffett, 2003). On the other extreme are those who argue that NCLB is a reasonable federal response to the inability of states and local school districts to provide appropriate education. Ross Weiner told the NCLB Task Force of the National Conference of State Legislators: "previously low-performing schools were not expected to teach as many students to proficiency as other schools, so their goals were adjusted downward accordingly. In far too many schools and communities, state accountability systems failed to set off alarms, even as the schools failed to educate most of their poor, minority, limited-English proficient, and disabled students" (Weiner, 2004, n.p.).

We believe there are many problems associated with NCLB, a chief one being its assessment system. One serious concern about this system relates to its narrow definition of reading and writing as pencil and paper activities measured through multiple-choice tests and inauthentic writing tasks. Today's teenagers live in a digital environment completely ignored by NCLB. According to research conducted by the Pew Internet and American Life Project (Fox & Madden, 2006), 87 percent of twelve- to seventeen-year-olds go online, 81 percent play online games, 75 percent send instant messages, 57 percent do research for school, 51 percent download music, and 49 percent have broadband Internet access at home. Amazingly, fully half of all twelve- to seventeen-year-olds have developed online content; for example, they have created a blog; designed a personal webpage; collaborated on a webpage for school with a friend or for an organization; shared original content such as artwork, photos, stories or videos online; or remixed content found online into a new creation (Lenhart & Madden, 2005). This disconnect from "competency" as defined by NCLB and what secondary students actually read and write is reinforced by the lack of evidence that secondary schools are graduating better citizens, college students, or workers. To date, the only evidence that achievement has improved comes from increases in the competency test scores themselves (Wood, 2004).

Even if one is to accept the narrow view of literacy embodied in NCLB, the current standard of bringing all children in all schools to proficiency level is unrealistic. Linn et al. (2002) argue that the goal of 100 percent proficiency is unattainable. A gain in proficiency of 1 percent per year was the original goal set by the House and Senate, but it was abandoned in favor of allowing states to set competency levels. Such a gain is probably not attainable on any valid measure of reading achievement, and, even if it were, no state would reach the 100 percent goal by 2014. Setting benchmark standards that must be reached periodically makes matters worse. As the AYP standards bar rises from year to year, more schools will be labeled as needing improvement. According to the NEA (January, 2006), studies in eleven states project, by the target year 2014, that from 75 to 99 percent of all schools will fail to meet AYP. For accountability systems to be effective, they must include achievable goals; unrealistic expectations are more likely to demoralize than inspire teachers (Linn, 2003).

Added to the problems related to AYP, states are given the responsibility of setting the standards and determining how they are to be measured. Test scores are placed above all other learning objectives, and the pressure to have schools meet AYP goals is immense. Some states have demonstrated that more of their schools are meeting AYP by modifying their own assessments. For instance, test cutoffs for "proficiency"' have been lowered; in other cases, tests have been revised to produce higher scores. As a result, the standards, taken as a whole, are essentially arbitrary. The NEA (January, 2006) notes how these modifications result in a dilemma for districts and confusion for parents: "For the second year in a row, many states amended their Title I accountability plans and implemented changes making it statistically easier to make AYP" (para. 5).

In spite of what appear to be attempts to "game the system," the number of schools failing to make AYP continues to rise. Many schools given high ratings on the state accountability measures failed AYP. For example, in Florida, 827 schools received an "A" rating according to state standards but failed to meet AYP goals. There are many reasons for this high level of failure, including the requirement that an increasingly larger percentage of students in each category pass the state assessment. Also, specified percentages of students in each grade take the assessments, which competes with parents (and students) who deliberately stay home on test day, as well as some reported anecdotal incidents of administrators advising students who are expected to fail to remain home on the day of the test. The NEA (January, 2006) concludes, "the picture presented so far by NCLB's system of test results and ratings is complex, muddled, and often misleading" (para. 1).

Paradoxically, the law that contains the phrase "scientifically based research" 111 times (Linn et al., 2002) mandates an assessment model that has no research base at all (Sternberg, 2004). As a result, states and local school districts must operate in an environment of high-stakes accountability that is essentially unpredictable. Equally troubling is Sunderman's (2006) observation that variations across states resulting from state-initiated policy changes limit the usefulness of any national data obtained from the NCLB legislation.

The problems associated with variability across states also extend to the issue of teacher quality. Despite the use of the term *highly qualified teacher* (HQT), NCLB does not distinguish between minimally and highly qualified teachers. It also demands a rapid implementation schedule and limited resources for teachers to meet HQT standards, and each state is able to define its own High Objective Uniform State Standard of Evaluation. There are alternative routes to teaching. In some instances, candidates only have to pass a computer-based test to demonstrate subject-matter knowledge. Most alternative routes require no classroom experience, such as student teaching, and no track record of success prior to certification. "This means that a novice teacher who has just a few weeks of training and no track record of success would be placed in the same *highly qualified* category as an accomplished teacher, like those certified by the National Board for Professional Teaching Standards (NBPTS)" (Berry, 2002, n.p.). These alternative routes to teacher certification have arguably trivialized the profession. No other profession would even consider labeling professionals "highly qualified" without a demonstration of necessary knowledge and proof that they can apply that knowledge effectively and in the best interest of their clients (Berry, 2002).

Without intention, legislation often privileges one group over another. For instance, a recent study from the Harvard Civil Rights Project found that predominantly white districts have been able to negotiate changes in NCLB and thus avoid penalties; districts serving blacks and other minorities have been less successful (Sunderman, 2006). The Supplemental Educational Services feature of NCLB that provides for tutoring, primarily by large private tutoring companies, is another example. In wealthier districts, parents are more likely to be informed about this option, can complete the application process, and can make arrangements for their children to attend tutoring sessions. Many districts with large concentrations of poor minority students have been less successful in gaining student participation, even with some of these districts now obtaining permission to do the tutoring rather than hiring a private firm. A study from Novak and Fuller (2003) of the Policy Analysis for California suggests that, because of its requirement to evaluate school progress on the basis of demographic subgroups, the law may disproportionately penalize schools with diverse student populations.

The National Center for Fair & Open Testing (FairTest) argues that standardized tests cause the most damage to high-poverty schools because those schools are the ones that most need to improve scores. According to FairTest's president, Monty Neil, "What happens with schools serving low income kids is they're supposed to make a huge amount of progress very quickly and they don't have the resources to do that job. They serve very needy children whose needs extend beyond anything a school can do. And so schools are going to get rather desperate to try to get the test scores up and they're going to do it by very narrow teaching-to-the-test. It won't work but that's what many schools are likely to do" (as cited by Myint, 2002, n.p.). This contention is supported by the Center on Education Policy's 2005 survey of those states that required a specific number of minutes in reading and math instruction. The Center found that these states had reduced the amount of time in social studies, science, art or music, and physical education by 27, 22, 20, and 10 percent, respectively (Center on Education Policy, 2005). A report based on extensive interviews in Native American communities observes that the NCLB regulations "do not fit or respond to the unique situations of Native communities and schools" (National Indian Education Association, 2005, p. 6).

Fallout from NCLB also includes diminishing opportunities to foster creativity. The increasingly massive and far-reaching use of conventional standardized tests is one of the most effective, if unintentional, vehicles this country has created for suppressing creativity (Sternberg, 2006). Because standardized tests are confined to multiple-choice questions, students develop the habit of looking for the "right" answer rather than thinking about multiple possibilities. With content knowledge prized over creative thinking, what students know becomes more important than what they can do with it. The importance of the innovative application of knowledge to real-world problem-solving contexts is lost. At a time in history when higher-order thinking skills are crucial, our schools have been reduced to preparation centers for low-level multiple-choice exams (Sternberg, 2004).

The loss of creativity in the classroom and diminution of teachers as professionals becomes even more evident in the wake of the Reading First scandals that have recently emerged. Reading First, a program funded through NCLB, awarded monies to states (and selected school districts) to implement scientifically based reading programs in schools. As NCLB has unfolded, questions have arisen about some of the relationships between the Education Department and publishers, professional developers, and awards granted (Lewis, 2007). The Education Department Education Inspector General's (IG) Office (USDOE, Office of the Inspector General, 2006) released one report about these relationships on September 22, 2006, and others have been released since then. The initial IG report on Reading First outlined unethical actions by several individuals who violated the intent and spirit of the Reading First statute in an ongoing and systematic manner. The IG's report directly quotes individual communications to establish that there was a plan to direct the outcomes of independent panels, stack those panels with those who already had formed a bias, and promote specific reading programs while eliminating others (IRA, 2006, para. 2–3).

Just recently, IRA's Board of Directors passed a position statement on Reading First (IRA responds to report on Reading First, 2006). While commending the teachers and others who have worked diligently to provide for the literacy needs of children, the paper opens with this strong admonishment:

> The Board of Directors of the International Reading Association (IRA) deplores the intentional mismanagement that occurred in the administration of the Reading First program by the U.S. Department of Education as detailed in the Final Inspection Report issued by the Office of the Inspector General. It is essential that all laws and regulations be closely adhered to in the administration of this program in order to implement it successfully, to protect its integrity among educators, and to ensure its continued public support. (para. 1)

The IG's report was supported by the GAO in March 2007, which released its own report that found that "Education Department officials and their contractors appear to have improperly backed certain types of instruction in administering a $1 billion-a-year reading program (Zuckerbrod, 2007, para. 1).

Teacher attrition may also be exacerbated by NCLB. The problem is more severe in poor and rural schools (National Indian Education Association, 2005). Morale is generally cited as a factor that affects teacher retention. According to a report from the Alliance for Excellent Education (2004), 1,000 teachers *a day*, excluding retirees, leave the profession and another 1,000 transfer to other schools. The cost is staggering: an estimated $2.2 billion for teacher dropouts and $2.7 billion for teacher transfers. New York City, for example, had 3,567 "regular" teachers leave in 2004, 936 more than the year before, and 1,100 above the previous three-year average. As Winerip (2005) notes, "these are not retirees or troubled teachers—they're certified teachers in good standing" (n.p.). A study conducted by the IRA (Mixed reactions to NCLB, 2005) found that slightly more than half of the 1,500 respondents surveyed believed that the accountability provisions of NCLB were appropriate, and 77.9 percent of the respondents agreed or strongly agreed that "children's reading achievement will improve when research-backed curriculum and instruction are fully implemented" (p. 1). But an alarming 78 percent reported that teacher morale had not improved as a result of NCLB. Richard Ingersoll (2004), author of *Who Controls Teachers' Work? Power and Accountability in America's Schools*, found that a lack of faculty influence over issues such as curriculum and discipline is leading ever increasing numbers of educators to leave the profession. He cautions, "Teachers by and large have very little input into and control over the key decisions that affect their jobs and workplaces. If NCLB simply increases the degree to which teachers are held accountable, without also increasing the resources and authority they need, this act may backfire. . . . Accountability and authority must go hand in hand" (University of Pennsylvania, 2004, n.p.).

The demoralizing effects of NCLB extend to students as well. Demands that ELLs and special education students be held to the same standards as all students are particularly unfair (Meier & Wood, 2004). But there appears to be widespread apprehension on the part of many children in high-stakes testing environments. In a particularly poignant study, children in grades 3–6 were asked to draw a picture about their experiences the day after completing their tests and then explain their pictures in writing (Triplett & Barksdale, 2005). Results clearly reflected high levels of nervousness, worry, and anxiety. In another study, sixth-grade students asked to rate twenty stressful life events only reported losing a parent or going blind as more stressful than being retained a grade in school. When the study was replicated in 2001, fear of retention had jumped to number one (Jimerson & Kaufman, 2003).

High schools are held accountable for graduation rates as part of setting AYP goals (USDOE, 2002). Many believe that the need for more students to achieve AYP has increased the dropout rate as well as the time it is taking students to graduate from high school. One problem is the lack of a set standard for calculating graduation rates; different states use different formulas. The Urban Institute and Harvard Civil Rights Project suggests an unintended consequence of this situation. In their view, "the need to show adequate yearly progress (AYP) in test scores creates a powerful incentive to eliminate low-performing students—schools face stiff penalties when they fall short. By eliminating low-performing students, test scores can increase dramatically without investing a dime in educational improvements!" (Orfield, Losen, Wald, & Swanson, 2004, n.p.). Although they could not offer hard data, they quote narratives from students who dropped out or felt "pushed out" from school. The researchers conclude that minority students across the nation are often administratively disenrolled for "lack of interest" when their tests scores are not up to snuff.

Advocating for Change

Although most of the attention of educators is currently on NCLB and elementary-level education, the need for advocacy for secondary schools, teachers, and students is clear. Although we often think of advocacy as arguing against something, it is actually defined as, "The act of arguing in favor of something, such as a cause, idea, or policy" (*The American Heritage College Dictionary*, 1993, p. 13). As we examine recent federal or state education legislation that impacts middle and secondary schools, we might be motivated to reverse unintended consequences through individual or group advocacy.

The history of the civil rights movement in the United States illustrates how a single individual can cause a groundswell of advocacy that produces landmark change. In the early 1950s, Reverend Joseph De Laine fought to secure a school bus for African American children of Clarendon County, South Carolina, including for his teenage son Joseph, who had to walk up to nine miles each way to their all-black school. The bus was denied. As a result, Reverend De Laine persuaded black parents to participate in *Briggs v. Elliott*, a 1954 lawsuit that became the first of five cases in *Brown v. Board of Education.*

A more recent example of the far-reaching effects of one individual's advocacy occurred in *Abbott v. Burke*, a case in New Jersey that the *New York Times* suggested "may be the most significant education case since the Supreme Court's desegregation ruling nearly 50 years ago." This case concerned the unfairness of local property taxes as the basis for funding schools. Kenneth Robinson was a student in Jersey City, New Jersey; his mother sued Governor William T. Cahill on the grounds that he wasn't enforcing the constitutional mandate of "thorough and efficient" education for all. The New Jersey Supreme Court agreed, but nothing changed, and the disparities between rich and poor schools persisted. The case, originally *Robinson vs. Cahill* but renamed *Abbott vs. Burke*, continued and resulted in more court orders, including rulings for school construction, full-day kindergarten, and a massive program of preschooling city children starting at age three (Mickle, 1973).

Effective advocacy also occurs outside the courts. Coalitions of individuals who share common concerns can work together to promote a cause, increase public awareness, and modify, support, or defeat proposed legislation. The Committee for Education Funding, for instance, is a nonpartisan group of more than 100 organizations representing diverse stakeholders. It focuses on federal policy, especially on funding issues, and the Committee works collaboratively for the good of all, allowing individual priorities to take a back seat to the fair financial treatment of all members. The Alliance for Excellent Education, another national coalition, writes position papers and works with legislators to draft bills, especially pertaining to middle and high school education, that are mutually beneficial (Lewis, Jongsma, & Berger, 2005).

On January 10, 2006, a coalition of more than forty organizations launched the "Campaign for the Education of the Whole Child" in Massachusetts. At its press conference, the group released a report that called for a change in the state's approach to school reform efforts, noting, "Unfortunately, current policies are pressuring educators into teaching the test instead of educating the whole child" (FairTest, 2006).

The New Jersey Reading Association, an affiliate of the IRA, has formed an Advisory Board for its Legislation Committee, comprised of members from the state legislature, State Board of Education, Department of Education, business, the media, and the Parents and Teachers Association. Together they draft position papers, mission statements, and plan conferences. Their chorus of voices has a wider range than the education community singing solo (Lewis et al., 2005). They have visited legislative offices, awarded state officials supportive of the association's goals, written letters to editors, organized press releases, and given testimony for and against pending legislation. Their work has made them visible; policymakers seeking information relating to literacy call on them for advice.

Influencing Legislation

Stakeholders can engage in advocacy at any time. Within the education community, advocacy tends to occur when legislation is being drafted, when regulations are being developed, and when unintended consequences become apparent. Advocates may frequent their state legislature website or consult with their state education association to learn of pending education legislation. The legislative committee considering the bill may hold hearings, and advocates can testify to support, oppose, or recommend changes to the bill before it is finalized.

Once a bill is signed into law, rulemaking begins to define how the law is implemented. There are public meetings, opportunities to offer written and oral testimony, and other ways to influence the outcome. Sometimes changes in federal law resulting from reauthorization can increase federal regulation. A case in point is IDEA. Earlier in this chapter, we described changes to this law resulting from input of stakeholders.

Even after regulations are written into the law, they can change, sometimes as the result of public outcry. NCLB offers several examples. Originally, this law stipulated a single statewide accountability system, and no allowances were made for children with severe cognitive disabilities; all children were to reach the same state standard. States now have some flexibility in determining reasonable expectations for these children. Also, all Limited English Proficiency (LEP) students were originally required to take the same assessment as other students, and their scores were to be counted in determining whether a school had made AYP. In 2004, Secretary of Education Rod Paige revised this requirement to give states the option to exempt any newly arrived immigrant student who had been in the United States for less than one year from taking the reading test. States were also given the option to count in the LEP subgroup, for AYP purposes, *exited* LEP students for as many as two years after they become proficient in English. Under a pilot program begun in 2005, as many as ten states were to be permitted to use growth models to evaluate school and school district progress in making AYP in the 2006 school year, charting how individual students are doing on standardized tests from one year to the next. In addition, teachers in rural schools were given three years to meet HQT requirements, and science teachers were given a broader scope for teaching,

State legislators can also call for changes in federal legislation, as occurred in Minnesota's Senate in March 2005, when Senator John Hottinger told the legislature that "the Federal government has taken a very improper and domineering role on this education mandate, and it seems as though NCLB is working against achievement gains for our kids instead of for them." He called for change. This action was similar to that of at least twenty-five other states whose legislators had called for more funding and greater flexibility in NCLB (Hottinger, 2005).

Becoming an Advocate

Although this brief section is not a complete primer for becoming an education advocate, we offer a few principles for effective advocacy. Most important, note that, when a systematic problem-solving approach is used for advocacy, it is more likely to succeed.

To begin your advocacy, conduct a self-assessment and do some homework. Personal likes or dislikes about an education policy are not enough to convince others that your reasoning is sound. Analyze and assess the key issues for you, your students, and your school. Ask yourself: What is the most important issue for you? Why? What is your point of view? What research supports your thinking? What research contradicts it?

After researching your issue, it is important to clarify what you want. Perhaps you would like class size to be reduced. Develop a reasonable way in which this might be accomplished so that you are part of the solution, not part of the problem. Be realistic in your vision, and address the concerns of your opposition as thoughtfully as you can so as to deflate their arguments. You also need to be clear about who can give you what you want so that you target the appropriate audience for action. Possibilities are your local or state school board, your state legislature, a parents group, the federal government, and your local or state business community.

Once you are clear on the issue and who needs to hear it, tell your story to others who might share your concerns. Evaluate how they respond to your message, what questions are asked for which you have few answers, and what points need additional clarification. From this process, you should be able to identify individuals or groups who might be willing to work with you on this advocacy initiative. There are many stakeholders in education; in fact, it is difficult to think of any individual or group who doesn't have a vested interest in the education of youth in the United States. What varies is how they see school issues being resolved; ideas range from putting more money into school resources that directly touch children in classrooms, more teacher-proof materials for instruction, or privatizing education through a voucher system. As an advocate, you want to identify stakeholders who share your view and to form a coalition with them.

If you know of pending legislation on your issue, begin your advocacy work as soon as you can. An effective advocate recognizes that the earlier in the lawmaking process that ideas and solutions are put forth, the greater is the likelihood of being considered. At the early stages, you have fewer legislators "standing their ground" on some point; give-and-take is understood in this early stage (Lewis & Cassidy, 2006).

Bear in mind the challenges and risks to collaboration. You might have to compromise, but be careful not to give away what is really important to you. Stay on point; groups can easily drift if the leader doesn't keep members focused. Involve partners only to the extent that they are willing to be involved. Some members of your coalition may be comfortable writing letters; others want to meet with policymakers; a few might prefer to talk to parents or work behind the scenes on preparing materials for distribution. Use each partner's talents so that each feels commitment to the effort.

If you are working with others, develop your advocacy plan collaboratively: setting your goals, deciding who needs to hear your message, and determining from whom the message should come. If you want to reach multiple groups, each group might need to hear from a different member of your partnership. A Chamber of Commerce, for instance, might be more accepting of your ideas if they come from someone in business, whereas the school board might be better listeners if a parent, perhaps the president of a Parent Teachers Association or Parent Teachers Organization, spoke to them. For obvious reasons, legislators listen best when they hear from voters from their own districts.

Conclusions

In this chapter, we have provided an overview of federal legislation that directly affects schools and school districts and, more important, students and teachers throughout the United States. There is grave concern among many educators about the negative consequences and ultimate outcomes of the mandates from Washington. We have provided an overview of many, but certainly not all, of the unintended consequences of the most enveloping of these laws, NCLB.

It has not been our intention to suggest that schooling in the United States is without its problems. But all education stakeholders must engage in open, critical dialogue that considers whether current federal educational initiatives can solve these problems. We suggest that, at the very least, considerable revision to the federal legislation is necessary if NCLB is to achieve its goals. To this end, we have tried to provide insight into how concerned citizens can influence legislative and regulatory processes. Although U.S. educators have not, historically, been effective political advocates, we hope that this chapter is a small step in changing that tradition.

References

Alliance for Excellent Education. (2004). *Tapping the potential: Retaining and developing high-quality new teachers.* Retrieved February 15, 2005, from http://www.all4ed.org/publications/Tapping ThePotential/TappingThePotential.pdf

Allington, R. L. (2002). Troubling times: A short historical perspective. In R. L. Allington (Ed.), *Big brother and the national reading curriculum: How ideology trumped evidence* (pp. 3–46). Portsmouth, NH: Heinemann.

The American Heritage College Dictionary. (3rd ed.). (1993). Boston: Houghton Mifflin.

Berry, B. (2002). *What it means to be a "highly qualified teacher."* Retrieved February 8, 2006, from http://wwwteacherleaders.org/ Resources/berryHQT.html. Now available at http://www.teaching quality.org/pdfs/definingHQ.pdf

Center on Education Policy. (2005, July). *NCLB: Narrowing the curriculum?* (NCLB Policy Brief 3). Retrieved February 10, 2006, from http://www.ctredpol.org/nclb/NCLBPolicyBriefs2005/CEPPB3web. pdf. Now available at http://www.cep-dc.org/_data/n_0001/ resources/live/CEPPB3web.pdf

Diamond, J. (1999). *Guns, germs, and steel: The fates of human societies.* New York: W.W. Norton.

Education Law Center. (n.d.). *About Abbott v. Burke.* Retrieved February 21, 2006, from http://www.edlawcenter.org/ELCPublic/ AbbottvBurke/AboutAbbott.htm

FairTest: The National Center for Fair and Open Testing. (2006, January). *Alliance for the education of the whole child.* Retrieved February 6, 2006, from http://www.fairtest.org/Whole%20Child/ Alliance%20PR.html

Farkas, S., Johnson, J., & Duffett, A. (2003). *Rolling up their sleeves: Superintendents and principals talk about what's needed to fix public schools.* New York: Public Agenda.

Foote, M., Linder, P., Sampson, M. B., & Szabo, S. *Stepping forward together: Voicing the concerns of teacher educators through practical applications and collaborative actions. The twenty-eighth yearbook of the* College Reading Association. Commerce: Texas A&M University.

Fox, S., & Madden, M. (2006). *Generations online.* Retrieved March 9, 2006, from http://www.pewinternet.org/PPF/r/170/report_display.asp

Hottinger, J. C. (2005, March 23). *NCLB changes moving forward in senate* [News Release]. Retrieved January 31, 2006, from http://www.senate.leg.state.mn.us/caucus/dem/membernews/2005/dist23/20050323_Hottinger_NCLB_in_Senate.htm

International Reading Association. (2006, November). *Position statement on Reading First.* Retrieved April 2, 2007, from http://www.reading.org/downloads/positions/ps0611_reading_first.pdf

IRA responds to report on Reading First. (2006). *Reading Today, 24*(2), 1. Retrieved February 22, 2007, from http://blog.reading.org/archives/oo2015.html. Now available at http://www.reading.org/publications/reading_today/samples/RTY-0610-readingfirst.html

Jimerson, S. R., & Kaufman, A. M. (2003). Reading, writing, and retention: A primer on grade retention research. *The Reading Teacher, 56,* 622–35.

Kennedy, E. M., et al. (2004, January 8). *Letter to Secretary Paige on the Bush Administration's failure to properly implement No Child Left Behind.* Retrieved March 1, 2006, from http://edworkforce.house.gov/democrats/paigenclbletter.html

Lenhart, A., & Madden, M. (2005, November). *Teen content creators and consumers.* Retrieved March 9, 2006, from http://www.pewinternet.org/pdfs/PIP_Teens_Content_Creation.pdf

Lewis, J. (2007). Federal and International Reading Association policies and initiatives for adolescent literacy. In J. Lewis & G. Moorman (Eds.), *Adolescent literacy instruction: Policies and promising practices* (pp. 35–36). Newark, DE: International Reading Association.

Lewis, J., & Cassidy, J. (2006). Advocating for effective federal literacy laws. In P. E. Linder, M. B. Sampson, J. R. Dugan, & B. A. Brancato (Eds.), *Building bridges to literacy: The twenty-seventh yearbook of the College Reading Association* (pp. 71–74). Commerce: Texas A&M University.

Lewis, J., Jongsma, K. S., & Berger, A. (2005). *Educators on the frontline: Advocacy strategies for your classroom, your school, and your profession.* Newark, DE: International Reading Association.

Linn, R. (2003). Accountability: Responsibility and reasonable expectations. *Educational Researcher, 32*(7), 3–13.

Linn, R. L., Baker, E. L., & Betebenner, D. W. (2002). Accountability systems: Implications of requirements of the No Child Left Behind Act of 2001. *Educational Researcher, 31*(6), 3–16.

May, M. (2003, April 8). Report critical of charter schools: Uncredentialed teachers, funding shortage, racial isolation cited. *San Francisco Chronicle,* A-15. Retrieved February 26, 2006, from http://sfgate.com/cgi-bin/article.cgi?f=/c/a/2003/04/08/BA199363. DTL

Meier, D., & Wood, G. (Ed.). (2004). *Many children left behind: How the No Child Left Behind Act is damaging our children and our schools.* Boston: Beacon Press.

Mickle, P. (1973). Sharing the wealth in school. *The Trentonian.* Retrieved Feb 26, 2006, from http://www.capitalcentury.com/1973. html

Mixed reactions to NCLB. (2005). *Reading Today, 22*(4), 1, 4.

Mock, D. R. (2007). The history and current trends surrounding high-incidence disabilities. In J. P. Stichter, M. A. Conroy, & J. M. Kauffman, *An introduction to students with high-incidence disabilities.* Upper Saddle River, NJ: Prentice Hall.

Myint, B. (2002, June). Testing the limits of No Child Left Behind. *Education Update Online.* Retrieved February 22, 2006, from http://www.educationupdate.com/archives/2002/jun02/htmls/spot_testing.html

National Education Association (NEA). (n.d.). *Teacher and paraprofessional quality.* Retrieved February 23, 2006, from http://www.nea.org/esea/eseateach.html

National Education Association. (NEA). (2005, March 20). *NCLB Testing Results Offer 'Complex, Muddled' Picture: Emerging Trends Under the Law's Annual Rating System.* Retrieved February 23, 2006, from http://www.nea.org/esea/ayptrends0305.html

National Education Association. (NEA). (2006, January). *More schools are failing NCLB law's "adequate yearly progress" requirements.*

Retrieved February 24, 2006, from http://www.nea.org/esea/ayptrends0106.html

National Indian Education Association. (NIEA). (2005). *Preliminary report on No Child Left Behind in Indian country*. Retrieved March 9, 2006, from http://www.niea.org/sa/uploads/policyissues/29.23.NIEANCLBreport_final2.pdf

Novak, J. R., & Fuller, B. (2003, December). *Penalizing diverse schools? Similar test scores, but different students, bring federal sanctions* (Policy Brief 03-4). Berkeley: Policy Analysis for California Education (PACE). Retrieved March 4, 2006, from http://pace.berkeley.edu/policy_brief_03-4_Pen.Div.pdf. Now available at http://pace.berkeley.edu/reports/PB.03-4.pdf

Orfield, G., Losen, D., Wald, J., &. Swanson, C. B. (2004, February 25). *Losing our future: How minority youth are being left behind by the graduation rate crisis*. Retrieved February 23, 2006, from http://www.urban.org/url.cfm?ID=410936

Robelen, E. W. (2005, April 13). 40 years after ESEA, federal role in schools is broader than ever. *Education Week*, pp. 1, 42.

Shannon, P. (2001). Turn, turn, turn: Language education, politics, and freedom at the turn of three centuries. In P. Shannon (Ed.), *Becoming political, too: New readings and writings on the politics of literacy education* (pp. 10–30). Portsmouth, NH: Heinemann.

Smith, N. B. (1965). *American reading instruction: Its development and its significance in gaining a perspective on current practices in reading*. Newark, DE: International Reading Association.

Sternberg, R. J. (2004, October 27). Good intentions, bad results: A dozen reasons why the No Child Left Behind Act is failing our schools. *Education Week*. Retrieved March 9, 2006, from http://www.edweek.org/ew/articles/2004/10/27/09sternberg.h24.html?querystring=good%20intentions,%20bad%20results&levelId=1000

Sternberg, R. J. (2006, February 22). Creativity is a habit. *Education Week*. Retrieved February 26, 2006, from http://www.edweek.org/ew/articles/2006/02/22/24sternberg.h25.html

Sunderman, G. L. (2006). *The unraveling of No Child Left Behind: How negotiated changes transform the law*. Cambridge, MA: The Civil Rights Project at Harvard University. Retrieved January 17, 2006, from http://www.civilrightsproject.harvard.edu/research/esea/NCLB_Unravel.pdf

Triplett, C., & Barksdale, M.A. (2005). Third through sixth graders' perceptions of high-stakes testing. *Journal of Literacy Research, 37,* 237–60.

University of Pennsylvania, Office of University Communications. (2004, January 14). *No Child Left Behind at the two-year mark.* Retrieved January 16, 2006, from http://www.upenn.edu/pennnews/ sourcesheet.php?id=77&print=1

U.S. Department of Education. (2004, June 18). *No Child Left Behind: Transforming America's high schools.* Retrieved February 23, 2006, from http://www.ed.gov/about/offices/list/ovae/pi/hsinit/papers/ nclb.pdf

U.S. Department of Education, Office of Elementary and Secondary Education. (2002). *No Child Left Behind: A desktop reference.* Retrieved February 23, 2006, from http://www.ed.gov/admins/lead/ account/nclbreference/reference.pdf

U.S. Department of Education, Office of the Inspector General. (2006). *The Reading First Program's grant application process.* Retrieved January 31, 2007, from http://www.ed.gov/about/offices/list/oig/ aireports/i13f0017.pdf

U.S. General Accounting Office. (2004, May). *Unfunded mandates: Analysis of Reform Act coverage* (pp. 23–24). Retrieved February 6, 2006, from http://www.gao.gov/new.items/d04637.pdf#search= Unfunded%20mandates%3A%20Analysis%20of%20Reform%20Act %20coverage

Werts, M. G., Tompkins, J. R., & Culatta, R. A. (2007). *Fundamentals of special education: What every teacher needs to know* (3rd ed.). Upper Saddle River, NJ: Prentice Hall.

Wiener, R. (2004, April 30). *Statement of Ross Wiener, Policy Director, The Education Trust, before the National Conference of State Legislatures Task Force on No Child Left Behind.* Retrieved January 15, 2006, from http://www2.edtrust.org/EdTrust/Press+Room/ ross+ncsl.htm

Winerip, M. (2005, June 1). New York's revolving door of good teachers driven out. *New York Times.* Retrieved March 1, 2006, from http://www.nytimes.com/2005/06/01/education/01education.html? ex=1275278400&en=d7aaa6922512dde6&ei=5090&partner=rss userland&emc=rss

Wood, G. (2004). A view from the field: NCLB's effects on classrooms and schools. In D. Meier & G. Wood (Eds.), *Many children left behind: How the No Child Left Behind Act is damaging our children and our schools* (pp. 33–50). Boston: Beacon Press.

Zuckerbrod, N. (2007, March 23). GAO: Reading program improperly managed. Retrieved March 24, 2007, from http://news.yahoo.com/s/ap/20070323/ap_on_go_ot/reading_program. Now available at http://www.newsvine.com/_news/2007/03/23/628309-gao-reading-program-improperly-managed

Literacy Research, Practice, and Other Never-Ending Stories

A. Jonathan Eakle
Johns Hopkins University

At about the time of the last publication of this series, Michael Ende (1979/1983) published *The Neverending Story*. The story begins when a young boy, Bastian, escapes from bullies into an archaic bookstore. There he encounters a man with a book about an adventure that never ends. Bastian steals the book, skips school, and begins reading it. As the story advances, he is magically engaged, becoming a main player in a text where memories are lost to a great "Nothing" (a force that threatens imagination). Bastian, a fitting name because he is the final fortification against the creeping "Nothing," confronts the force with will and imagination. And, as in many such tales, creativity triumphs and heroes are made. This brief opening of a never-ending story frames what I think is fitting for the closing pages of the present volume about literacy research and practice.

Literacies and Memories

As in heroic tales, educators and researchers often look to the past for futures and possibilities. In best cases, as did Bastian, they use imagination and memories for creative teaching practice. Comparisons of earlier books in this series about literacy research and practice with the present text underscore that memories can endure, are recycled, or fade. Smith, Carey, and Harste closed a chapter in the 1982 volume of this series with a vignette showing that memories are not simply bits of data like books on a shelf to be neatly arranged and retrieved; memories are always moving and elusive: "what happens to most of what we comprehend at a given moment loses its own distinctive features and becomes part of something else" (p. 35). Opportunities for educators to reflect and act on how readers and writers become part of "something else"—and how imaginative forces of literacy education, as in *The Neverending Story*, stand against the "Nothing"—make teachers important bastions of what is, or should be, memorable in the education of adolescents.

Coeditor Allen Berger remarked as we compiled this volume, "nothing comes from nowhere," which is shown in the introductory bookend through the histories of this collection of writings and the many influences on it. Now, in this other bookend, I turn to memories of literacies, using as catalysts the 1982 version of this book, well aware that what I write is absorbed in a continuing, never-ending story of this half-century-old series.

Enduring Memories

Theories

The earlier version of this book was published at the apex of what is known as the Cognitive Revolution, a response to Behaviorism, which, in its most radical form, rejected all internal processes of mind. The Revolution predisposed literacy education and research enormously in the 1980s, and the 1982 book offered many examples of these influences. One such influence was Developmental Theory and, under its umbrella, the recycled 1920s concepts of Vygotsky, who, rather than focusing exclusively on external behavioral matters, formulated ideas about the mind that included internal speech and zones of development. Recycled constructivist ideas endure in the thoughts and works of teachers, researchers, and teacher educators today, and those ideas reappear in the present volume. Perhaps a reason that constructivist notions endure through decades is that supporting learners with concepts and material within their range of capability is simply what good sensible teachers know to do.

The Transactional Theory of Reading (Rosenblatt, 1938) is another frame rediscovered in the 1970s and 1980s that endures

in the present volume. Instruction in reading for different purposes (e.g., reading a sonnet compared to reading a physics text)
is a notion that makes sense, especially to good secondary school
educators. These theories and practices are hinged on the belief
that literacy is an act that involves the construction of meaning
by the reader, and transactional themes are so much a part of
current thinking in literacy circles that anything to the contrary
is, at best, a distant faded memory. As literacies today are enacted in various forms, returning to Rosenblatt's theories especially reminds us that it is what teachers, researchers, policymakers,
and, perhaps most important, students choose to construct as
meaningful that makes literacies and schooling memorable, or
not.

Progress and Achievement

Another driving force that endures in literacy education is the
Modern Ideal of Progress. In one sense, this ideal can be understood through the work of John Dewey, whose progressive education reform movements during the early part of the last century
are often equated with recent liberal pedagogies. Although mentioned only briefly in the present volume, Dewey's inquiry-based
stance on learning underpins much of what occurs today in progressive classroom practices and research.

On the other hand, notions of progress in education have
taken on new meanings during recent years, as suggested throughout the present book. Currently, public school teachers and administrators are most concerned with the measurements and
surveillance of their achievements, marked in adequate yearly
progress (AYP) reports, adherence to various standards, school
funding, and rules of the state. Although few educators would
argue that any child, regardless of background or experience,
should be left behind others, if we listen closely to some of our
best and most experienced teachers and literacy researchers, something is sorely wrong in these present accounting practices. Today, the phrase "teaching to the test" rolls regularly and much
too smoothly from the tongues of many educators.

Out of developmental notions of progress, many of the writings in the 1982 book were based on concepts of lack: what ado-

lescent readers are developmentally capable of mastering, given proper education training and resources, but have not achieved and need to be taught. Petrosky began the 1982 volume by reviewing the 1979–1980 National Assessment of Educational Progress (NAEP) report, which was dismal. He questioned how education practices of that time could lead to adolescents accomplishing anything but the "most basic performance" (p. 16), words that echo current literacy policy debates.

At the center of these issues, Petrosky (1982) pointed out achievement gaps of students from "disadvantaged-urban communities" compared with those of other adolescents (p. 12). Allington and Mathson (this volume) relay that, after a quarter of a century, these trends and gaps endure, despite enormous federal education expenditures and pressures applied for schools to meet AYP goals. Where does the money and effort go? Why are teachers often frustrated that their adolescent students do not perform better? An enduring critical response, as Tatum (this volume) argues, is that poverty, low-quality education, community conditions, and race-based treatment are root causes for much of these enduring conditions and low literacy scores. To be sure, critical responses to achievement issues hold fast in many corners of the education community.

These issues are especially relevant in the wake of purported improprieties involving reading research, federal and commercial reading programs, and questionable education practices that are becoming visible as the present book goes to press (Grunwald, 2006). Certainly, policy, politics, commercialism, mandates, standards, and achievement tests have become, more than ever, a part of everyday life in literacy education. And perhaps this complex of forces will be the most memorable of our time. Close readings of works, such as the chapter written by Lewis and Moorman (this volume), may provide a more encouraging future for adolescent literacy education as (or if) more educators and academics advocate for literacy policy and pedagogical change.

Strategies

Research of the Cognitive Revolution provided teachers with a wide range of approaches and resources that, according to conventional wisdom, should have made a difference in adolescent literacy achievement over the past twenty-five years. In the 1982 book, a principal focus was on reading strategies. Although similar reading strategies may seem comparatively less evident in the present volume, the word *strategies* appears over 200 times in these pages; with no doubt, particular strategic methods and uses of texts very much endure in secondary schools and teacher education.

Take, for instance, the reading process strategies tabulated by Judith Langer (1982), marking off literacy domains such as background knowledge, prediction, and text organization that occur "before, during, and after reading" (p. 47), processes that were also taken up in chapters authored by Page (1982) and Tierney (1982). Furthermore, Vaughan (1982) elaborated strategic uses of SQ3R (Survey, Question, Read, Recite, Review) and its "innumerable modifications" (p. 67), Directed Reading and Thinking Activities (DRTA), and Sustained Silent Reading (SSR), which are more or less entrenched in the lexicons of many secondary school teachers.

Tierney (this volume) extends strategic learning and teaching methods considerably beyond what were and remain, in most corners of literacy education, mainstays of the Cognitive Revolution. Many good teachers agree with him: "whereas most models of strategic readers and writers emphasize mastery and independence, we see a need to emphasize inquiry-oriented learning, including *the agency of the learner as navigator, designer, collaborator, and communicator*" (p. 29, emphasis added). Readers of the present volume would do well to study Tierney's revisited strategic stance closely and to consider carefully, as Beach and O'Brien (this volume) suggest, that reading and writing strategies are not simply the stuff that fills instructional time, but are only temporal devices for skillful mastery of literacies.

Fading Memories

Indeed, some memories endure and are recycled. Others fade. Sometimes our memories of literacies are tied to particular terms, images, and concepts. For instance, in the 1982 book, "meta" processes and descriptions were fashionable. Certainly, notions of metacomprehension (or "metacognition")—the "third eye permitting readers to check information that the ideas in text make sense and are consistent with one another" (Langer, 1982, p. 44)—endure in literacy education, but such specific descriptions are largely absent in the present volume. As well, the slots and mappings of Schema Theory that carried much weight in the 1982 book have faded in the more recent text, along with names of Cognitive Revolution pioneers, such as Rummelhart, Piaget, and Ausubel.

Similarly, formulas that charted and measured text readability, as described at length by Estes (1982), and extensive foci on text structures are relatively set aside in the present volume and merely mentioned in the context of more holistic practices (e.g., by Beach and O'Brien and by Hinchman). These points signal the shift over the past quarter of a century from reading and writing as discrete and structured processes to a broader sense of what counts as literacies (Alvermann & McLean, this volume).

Of related topics, explicit references to whole-language processes have faded during recent years, even though these approaches underpinned arguments of many contributors to the 1982 volume and continue on in many exemplary literacy practices. Furthermore, issues regarding relations of reading and intelligence that appeared in the 1982 book (e.g., Johnston & Pearson) are largely absent in mainstream literacy education studies and in the present volume. Perhaps these absences are because of "political correctness," an expression that entered the popular lexicon in the 1980s. As well, eye movement studies, memory for digits, rapid naming memory, long-term memory storage, and so forth are domains that are fading in the conventional literature of literacy education and now are topics more typically taken up in other venues, such as neuroscience publications.

Palaces for Future Memories

Never-Ending Theories

In *Through the Looking Glass*, Lewis Carroll (1871/2005) wrote, "It's a poor sort of memory that only works backwards" (n. p.).

Although many past concepts and practices in secondary literacy research and education endure and some fade, the present volume clearly points out that the field is changing. In part as a reaction to agenda set forth during the Cognitive Revolution, there was a groundswell of research in the late 1980s and 1990s that pushed against dominant cognitive psychological notions. As Alvermann and McLean detail in the present volume, tied to this resistance are arguments that literacy is principally a sociocultural phenomenon. Furthermore, as many authors detail earlier in this book, the lives and literacies of adolescents today are increasingly complex.

In recent research, these complexities center on what it means for young people to use and produce texts and how this is connected with their identities, which can by no means be easily categorized, as pointed out by the authors of the present book (Alvermann & McLean; Damico, Campano, & Harste; Hinchman; Leander & Zacher; Tatum). In this vein, running through many of the previous pages are influences of pioneering thinkers of the late twentieth century, such as Bourdieu, Foucault, Giroux, and Lefebvre. An examination of the chapter by Underwood, Yoo, and Pearson (this volume) shows how contemporary thoughts about literacies are shifting and reforming particular models of research and practice. Often, contemporary approaches to literacies involve power and power relations; in many cases, issues of the 1980s, such as text structure, have given way to studies of twenty-first-century power structures. Perhaps of greatest importance in these studies is that, too often, power structures deprive students, especially those of particular language and social backgrounds, of their legitimate speaker status (Jiménez & Teague, this volume).

New Literacies

Taking a center stage in much recent literacy research are "broader" notions that connect multiple communicative forms to acts of reading and writing (Flood, Lapp, & Heath, in press; Pahl & Rowsell, 2006). Threaded through the present text are writings about the multiple literacies of space, time, and novel education practices involving, as Leander and Zacher point out,

"multivoices, multicultures, multimodalities, multisites of practice, and multiscales" (p. 161). Without doubt, "multiples" are
on the cutting edges of literacy research and practice.

A preview to some notions of "new literacies" can be found
in the 1982 book, during the erection of another signpost in the
never-ending story of literacies: The Digital Revolution. In the
earlier book, Singer, Dreher, and Kamil reviewed the evolution of
technologies and literacies, taking readers from chalk and black-
boards through Gutenberg's press and into the late 1970s–1980s
Computer Age. Key points to be remembered from their text are
references to the then novel areas of "computer-assisted instruction" and "computer-managed instruction." Furthermore, as
Early suggested in the final pages of the 1982 book, many educators viewed new technologies as a distraction and as competition
to print-based literacies. Today, although secondary school classrooms remain principally print-centric and earlier notions of what
is most valued in literacy classrooms survive, there is little doubt
that digital technologies are key in present and future literacies.
And, as authors of the present volume suggest, youth are often
much more savvy in their uses of sophisticated digital literacies
than are their elders.

Even so, the boundaries between print-based and other
literacies are blurring. Since publication of the 1982 volume of
this series, for example, Ende's (1979/1983) *The Neverending
Story* has been transformed into a trilogy of movies, computer
games, a television series, and a line of commercial merchandise.
Furthermore, earlier in this volume, Leu and his colleagues direct
readers off the printed page and into the Internet cybersphere to
examine digital case study videos about literacy. As well, opening this section is a classic "looking-glass" quote taken from an
online digital text that can be downloaded into handheld digital
communication devices and read virtually anywhere. Mass information can be retrieved through wireless networks and jump-
driven into miniature memory systems that make memory for
discrete facts and details seem, at best, part of a cluttered literacy
past. These issues point to shifting roles of teachers and their
importance in guiding students in creative uses of literacies, as
well as examining social, economic, and political assumptions
and consequences of particular texts. When the present book is

reviewed in the future, it may be found that practicing what we now call "new literacies" will have led students, teachers, and researchers, like Bastian, into novel, engaging streams of never-ending stories.

References

Carroll, L. (2005). *Through the looking glass*. [Project Gutenberg Ebook, online]. Retrieved November 17, 2006, from http://www.gutenberg. org/dirs/etext91/lglass19.txt

Early, M. (1982). Epilogue: New students, new teachers, new demands. In A. Berger & H. A. Robinson (Eds.), *Secondary school reading: What research reveals for classroom practice* (pp. 193–202). Urbana, IL: National Council of Teachers of English, National Conference on Research in English, and ERIC Clearinghouse on Reading and Communication Skills.

Ende, M. (1983). *The neverending story* (R. Manheim, Trans.). Garden City, NY: Doubleday. (Original work published 1979)

Estes, T. H. (1982). The nature and structure of text. In A. Berger & H. A. Robinson (Eds.), *Secondary school reading: What research reveals for classroom practice* (pp. 85–96). Urbana, IL: National Council of Teachers of English, National Conference on Research in English, and ERIC Clearinghouse on Reading and Communication Skills.

Flood, J., Lapp, D., & Heath, S. B. (Eds.). (in press). *Handbook of research on teaching literacy through the communicative and visual arts* (Vol. 2). Mahwah, NJ: Erlbaum.

Grunwald, M. (2006, October 1). Billions for an inside game of reading. *The Washington Post*. Retrieved November 17, 2006, from http://www.washingtonpost.com/wp-dyn/content/article/2006/09/29/AR2006092901333.html

Johnston, P., & Pearson, P. D. (1982). Assessment: Responses to exposition. In A. Berger & H. A. Robinson (Eds.), *Secondary school reading: What research reveals for classroom practice* (pp. 127–141). Urbana, IL: National Council of Teachers of English, National Conference on Research in English, and ERIC Clearinghouse on Reading and Communication Skills.

Langer, J. A. (1982). The reading process. In A. Berger & H. A. Robinson (Eds.), *Secondary school reading: What research reveals for class-*

room practice (pp. 39–51). Urbana, IL: National Council of Teachers of English, National Conference on Research in English, and ERIC Clearinghouse on Reading and Communication Skills.

Page, W. D. (1982). Readers' strategies. In A. Berger & H. A. Robinson (Eds.), *Secondary school reading: What research reveals for classroom practice* (pp. 53–66). Urbana, IL: National Council of Teachers of English, National Conference on Research in English, and ERIC Clearinghouse on Reading and Communication Skills.

Pahl, K., & Rowsell, J. (Eds.). (2006). *Travel notes from the new literacy studies: Instances of practice.* Clevedon, UK: Multilingual Matters.

Petrosky, A. R. (1982). Reading achievement. In A. Berger & H. A. Robinson (Eds.), *Secondary school reading: What research reveals for classroom practice* (pp. 7–19). Urbana, IL: National Council of Teachers of English, National Conference on Research in English, and ERIC Clearinghouse on Reading and Communication Skills.

Rosenblatt, L. M. (1938). *Literature as exploration.* New York: Appleton-Century.

Singer, H., Dreher, M. J., & Kamil, M. (1982). Computer literacy. In A. Berger & H. A. Robinson (Eds.), *Secondary school reading: What research reveals for classroom practice* (pp. 173–192). Urbana, IL: National Council of Teachers of English, National Conference on Research in English, and ERIC Clearinghouse on Reading and Communication Skills.

Smith, S. L., Carey, R. F., & Harste, J. C. (1982). The contexts of reading. In A. Berger & H. A. Robinson (Eds.), *Secondary school reading: What research reveals for classroom practice* (pp. 21–37). Urbana, IL: National Council of Teachers of English, National Conference on Research in English, and ERIC Clearinghouse on Reading and Communication Skills.

Tierney, R. J. (1982). Learning from text. In A. Berger & H. A. Robinson (Eds.), *Secondary school reading: What research reveals for classroom practice* (pp. 97–110). Urbana, IL: National Council of Teachers of English, National Conference on Research in English, and ERIC Clearinghouse on Reading and Communication Skills.

Vaughan, J. L., Jr. (1982). Instructional strategies. In A. Berger & H. A. Robinson (Eds.), *Secondary school reading: What research reveals for classroom practice* (pp. 67–84). Urbana, IL: National Council of Teachers of English, National Conference on Research in English, and ERIC Clearinghouse on Reading and Communication Skills.

INDEX

EDITORS

Leslie S. Rush is assistant professor of English education at the University of Wyoming, where she teaches courses in adolescent literacy, young adult literature, and English language arts pedagogy. Her research interests include multiliteracies, critical literacy, and content area literacy. Rush taught high school English for twelve years in California, Texas, and East Africa. An active member of NCTE and its affiliate organization, the Conference on English Education, Rush has published in *Reading Research and Instruction*, *Reading Online*, and the *Journal of Literacy Research*. In addition, she serves on the editorial review board for *Reading Research Quarterly*, *Journal of Literacy Research*, and *The Qualitative Report*.

A. Jonathan Eakle is assistant professor and reading program director in the Johns Hopkins University School of Education. His research addresses multiple literacies in classrooms and out-of-school settings, digital communication, creativity, and museum literacy practices. Eakle teaches courses in cross-cultural studies and content area literacy, supervises clinical practices at Johns Hopkins, is principal investigator of literacy grants, and is an editor for literacy publications. His recent work appears in *Reading Research Quarterly*, *The Reading Teacher*, *Reading Online*, and other venues.

Allen Berger is professor emeritus and was Heckert Professor of Reading and Writing (1988–2006) at Miami University. He is the author of approximately 400 articles on literacy education and has coedited and coauthored some ten books for NCTE and IRA. He chaired NCTE's Resolutions Committee and, for seven years, edited NCTE's quarterly, *English Education.* He has chaired IRA's Studies and Research Implementation Committee, as well as IRA's Professional Standards and Ethics Committee, and served on an eight-person IRA task force to update the new *Standards for Reading Professionals* (2004) and on a newer task force to explore IRA's involvement in program accreditation. In 2005, Berger received the Laureate Award from the College Reading Association. He is currently president-elect of the Ohio Council, IRA. He is a winner of statewide literacy awards from the Ohio Council, IRA, and the Ohio Council of Teachers of English Language Arts, NCTE. Prior to teaching, Berger was a newspaper reporter in Rome, New York, and a newspaper reporter-photographer in Lynchburg, Virginia. He taught high school reading and English for five years in Utica and Rochester, New York, and has been a tenured faculty member at Southern Illinois University, the University of Alberta, the University of Pittsburgh, and Miami University. He earned his doctorate from Syracuse University under the direction of NCTE past president Margaret J. Early and studied with College Reading Association past president Leonard Braam and IRA past president William D. Sheldon. His home is in Savannah, Georgia.

CONTRIBUTORS

Richard L. Allington is professor of education at the University of Tennessee. He is a past president of IRA and the National Reading Conference and author of more than 100 articles and several books, including *What Really Matters for Struggling Readers: Designing Research-Based Interventions* and *Big Brother and the National Reading Curriculum: How Ideology Trumped Evidence*.

Donna E. Alvermann is University of Georgia-appointed distinguished research professor of language and literacy education. Formerly a classroom teacher in Texas and New York, her research focuses on content-area literacy instruction and youth-initiated forms of engagement with digital media. Her coauthored and coedited books include *Content Reading and Literacy: Succeeding in Today's Diverse Classrooms* (5th ed.); *Reconceptualizing the Literacies in Adolescents' Lives* (2nd ed.); *Bridging the Literacy Achievement Gap, Grades 4–12*; and *Adolescents and Literacies in a Digital World*. Past president of the National Reading Conference (NRC), she serves on the Adolescent Literacy Advisory Group of the Alliance for Excellent Education. Alvermann was elected to the Reading Hall of Fame in 1999 and is the recipient of NRC's Oscar Causey Award for Outstanding Contributions to Reading Research, NRC's Kingston Award for Distinguished Service, College Reading Association's Laureate Award and the Herr Award for Contributions to Research in Reading Education. In 2006, she was awarded IRA's William S. Gray Citation of Merit.

Manju Banerjee is a doctoral student in special education in the Department of Educational Psychology at the University of Connecticut. She is a research consultant for the Educational Testing Service and an editorial board member for the *Journal of Postsecondary Education and Disabilities*.

Richard Beach is professor of English education at the University of Minnesota, where he studies responses to literature and the media. He is author of *Teachingmedialiteracy.com: A Resource Guide to Web-based Links and Activities* and coauthor of *Teaching Literature to Adolescents*; *Engaging Students in Digital Writing*; and *High*

School Students' Competing Social Worlds: Negotiating Identities and Allegiances through Responding to Multicultural Literature; he is also coeditor of *Multidisciplinary Perspectives on Literacy Research.*

Gerald Campano is assistant professor at Indiana University. He is a Carnegie Scholar and a former elementary school teacher. He recently published *Immigrant Students and Literacy: Reading, Writing, and Remembering.*

Marcia Carter was an elementary and high school teacher for over thirty years and has served as adjunct faculty in education at California Polytechnic State University. Currently, she is a consultant for the Region 8 Advancement Via Individual Determination (AVID) program in four California counties. She is a state and national presenter for the AVID program and is a former College Board consultant and current staff developer.

Jill Castek is a doctoral student in cognition and instruction in the Department of Educational Psychology and a member of the New Literacies Research Team at the University of Connecticut. She is interested in cross-cultural telecollaborative learning through the creation of online partnerships with classes around the world.

James S. Damico is assistant professor at Indiana University. Winner of an AERA Outstanding Dissertation award, his published work includes articles in *Language Arts, Theory into Practice,* and *Journal of Adolescent & Adult Literacy,* as well as coauthored chapters in several edited books. Currently, as creator and co-director of the Critical Web Reader project (http://cwr.indiana.edu), he is creating Web-based tools that facilitate strategic Internet reading, and he is studying the ways teachers and students use these tools to engage with Internet texts and technologies.

Danielle V. Dennis is assistant professor of elementary education at the University of South Florida.

Jerome C. Harste is professor emeritus of language education at Indiana University, where he held the Martha Lea and Bill Armstrong Chair in Teacher Education. His book, *Language Stories and Literacy Lessons,* coauthored with Carolyn Burke and Virginia Woodward, was awarded the David H. Russell Research Award for Outstanding Contributions in the Teaching of English. He served on the board of the International Reading Association and is past president of the National Reading Conference, the National Conference on Research in Language and Literacy, the Whole Language Umbrella, and the National Council of Teachers of English.

Contributors

Anita Hernández serves as associate professor in the College of Education at California Polytechnic State University, San Luis Obispo. She teaches reading and language arts methods and bilingual literacy methods courses to future teachers. She is a former classroom teacher and coordinated a program for college migrant students. She is a project director of a national professional development program for teachers of English learners. She is a coauthor of *Theme-Sets for Secondary Students: How to Scaffold Core Literature*.

Kathleen A. Hinchman is professor and chair of the Reading and Language Arts Center at Syracuse University. Once a middle school teacher, she teaches undergraduate and graduate classes in childhood and adolescent literacy. She has published in *The Reading Teacher, Language Arts, Reading Research Quarterly*, and *Journal of Literacy Research*, and has coauthored or coedited *Reconceptualizing the Literacies in Adolescents' Lives, Principled Practices for a Literate America, Teaching Adolescents Who Struggle with Reading*, and *Tutoring Adolescent Literacy Learners*. She served as president of the Central New York Reading Council and the New York State Reading Association and as a member of the Board of Directors of the National Reading Conference, which she will serve as president in 2009.

Brian C. Housand is currently a University of Connecticut doctoral student at the Neag Center for Gifted Education and Talent Development. He is studying the needs of high-ability readers and how the Internet can be used to best meet these needs.

Robert T. Jiménez is professor of education in the Department of Teaching and Learning, Peabody College, Vanderbilt University (Ph.D. 1992, University of Illinois at Urbana-Champaign). A former bilingual education teacher, he is now conducting research on how written language is thought about and used in contemporary Mexico. His most recent book is *Race, Ethnicity, and Education: Language and Literacy in Schools*. His work has also appeared in numerous journals.

Kevin M. Leander is associate professor in the Department of Teaching and Learning, Peabody College, Vanderbilt University. Prior to graduate study, he was a middle and high school English and French teacher in the United States and Italy. He has published in *Cognition and Instruction, Research in the Teaching of English, Ethos, Reading Research Quarterly, Discourse Processes*, and other venues.

Donald J. Leu is the John and Maria Neag endowed chair in literacy and technology at the University of Connecticut and director of the

New Literacies Research Lab (http://www.newliteracies.uconn.edu/). He is a graduate of Michigan State, Harvard, and Berkeley. He is a former ESL teacher, elementary teacher, and reading specialist. He is also a former president of the National Reading Conference and is currently a member of the Board of Directors of the International Reading Association. Leu's scholarship focuses on the new literacies of online reading comprehension and learning. He currently co-directs a major, federal research grant, Teaching Internet Comprehension to Adolescents (http://www.newliteracies.uconn.edu/iesproject/index.html) that studies how best to teach online reading comprehension to adolescents in urban districts in Connecticut and rural districts in South Carolina. He has more than 100 publications and twenty books, including coauthor of *Teaching with the Internet: New Literacies for New Times* (4th ed.) and *Effective Literacy Instruction* (5th ed.) and coeditor of *Handbook of Research on New Literacies.*

Jill Lewis is professor of literacy education at New Jersey City University. She has served on IRA's board of directors. She began her teaching career in public schools, grades 7–12. She has chaired IRA and NJRA's Government Relations Committees and was a recipient of New Jersey Reading Association's Distinguished Service Award. She recently completed a second term as board of directors chair of the American Reading Forum. She has authored numerous professional articles on professional development, advocacy, and adolescent and content literacy. She is lead author of IRA's publication *Educators on the Frontline: Advocacy Strategies for Your Classroom, Your School, and Your Profession* and author of *Academic Literacy: Readings and Strategies* (4th ed., 2007). She is a volunteer consultant for the Secondary Education Reform Activity program in Macedonia and has also worked in Macedonia, Kazakhstan, and Albania for IRA's Reading and Writing for Critical Thinking Project.

Yingjie Liu is a doctoral student at the University of Connecticut in the learning technology program. She conducts research on technology-assisted students' informal science learning.

Cheryl A. McLean is a doctoral student and teaching and research assistant of language and literacy education at the University of Georgia. Formerly a secondary school teacher in Trinidad and Tobago, her research interests include adolescent literacy and narrative inquiry. She is currently coeditor of the *Journal of Language and Literacy Education* (http://www.coe.uga.edu/jolle/). In 2006, she was awarded the Jackson Carson Memorial Scholarship for excellence in teaching.

Gary Moorman is professor of education and reading/language arts program coordinator at Appalachian State University. He has published in the *Reading Research Quarterly, Reading Research and Instruction, Journal of Reading, The Reading Teacher, Reading Psychology*, and *Review of Research in Education*. He has written three books, *Learning to Teach Reading, Designing Reading Programs*, and *Researching Online for Education*. Most recently, he is the coeditor of *Adolescent Literacy Instruction: Policies and Promising Practices*. He served as the online communities director for *Reading Online*, the International Reading Association's online journal, and as an editor of the *Yearbook of the American Reading Forum*. He has participated in international projects with Adam Mickiewicza University in Poland, the Secondary Education Activity Project in Macedonia, and as a consultant to Qatar University.

Elizabeth Noll is associate dean of graduate programs and faculty development, School of Education, University of New Mexico. She has served as publications chair for the National Conference on Research in Language and Literacy (NCRLL).

David G. O'Brien is professor of literacy education and an associated faculty member at the Minnesota Reading Research Center, University of Minnesota, Twin Cities. A former junior high teacher, his scholarship and teaching focus on the literacy practices of adolescents, particularly the engagement of "struggling" readers with digital literacies and how adolescents use literacy to learn content across the disciplines. His research appears in a range of education and literacy journals as well as in books and book chapters.

Maureen O'Neil is a doctoral student in communications at the University of Connecticut.

P. David Pearson is dean of the Graduate School of Education at the University of California, Berkeley, and is a faculty member in the language, literacy, and culture program. He has served the reading and literacy education profession in a range of roles: as editor of *Reading Research Quarterly* and the National Reading Conference *Yearbook*, as president of NRC and member of the IRA board of directors, and as the founding editor of the *Handbook of Reading Research*. Those contributions have earned him several awards: IRA's William S. Gray Citation of Merit (1990) and Albert Harris Award (2005), NRC's Oscar Causey Award (1989), NCTE's Alan Purves Award (2003), and the University of Minnesota Award for Outstanding Alumni Contributions. Before coming to UC Berkeley, Pearson served on the reading education faculties at Minnesota, Illinois, and Michigan State.

Jeannine D. Richison has been teaching for thirty-one years, twenty-three of them at the secondary level. She is associate professor and coordinates English education for secondary teacher candidates at California Polytechnic State University. She has worked with the American Board for Certification of Teacher Excellence, California Commission on Teacher Credentialing, and is coauthor of *Theme-Sets for Secondary Students: How to Scaffold Core Literature*.

Alfred W. Tatum is associate professor and director of the Reading Clinic at the University of Illinois at Chicago. He has published in *Reading Research Quarterly, The Reading Teacher, Journal of Adolescent & Adult Literacy, Educational Leadership, Journal of College Reading and Learning,* and *Principal Leadership*. His book, *Teaching Reading to Black Adolescent Males: Closing the Achievement Gap*, received NCTE's James Britton Award. He earned his Ph.D. from the University of Illinois at Chicago. He began his career as an eighth-grade teacher on the South Side of Chicago.

Brad L. Teague is a doctoral student in the language, literacy, and culture program at Vanderbilt University. He holds a B.A. in Spanish and linguistics from the University of North Carolina at Chapel Hill and an M.A. in applied linguistics from the Universidad de las Américas in Puebla, Mexico. His primary area of interest is second language and literacy learning.

Robert J. Tierney is dean of the Faculty of Education at the University of British Columbia and professor in the Department of Language and Literacy Education. He is also past president of the Association of Canadian Deans of Education (ACDE) and current president of the Reading Hall of Fame. As an international scholar, he has authored books and articles on literacy education, educational assessment, teaching, and learning. His recent writing focuses on discussions of professionalism and meeting student needs in the current political climate of accountability. As a teacher educator, researcher, administrator, and former classroom teacher, Tierney is active in education initiatives throughout Canada, the Asia Pacific Region, and the United States.

Terry Underwood is professor in literacy education and a graduate program coordinator at Sacramento State University. He won an NCTE promising researcher award in 1996 for his dissertation, *A Study of Students' Literacy Achievement and Academic Motivation in a Context of Portfolio Assessment in Middle School English Classrooms*. In the early 1990s, he served as a member of the team in California that developed and field tested the CLAS reading test.

Contributors

Monica S. Yoo is a doctoral student in the Graduate School of Education at the University of California, Berkeley. Her research interests include adolescent literacy, reading comprehension, students' use of reading and writing strategies, and the social and cultural contexts of students' literacy practices. Currently, she is investigating how students' personal reading and writing strategies intersect with the strategies taught in the classroom.

Jessica C. Zacher is assistant professor in Teacher Education and Liberal Studies at the California State University, Long Beach. She recently received her Ph.D. from the University of California, Berkeley Graduate School of Education. She is currently investigating the ways that urban children, including second language learners, experience highly structured language arts curricula in high poverty schools.

Lisa Zawilinski is a doctoral student in the Department of Curriculum and Instruction and a member of the New Literacies Research Team at the University of Connecticut. She is interested in ways in which Internet communication technologies such as wikis, blogs, and instant messages can enhance student learning.

This book was typeset in Sabon by Electronic Imaging.
Typefaces used on the cover include ITC Lubalin Graph Demi
and Swiss 721 BT.
The book was printed on 50-lb. Williamsburg Offset paper
by Versa Press, Inc.